# THE LA COSTA PRESCRIPTION FOR LONGER LIFE

R. Philip Smith, M.D.
and
Patrick Quillin, Ph. D., R.D.

FAWCETT CREST • NEW YORK

To Gerry, my wife, and to Bopi and Becky.

—R. Philip Smith

For my wife and best friend, whose talents and supportive love nurtured this book from a vague dream into reality. You are the wind in my sails. God bless you, Noreen.

—Patrick Quillin

A Fawcett Crest Book
Published by Ballantine Books
Copyright © 1985 by R. Philip Smith & Patrick Quillin

Library of Congress Catalog Card Number: 83-063201

ISBN 0-449-21033-2

This edition published by arrangement with Roundtable Publishing, Inc.

Manufactured in the United States of America

First Ballantine Books Edition: November 1986

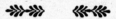

# Contents

# Acknowledgments

The completion of this book required a supportive cast of many. We wish to express our sincere appreciation to all of those who have made it possible: To friends and families who tolerated our absences while we were preoccupied with putting together this manuscript. To our co-workers who helped us to assemble and to check the many details that are required by a work of this nature. To the thousands of scientists whose laboratory work has made it possible for us to assemble the facts that are the basis of our prescriptions. To the many librarians, particularly those at the UCLA biomedical library, who helped us tirelessly and patiently. To our editor Jim Neyland and the staff at Roundtable Publishing, especially Laura Wilson, for their relentless dedication. And to the thousands of people who have contributed to this book by their experiences. Thank you all.

# Preface

It has been said that the ultimate human being would have the body of a twenty-five year old athlete and the mature functioning mind of a seventy year old. As we age, we gain knowledge, patience, judgment, self-acceptance, friends, family, and sometimes material wealth as well—all things that make living more enjoyable. Bertrand Russell, the famous mathematician and philosopher, stated that he had often contemplated suicide when he was in his teens and early childhood, but that he had eventually become enraptured with life and could not get enough of living. Indeed, for most people, just when life is becoming enjoyable, health begins to fail, both physically and mentally. They are robbed of the most salient moments of life through premature death. That needn't be the case.

The principles that are set out in the following pages are intended to help you to avoid illness, increase your mental, physical, and sexual powers, help you live longer, and—most importantly—make those extra years or decades well worth living.

There have been many books written on health and longer life. What makes this one different? A great many of them—particularly recent books—have recommended strange and esoteric solutions, from ingesting large quantities of chemicals to freezing or starvation. Our program is much more practical and considerably more reliable. The prescriptions we offer for longer life are based on experience, proven facts, and the results of laboratory experiments. Ours is a clear-cut program that tells you exactly what to do, how to do it, when to do it, and why.

Our knowledge has been drawn from years of study and many more years of clinical practice. We have included numerous case histories to illustrate our points, and to show you that other people have faced the same problems that you experience. Many of them have succeeded in adding decades of enjoyment to their lives.

They came to us because they asked the questions you may be asking yourself: "I wonder if my life could be better, with more energy and less sickness? Am I doomed to become a semi-invalid when I am in my 60s, then face death in my 70s? Is there some way I can put more years in my life and more life in my years?"

There are positive answers to all of those questions, and they are surprisingly simple. Once you understand and follow the prescriptions we offer, you can look forward to a healthier, happier, and longer life. Some can expect zestful living into their eighties, some into their nineties, and some even well beyond 100.

R. Philip Smith, M.D.

Patrick Quillin, Ph.D., R.D.

꧁꧂ **1** ꧁꧂

# Health and Longevity

"May you make lots of money—and spend
it all on doctor bills."

—OLD CURSE

[• As our ability to conquer disease increases, we obstruct
our potential for longer life by personal habits • The United
States is leading the western nations down the suicidal path
• Everybody pays for poor health, including the healthy •
Happy, healthy life is possible past 100 • Normal health vs.
optimal health • Good health does not require abstinence,
but it does require commitment]

Every day, millions of business executives, men and women,
will spend most of their daytime hours seated at desks, often
under intense stress. They will wash down calorie-rich lunch-
eons with several alcoholic drinks and go home at night to
have more of the same. Millions of others will eat one or two
meals at a fast food restaurant and get no exercise whatsoever.
Many become accustomed to six cups of coffee and assorted

1

pastries in the morning, with a frozen macaroni dinner warmed up at the end of the day. Hundreds of thousands of stay-at-home people will spend today indulging in orgies of junk-food while doing housework or watching television. Tomorrow they plan to start the latest popular diet that awkwardly limits food intake—hoping that this one, finally, will work magic. When their children come in from school, they will grab snacks of potato chips, soda pop, and candy bars.

If you can identify with any of the above descriptions, you are one of a vast number of people in the developed world who may have a shortened lifespan because of a suicidal lifestyle.

It is a curious paradox of our modern technological world that, as our ability to conquer deadly diseases increases, we obstruct our potential for longer life by our personal habits. In 1347 A.D., the bubonic plague killed 75 million people, about half of the population of the known world. As recently as 1918, an influenza epidemic left over 21 million people dead. By the 1980s, however, inoculations, vaccines, and improved sanitation had neutralized the dreaded epidemics of the past. Scientific advances in medicine had produced surgical procedures that enable us to replace worn-out or damaged organs—hearts, kidneys, livers, and others—and to perform other procedures that once would have been considered miracles. And a large part of the world is fortunate enough to possess an excess of food supplies, so that malnutrition is unnecessary.

But there are drawbacks to our wondrous age. We live at a fast pace, eating too much or making poor food choices just to keep going. We have machines to do our manual labor, allowing us to lead sedentary lifestyles. The family structures that once supplied emotional sustenance are eroding. The abuse of alcohol, drugs, and tobacco is escalating. Our technology is producing an increasing number of toxic waste products.

At one time we thought that abundant food, plenty of leisure time, scientific advances, and great wealth would produce a peak of human health. But this is not the case. Suicide from lifestyle has replaced homicide from microorganisms as the principal cause of death in the developed world.

Although Finland has a higher incidence of heart disease and Japan has a higher incidence of stroke, the United States is leading the other developed nations down the suicidal path. The following set of statistics is selected from what is known about the health condition of the people of the United States, but they apply in some degree to all of the nations of the technological West:

- Almost 3,000 people per day die from vascular diseases (heart disease, stroke).
- Over 1,000 people per day die from cancer.
- Thirty-five million people suffer from hypertension (high blood pressure).
- One out of nine people is severely limited in activity because of a chronic health problem. (This number is increasing.)
- One out of four people over 65 years of age is limited in activity by arthritis.
- Fifteen percent of the population (over 24 million people) needs some kind of mental health care.
- Thirty billion dollars was spent in 1977 on liquor and tobacco, while medical research was given only $4 billion.

- In 1981, 485 million workdays and 204 schooldays were lost because of poor health.
- There are conservatively fifteen million alcoholics. Thirty percent of all drinkers consume five or more drinks at one sitting.
- One-third of the adult population smokes. That's over 52 million people.
- One-fourth of the population eats no breakfast.
- There are six million known diabetics, with millions of others who are borderline cases.
- In 1979, over 109,000 Americans died from cancer of the gastrointestinal tract, a disease that is relatively rare in underdeveloped nations.
- Ninety percent of the population depends on prescription lenses to see.
- With sales of *legal* drug prescriptions well over $10 billion per year, we are rapidly becoming a society of drug abusers.

In the nations of the West, a great deal of money is spent each year for health care—for individual doctor bills, for medical insurance, and for government programs. In 1982, health care expenditures in the United States reached 11 percent of the gross national product—a total of $322 billion. Over 25 million operations were performed in American hospitals in 1980, and the average cost of a hospital visit that year was $2,261. Over 100,000 coronary bypass operations are performed yearly at a price of $50,000 each.

Even if you were healthy and had no need of a doctor or a hospital last year, you probably paid for poor health through taxes and/or insurance premiums. Since government health-

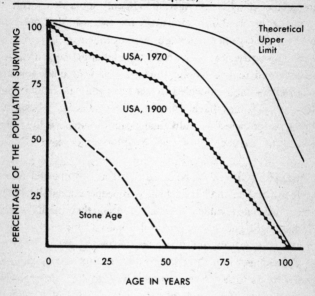

**FIGURE 1.1**

**LONGEVITY CURVES FOR HUMANS**

(Past and Projected)

care and insurance programs are merely a redistribution of
health expenses, each person contributes about $1,400 per year
for the poor health of the general population.

What does all this have to do with longevity? Everything.
The longevity curve in Figure 1.1 shows that there has been
little improvement in average lifespan in the past few decades
of impressive medical advances. Because of the progress in
medical science, we should be able to live longer and happier
lives, and we can do so if we choose. It is—very clearly—a

5

matter of choice. Longevity is a matter of good health and good health practices.

Bob Hope has said that very few people want to be eighty years old—except those who are 79. Actually, most people are interested in living longer, though only some are concerned about getting healthier. However, the two—health and longevity—go together. They are interdependent.

A constantly sick, overweight, and lethargic person cannot be expected to live a long time. If you wait until you are incapacitated and enfeebled to ask how you can extend your lifespan, you may have waited too long. Just as a beautiful forest is composed of individual beautiful trees, a long and healthy life is made up of many health-oriented days.

CASE HISTORY: J.V. believed that she had married into a perfect life. She and her husband had been reasonably healthy and in their late twenties when they had said their marital vows. He had just begun his career on the bottom rung of the ladder of a large law firm, and the future seemed bright.

The changes in their relationship and health during the next twelve years were subtle. She gave birth to three children and devoted herself to the role of wife and mother. Now, J.V. was always tired, often sick, sometimes depressed—and forty pounds overweight. Her lifestyle was all-too-typical—rushing through nonnourishing meals, eating frequent dinners out, often only fast foods, getting little exercise, suffering emotional distress, with excess alcohol intake, heavy smoking, and desperate dabbling in prescription drugs to control her weight and moods.

When her husband was attending a convention at La Costa, J.V. checked into the spa program. She listened intently during her medical examination and the evening health seminars, and as a result she determined that she would do something about her situation.

She was put on a program to stop smoking. She was given an 800-calorie per day diet with high-potency vitamin and mineral supplements and extra ascorbic acid to help reverse the effects of smoking. She agreed to go without alcohol for the first two weeks and thereafter to have no more than one or two small drinks a day. She began an exercise routine and found that she enjoyed it. Swimming, walking, and playing volleyball became exciting to her.

Two weeks later, J.V. checked out of La Costa looking and feeling better.

When she returned for a visit eight months later, she was 125 pounds of lean, dynamic, happy woman. She had also just learned that she was pregnant with her fourth child. She had progressed further with the program she had begun on her first visit, discovering that some of her troubles had stemmed from society's view of women without careers. Her feelings had changed. She acknowledged that she liked children, and decided that her career as a wife and mother was as important and satisfying as the careers of "working women." The changes she had made in her diet, exercise, attitude, and physical environment had made an incredible difference in her health, energy level, and appearance.

Her dynamic transition in health and happiness had inspired her husband to follow her example. They made a handsome pair, the picture of the ideal couple they had started out as. It happened because J.V. determined that she would make the change in her life. She accomplished it herself. We merely showed her the way.

\* \* \*

That is the one most important factor in good health and in longevity—you are the one who has to accomplish it. We can only guide you. It is through ignorance or apathy that many of the people of the developed nations of the world eventually develop disabling diseases. Some are fortunate enough to reverse their destructive lifestyles before it is too late. We would like to see those numbers increase. It is the objective of this book to show you how you can join the ranks of those who will live longer, happier lives than their neighbors. (And maybe you can take your neighbors along with you in the process.)

You must weigh the alternatives and make the decision and the commitment. Your awareness and acceptance of the responsibility in extending your lifespan is essential to success. The best medical advice is useless without it.

In a study done at Mount Sinai Hospital in Chicago, sixty percent of the people polled recognized the seriousness of the major killing diseases, and they could identify the symptoms. However, most of these respondents did not feel that they were themselves vulnerable to heart disease, cancer, and stroke. A great majority of them recognized that diet and exercise were related to health, and they were aware of the hazards of smoking and stress and sedentary lifestyle. All of the people surveyed acknowledged that those lifestyle practices were subject to voluntary control, yet this awareness did not alter their habits. Many smoked, overate, and led sedentary lives. They believed that any condition that might develop from their suicidal practices could be cured by doctors.

It is true that medical science can achieve much in the way of repairs to the human organism, but most of these do not extend healthy life; they merely prolong death. True longevity is to live younger longer, not to maintain the feeble and dying for interminable lengths of time on complex life-support systems.

Happy, healthy, productive lives are possible well beyond the century mark, but the key word in this is "healthy." We have numerous examples of those who have remained vigorous and creative past the average lifespan. The following are only a few:

- Grandma Moses was still painting at age 100.
- Eubie Blake could still play excellent piano at age 100.
- Bertrand Russell led international peace drives at age 94.
- George Bernard Shaw wrote the play *Farfetched Fables* when he was 93.
- Eamon DeValera was serving as president of Ireland at age 91.
- Pablo Picasso was drawing and engraving at age 90.
- Artur Rubinstein gave one of his greatest recitals at Carnegie Hall when he was 89.
- Michelangelo designed the Church of Santa Maria degli Angeli when he was 88.
- George Burns won his first Academy Award when he was 80.

The key is good health, and the choice for good health is yours to make. No one can do it for you, and the sooner you make the choice, the easier it will be to achieve. Delay merely prompts further delay. In a recent poll of retired executives of Fortune 500 companies—people who have had money, prestige, and power—the question was asked: "If you had it to do over again, what would you do differently?" Two answers were almost unanimous:

9

- I would have taken better care of my health.
- I would have spent more time with my family.

Both answers express regrets at allowing time to pass while ignoring health and loved ones, the truly important things in life.

What most people do not realize is that a healthy lifestyle is not a struggle. It is not an existence of self-denial, nor is it the end of pleasure.

There are varying degrees of health, so it is important for us to define what we mean by a healthy lifestyle. It is possible to talk about "good health" and "normal health," but these terms are inadequate without placing them in relative position on a scale. In Figure 1.2, we have divided health into a range of levels between death and "optimal" health, with the currently acceptable norm representing the largest percentage of the population.

Normal health is not what you want. Unfortunately, these days, the normal person is overweight, wears glasses, has dentures by age 50, has six colds a year, and is likely to die from heart disease or cancer. Truly ideal or perfect health is a potential that few people achieve, just as the ultimate limits of longevity are difficult to calculate. Einstein, one of history's most brilliant men, estimated that even geniuses use only ten percent of their intelligence potential. It is possible that we have as yet tapped only a small percentage of the human physical potential as well. Before Roger Bannister ran the mile in less than four minutes, it was thought that the human body could not withstand the physical exertion necessary to accomplish this.

## FIGURE 1.2
## HEALTH STANDARDS OF THE GENERAL WESTERN POPULATION

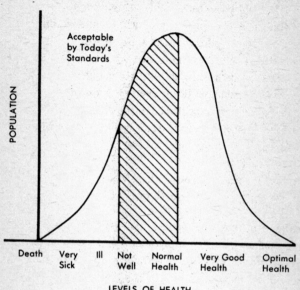

For that reason we use the term "optimal" health—a degree of health and fitness that permits utilization of an individual's full potential under present conditions. How does one recognize optimal health? We would consider you to be in optimal health if you are:

• Trim and physically fit, able to participate in sports.
• Full of energy and vigor; rarely tired.

- Free from minor complaints of insomnia, headaches, constipation, and indigestion.
- Active and creative.
- Alert and clearheaded; able to concentrate.
- Radiant with clear skin, glossy hair, and sparkling eyes.
- Confident, optimistic, and self-assured.
- Relaxed and free from worry.
- Satisfied with work and life's direction.
- Assertive without being overly aggressive.
- Satisfied with sexual relationships.
- Free from destructive health habits such as smoking, excessive eating, and drinking.
- At peace with self.
- Rarely sick and quick to heal from injury.
- Living a quality life until age 100 or more.

Sound impossible? Don't believe it. It is a very realistic goal. And an improved lifestyle does not mean the end of fun in your life. If anything, it permits you to enjoy your life to the fullest.

Humans naturally seek out pleasure and avoid pain. Both pleasure-seeking and pain-avoidance serves a purpose in life. If eating were not a pleasurable experience, people would die from malnutrition. If sex were not enjoyable, humans would not propagate. If sleep were unpleasant, humans would avoid it, and physical strength and endurance could not be maintained.

Pain-avoidance is part of the instinct for self-protection and survival. The burning sensation from fire tells the human to beware. Painful injuries force us into a much needed rest.

However, some degree of discomfort in life is necessary to

achieve any important goal. (See Figure 1.3.) Anyone who has the parental pride of successfully rearing children is aware of the strains and difficulties involved. The athlete receiving an Olympic medal has spent thousands of hours training for the event, and will at that point acknowledge that it was worthwhile. Anyone who has been successful at business will admit that it took hard work and sacrifice to realize the dream.

This same kind of effort is necessary for achieving a longer and better life. The amount of change, effort, or sacrifice you will have to make to add fulfilling decades to your lifespan depends on how far you have strayed from the path of health. The greatest effort, time, and discomfort will have to be invested by those who are heavy smokers or are obese. If you are a sugar or salt addict, a "sofa jockey" or a person who is overly intense, you may also have to endure some discomfort in rearranging your habits.

This does not mean, however, that you will be required to endure a life of abstinence. Thousands of satisfied guests at La Costa have agreed that nourishing food, when properly prepared, is far more tasty than the nonfoods that had constituted their diets before. Once your body passes through the initial efforts to become well toned, you will find that you anxiously look forward to your exercise periods. Once you have made adjustments in your attitude toward yourself and your life, you will find your days pass much more enjoyably.

Think of your goal of good health and long life as something you have to earn by effort, and you can achieve it. If necessary, offer yourself tangible rewards for various stages of your accomplishment—new clothes, a set of golf clubs, a vacation, or a record album—and this may serve as positive reinforcement for those moments when your determination may waver.

**FIGURE 1.3**

**PLEASURE AND PAIN ENCOUNTERED AS LIFESTYLE CHANGES**

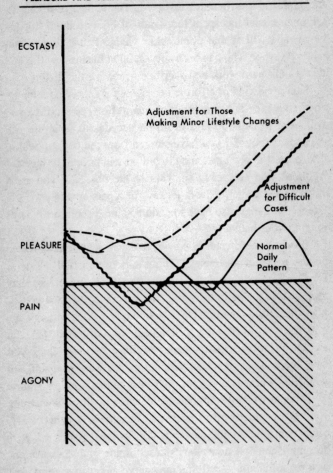

But the important thing to remember throughout the process is that change requires effort, commitment, and sometimes discomfort. With this kind of investment, you can achieve a longer, healthier, and happier life.

## 2

# Preventive Medicine

"An ounce of prevention is worth a pound of cure."

—EVERYONE'S GRANDMOTHER

[• Do you treat your body as well as you do your automobile?
• The tenacity of youth and organ reserves • What is aging?
• The six key factors of preventive medicine—genetics, nutrition, exercise, attitude, environment, and body maintenance • Prescriptions for prevention.• Changing the attitude of our pill-oriented and throw away society]

How would you treat your automobile if you were told it would be the last one you could ever own? You would probably treat it with care, protecting it and maintaining it to the best of your ability.

Do you realize that you are currently "driving" the one and only body you will ever have?

Comparing your body to your automobile is not inappropriate. Preventive automobile maintenance and preventive medicine have much in common; there is only one significant difference—although it's possible to buy a new car when the old one wears out, most people treat their automobiles better than they do their bodies. Far too many people wait until their bodies flash danger signals before seeking help. By then it is sometimes too late. It is a lot easier to add a quart of oil to a car or replace a battery than it is to cure cancer or replace a heart.

CASE HISTORY: W.E. was a very wealthy man. He was also a very sick man. He had been to La Costa several times in the past, but each visit was brief and hurried. He was sincere about his desire to lose weight and get his body into shape, but always business called him urgently back. When he was younger, he had inherited his father's small manufacturing plant and—over a period of some years—had built it into a Fortune 500 company. W.E. had great talents, and he had the drive and determination necessary for success. But to achieve his goals, he had endured years of stress, poor diet, excessive drinking and smoking, with a sedentary lifestyle.

During these years, he had constantly promised himself, "As soon as I get my company moving right, I'm going to take some time off and look after my health."

He had waited too long. This latest visit was one of desperation.

At 62 years of age, with every reason to live, W.E. was suffering from two dreaded diseases—cancer of the prostate (which had metastasized) and emphysema. There were at least ten factors in his lifestyle that could have caused these conditions, including smoking, a high-fat diet, and no exercise. He should have done something about them earlier. He had noticed labored breathing developing slowly over a period of two years, but had ignored it. His mind had been on business.

When he came to La Costa seeking help, we had to tell him that we were not equipped to handle patients in the final stages of the diseases he had.

W.E. misunderstood. Tearfully he pulled out his checkbook and said, "If money is the problem, I can take care of that."

We had to explain to him that money had nothing to do with it, that we were involved in preventing diseases more than with curing them. At his stage of physical degeneration, he would be better off with his own physician and with the treatment programs his doctors had already begun. Because his cancer had already spread to other parts of his body, the outlook was not good for W.E.

## The Tenacity of Youth

The attitude of "I'll worry about that tomorrow" can be a deadly one. There is much in our western society that encourages us to think that way. We look upon doctors the same way we look upon automobile mechanics. Medical science has made great strides in recent decades—chemotherapy, radiation therapy, coronary bypass surgery, heart transplants, open heart surgery, drugs. We abuse our bodies, and then take them in to our doctors and say, "Fix it."

Doctors will do whatever they can to make necessary repairs; that's their job. They aren't paid to stand over your shoulder to tell you when you're abusing your body or taking risks. They can't be paid to do that. That's your job.

You have to learn that your body can take only so much

abuse before it begins to deteriorate or react in some way. This is one serious lack in our educational process. We spend the first twenty years of life—the period of youth and vigor—preparing for "life." During these years we feel indestructible, and we aren't taught otherwise. We can tolerate all sorts of abuses and still bounce back vigorously. We can eat more and not get overweight. We can exercise strenuously and not be sore the next day. We can drink heavily and not regret it the next morning.

Then we set out on our lives at about the time when the body's resiliency begins gradually to fade. No one really tells us this is going to happen. We're prepared to go on for many years abusing our bodies and expecting them to bounce back as if we were in our teens.

Most of us are in our thirties when we notice things aren't quite what they used to be. We discover we can't stay up as late or drink and eat as much without feeling the effects the next day. We find that we have to stretch our muscles before performing exercise to avoid injuries. What our bodies are trying to tell us is that we are beginning to deplete our organ reserves.

What are "organ reserves"? At birth your body receives a capability to tolerate abuses committed upon it. The degree of tolerance you receive is based upon your genetic background combined with environmental nourishment (nutrition, emotional support, etc.) during the prenatal and early infancy period. No one has unlimited organ reserves. When you have depleted your reserves, they're gone and cannot be replenished.

Your ability to hold onto youth is dependent upon maintaining your organ reserves as long as possible. We speak of this ability as the "tenacity of youth," and we can compare it to a pair of jeans. In the old days, there was a slogan, "Blue jeans never wear out." This wasn't quite true, but jeans do have a way of seeming indestructible; it's why they are so popular. After years of abuse, they become faded and thin, tending to fray in well-worn places. At this point you have to be careful with them or they'll tear. However, if you have been careful with them from the beginning, they may last twice as long.

The same is true of your body. If you abuse it early and intensely, as some alcoholics and drug addicts do, your middle age may seem more like old age. If you habitually consume too much salt, your body may tolerate it for years, even decades; but eventually the kidneys will lose their ability to excrete the excess sodium and you will develop high blood pressure.

Eventually in all of us, the tenacity of youth gives way to the semistability of middle age, which in turn gives way to the easily upset balance of older years. At precisely what age your particular body will do this depends on how you treat it.

This is not to suggest that you must pamper your body throughout your life in order to get full use out of it. There wouldn't be much point in that. What we want to suggest is that you replace abuses to your body with challenges. Exercise challenges the cardiovascular system. Fiber challenges and cleanses the digestive system. Learning and meditating challenge the mind. The body needs challenges of diet, exercise, attitude, and more. That is what keeps it invigorated and functioning well. Abuses deplete organ reserves and increase aging; challenges create vitality and extend the tenacity of youth.

## The Six Key Factors of Preventive Medicine

With optimal care, the human body can last far longer than the current average lifespan. According to Roy Walford, M.D., researcher in gerontology at UCLA, the human body should be able to live vigorously for 100 to 140 years. This optimal care is essential for anyone hoping to reach that potential. It is also preventive medicine.

We divide preventive medicine into six key factors that the individual practitioner must be aware of—genetics, nutrition, exercise, attitude, physical environment, and body maintenance. Each one of these factors influences each of the 60 trillion cells in your body. Each also interacts with the others, making the processes of life—and the extension of life—highly complex. For example, exercise is directly beneficial to health and longevity; it also interacts with your intake of nutrients, consumption of calories, and efficiency of absorption.

*Genetics* is the one factor that we can't do much about. We can't go back and change our parents to give us better inherited characteristics. Some may choose to alter some of the relatively unimportant details, such as hair color or length of nose. As yet we can do nothing about the more important characteristics, such as genetic susceptibility toward diseases like cancer, diabetes, and heart disease.

Some genetic characteristics, however, have a range or differential within which you may improve upon the condition of your parents. For example, with improved diet, a child may grow to be taller and/or more intelligent than either mother or father.

22

Genetics may be considered the blueprints for your body; diet or *nutrition* provides the raw materials for building it. It is one of the most important keys for planning a longer and healthier life. Food is a complex collection of chemicals that can do amazing things. Your body can be described as the same. Given a healthy set of blueprints (DNA) and the proper quality and quantity of raw materials (food), your body deftly performs hundreds of millions of complex chemical reactions every second of your life.

*Exercise* is of equal importance with nutrition. Humans evolved as highly active creatures. Only in recent years have we become sedentary, not heeding the warnings of biologists to "use it or lose it." This admonition applies to all of our bodily functions—not just to muscles, but everything from brain activity to sexual ability. Many "dis-eases" common today may develop from "dis-uses" of the body. It is critical to remember that active individuals tend to live far longer than those who are sedentary or inactive.

One factor that may surprise you is *attitude*. Happy people, those who have positive attitudes about themselves and who are interested in other people, tend to live longer than those who are pessimists or loners. Your mental attitude does affect your physical health and well-being. It affects the way you feel each day, and it has a cumulative effect over your entire lifespan. Your mind can cause diseases, and it can prevent or cure them as well.

Your *physical environment* is also a key factor in your health. We are all aware that viruses and bacteria exist in the environment, causing diseases. But smog, noise, light, chemical pollutants, and smoke affect us as well, causing illness and disease and influencing our lifespans.

The final factor is *body maintenance*, looking after the little details of cleanliness, comfort, and hygiene to keep everything in good working order. Bunions, cavities, and aching backs may seem like relatively unimportant matters, but what good is living longer if you are beset with aches and pains constantly? Giving care to these details is a sign that you respect your body and want to keep it functioning at top form.

All of these six key factors are interrelated, each affecting the others in ways large or small. Attitude may affect nutrition. If you are bored or depressed, you may lose your appetite or over-eat. By the same token, nutrition may affect attitude. Certain foods or additives may cause you to feel irritable or lethargic. Certainly your physical environment affects exercise. Smog limits exercise, as does smoking.

Within the six categories there are risks you may encounter, some more avoidable than others. Of course all should be avoided if possible, but all are not equal in importance. Table 2.2 ranks the relative risks within each category. Those interested in health and longevity should certainly endeavor to avoid all of the high risks.

It isn't advisable to give up all the low risks, thinking they will compensate for one high risk factor. Avoiding fresh produce because of the pesticides used while continuing to smoke cigarettes is foolish. Buying all the best nutritional supplements while getting no exercise will hardly keep you off the sick list.

## Prescriptions for Prevention

Preventive medicine works. Followed properly, it keeps people healthier longer, saves everyone time and money, and

**TABLE 2.1**

| Risk Level | Genetics | Nutrition | Exercise |
|---|---|---|---|
| High | Genetic diseases (Tay Sachs, Cystic Fibrosis, Sickle Cell Anemia) | | |
| Moderate to High Risk | | Obesity<br>High Fat<br>Low Fiber<br>High Salt<br>High Sugar<br>High Cholesterol<br>Excess Alcohol<br>Low Vitamin C | Sedentary Lifestyle<br>Weekend Athletics |
| Moderate Risk | Family tendency toward Short Life, Obesity, Heart Disease, Diabetes, Cancer | Low Iron<br>Low Chromium<br>Low Selenium<br>Low Calcium<br>Low Magnesium | Contact Sports<br>Extreme Activity<br>Improper Shoes |
| Low to Modate Risk | | Low Zinc<br>Low Flouride<br>Low Protein<br>Hydrogenated Fat<br>Low Potassium | Climbing and Diving Sports<br>Poor Equipment |
| Low Risk | | Food Additives<br>Saccharin | |

# THE LA COSTA PRESCRIPTION FOR LONGER LIFE

## RELATIVE RISKS OF SIX HEALTH FACTORS

| Risk Level | Physical Environment | Body Maintenance | Attitude |
|---|---|---|---|
| High Risk | Smoking Tobacco | | Loneliness<br>Distress<br>Tension |
| Moderate to High Risk | Certain Pesticides<br><br>Second Hand Tobacco Smoke | | Hate<br>Pessimism<br>Wrong Pace<br>Feeling Useless<br>Vindictiveness<br>Despair |
| Moderate Risk | Accidents<br><br>Toxins | | Low Self Esteem<br>Stifled Creativity<br>Lack of Direction<br>Lack of Laughter |
| Low to Moderate Risk | Polluted Water<br>Noise<br>Microorganisms<br>Sunlight<br>Air Pollution | Lack of Care of Back, Feet, Teeth, Gums, Ears, Gastrointestinal Tract, Eyes, Sinuses, Hair, Skin | |
| Low Risk | Radiation<br>Some Pesticides | | |

prevents needless suffering. Why then hasn't preventive medicine been more abundantly practiced? There are a number of reasons.

The most obvious reason is that most people wouldn't think about going to see a doctor to learn how to stay well. We don't generally call our doctors until we get sick, and even then many hesitate because of the cost. If we aren't suffering pain or fever, we occupy our thoughts with immediate concerns.

There is also the fact that conventional medicine is geared not toward prevention but toward emergency practice, dealing with serious and acute situations that need immediate correction. Infections, wounds or injuries, shock—all these have an urgency that must be met to save lives. Considered along with these, helping patients to avoid future illness and disease becomes less important. Besides, most doctors have difficulty getting patients to obey instructions for acute treatments; when it concerns recommendations for future good health they have serious doubts about patient compliance.

There are also a number of societal attitudes that have impeded acceptance of preventive medicine in the developed nations. We are a "throwaway" society. If something doesn't work, our reaction is not to repair it but to throw it away and buy something new that will work. Advertising encourages us to think this way, and that thinking carries over to things other than products. Even the divorce rate indicates that husbands and wives consider it easier to get a new partner than to salvage the old marriage.

We have also become pill-oriented. We seek instant relief for any problem, and we are led to have that attitude from earliest childhood—with orange-flavored aspirin, red cough syrup, and sweet chewable vitamins shaped like animals or cartoon characters. When we become adults, we look to sleeping pills, stimulants, diet pills, appetite suppressants, and even recreational drugs to feel happy and sociable. If it is not something we take, we find it hard to look upon as medicine.

We also have been reared with the idea that our own health is someone else's responsibility. This is a legacy from attitudes of childhood, expecting others—whether doctor, spouse, parent, employer, or friend—to take responsibility for our various needs.

Preventive medicine requires becoming master of your own body and mind so that you control what goes into them, what surrounds them, and what they do with, to, and for themselves.

We hope you are interested in taking charge of your life and doing something about improving your chances for longevity. In the pages that follow, we offer you specific and detailed prescriptions you can follow in the practice of preventive medicine to help you be younger longer.

# ⊰⊱⊰⊱ 3 ⊰⊱⊰⊱

# Rate Your Health

"To me old age is always fifteen years older than I am."

—BERNARD BARUCH

[• The means for determining your level of wellness • How nourishing is your diet? • How physically fit are you? • What is your stress/distress level? • Is your attitude affecting your health? • Are there problems in your physical environment? • What is your genetic assessment? • What is your level of body maintenance? • What are your chances of living to 100?]

**M**odern medicine has developed some rather impressive devices. Fiber optics allow today's physician to look inside the human body. CAT-scan X-rays provide detailed maps of the central nervous system. The cardiologist can determine occlusions in your blood vessels through the use of the angiogram. All of these new developments help to uncover and treat disease.

Only recently have means been developed to help determine your level or degree of "wellness." Many of these are not instruments but written tests you can take. By means of detailed personal information, the health care practitioner can determine your likelihood of encountering illness in the near future. Computers can analyze your diet to uncover areas of nutritional concern. The cardiologist's treadmill test reveals details about the condition of your heart, lungs, and circulatory system. The exercise physiologist has methods of determining your strength and flexibility.

Of course these tests cannot be self-administered. However, there are a few simple tests you can take that will enable you to assess your health and prospects for living beyond the normal allotment of years. In the following tests, answer the questions honestly and truthfully. When you have finished, add up your points for each test. Then add the total of all the tests to determine your chance of enjoying a birthday cake with 100 candles.

## HOW NOURISHING IS YOUR DIET?

For each question, circle the answer that most closely applies to you.

POINTS      SCORE

1) The largest skinfold thickness I
   have on the back of my arm,
   just above my hip bone, or on
   my midthigh measures:

a) 3 or more inches.                    −2
b) 2 to 3 inches.                         0
c) 1 to 2 inches.                         3
d) Less than 1 inch.                      6          _____

2) I eat breakfast: (Coffee and
   doughnuts do not count)

   a) Rarely.                             1
   b) Sometimes.                          2
   c) Usually.                            3
   d) Almost always.                      4          _____

3) My meal pattern is:

   a) I skip many meals, eat a
      few large meals.                    1
   b) I skip some meals, eat a
      few large meals.                    2
   c) I eat much, often.                  3
   d) I eat small frequent meals.         4          _____

4) Before swallowing, I chew my
   food:

   a) Less than 5 times.                  1
   b) 5 to 10 times.                      2
   c) 10 to 20 times.                     3
   d) 20 or more times.                   4          _____

5) I have tried:

   a) Many diets, but few work.           1

   b) Some diets, lose weight,
      then gain it back.          2

   c) No diets.                  3

   d) No diets, am at perfect
      weight.                 4       \_\_\_\_\_

6) I usually eat the following type
   of foods:

   a) Fried, deep fried, boiled,
      canned, prepared.      1

   b) Baked, canned, frozen.   2

   c) Broiled, steamed, micro-
      waved.               3

   d) Unfried, with minimum
      grease, drained of oils,
      mostly fresh, or unpro-
      cessed foods.         4       \_\_\_\_\_

7) In my budget the buying of
   wholesome foods rates:

   a) Low priority; can't afford
      it.                   1

   b) Only when guests are com-
      ing.                 2

   c) Relatively high priority.   3

   d) Very high priority.       4       \_\_\_\_\_

8) I salt my food:

   a) Always at the table; some-
      times while cooking too.   1

b) Always but lightly.      2
c) Sometimes.      3
d) Very rarely.      4     _____

9) Snack and dessert foods—such as carbonated soft drinks, candy, pastry, sweetened breakfast cereal, and potato chips—are in my diet:

a) At least one of these each day.      1
b) Sometimes one of these a day.      2
c) Only a few times each week.      3
d) Rarely.      4     _____

10) My consumption of alcoholic beverages is: (1 drink equals 1 ounce distilled spirits, 4 ounces of wine, or 12 ounces of beer.)

a) 4 or more drinks each day.      1
b) 3 to 4 drinks each day.      2
c) 2 to 3 drinks each day.      3
d) 2 drinks or less each day.      4     _____

11) The following identifies my consumption of dairy products:

a) I don't eat many dairy products.      1

b) I eat high-fat cheeses and whole milk with some occasional butter and ice cream. 2

c) I eat some butter and ice cream, but mostly low-and nonfat milk. 3

d) I eat three or more servings each day of low and nonfat milk, yogurt, or cottage cheese, with rare samplings of high-fat dairy products. 4 _____

12) The following identifies my consumption of fruit and vegetables:

a) I eat canned vegetables with sauces, some fruit. 1

b) I eat one or two servings of vegetables or fruit each day, usually canned or cooked. 2

c) I eat usually two servings each day of canned or fresh fruit or vegetables. 3

d) I eat four or more servings each day, usually fresh fruit or vegetables. 4 _____

13) The following identifies my consumption of fats: (Nuts, oils, bacon, salad dressings,

margarine, butter, fried foods, etc.)

a) I like these foods, eat them often, and am overweight.     −2

b) I like fried foods and use dressings, gravies, and margarine regularly, but I'm not overweight.     0

c) I try to restrict my intake of these.     3

d) My low intake is primarily from vegetable oils (not hydrogenated) and nuts, and I am not overweight.     6     _____

14) My consumption of the protein group would be best described as:

a) Red meat, eggs often.     1

b) A little of every kind of meat, often fried.     2

c) I restrict red meat to small servings a few times each week, eating fish and poultry the rest of the time.     3

d) My diet is principally "vegetarian" with some animal protein as supplement; I know how to match proteins.     4     _____

15) My intake of breads and grains would best be described as:

a) Usually white bread, instant potatoes, crackers, etc.  1
b) Sporadic, these make me fat.  2
c) Usually whole grain.  3
d) Almost always whole grains, consumed often for fiber and protein source.  4  _____

16) I take vitamin and mineral supplements:

a) Never.  1
b) Daily in large quantities.  2
c) Sometimes.  3
d) A broad spectrum (multiple vitamin/mineral) in low potencies on a regular basis.  4  _____

17) My eating environment is usually:

a) Away from home and hectic (restaurant, plane, etc.)  1
b) Equally divided between home and away.  2
c) Mostly at home, sometimes with others.  3

d) Usually at home in a
   relaxed, pleasant surround-
   ing.                                    4          _____

TOTAL                                                 _____

EVALUATION:

*Score:*      *You are:*

11–34      At high risk nutritionally—you probably need sup-
           plements and a more in-depth nutritional analysis.

35–51      At moderate risk—your diet could be improved
           considerably, and supplements would be a good
           idea.

52–72      Low to very low risk—supplements may be of
           value, keep up the good work.

Generally, the higher your score, the lower your dietary risks.


## PHYSICAL FITNESS

|  | POINTS | SCORE |
|---|---|---|
| 1) My systolic blood pressure is: | | |
| a) 145 or more. | 1 | |
| b) 130 to 145. | 2 | |
| c) 112 to 129. | 3 | |
| d) 111 or less. | 4 | _____ |

2) My diastolic blood pressure is:

    a) 100 or more.               1
    b) 88 to 99.                  2
    c) 75 to 87.                  3
    d) 74 or below.              4     _____

3) My resting heart rate is:

    a) 110 or more.           −2
    b) 90 to 109.               0
    c) 65 to 89.                 3
    d) 64 or below.             6     _____

4) My job involves primarily:

    a) Sedentary work.          1
    b) Mostly sedentary, some
        walking.                 2
    c) Movement for about half of
        the day.                3
    d) Vigorous activity most of
        the day.               4     _____

5) The total number of push-ups
or pull-ups I can do is:

    a) 2.                        0
    b) 2 to 5.                 2
    c) 5 to 10.               3
    d) 10 or more.           4     _____

6) In twelve minutes, I could run:

    a) Less than a mile.        1

b) About a mile.      2
c) 1 to 1½ miles.      3
d) 1½ miles plus.      4     _____

7) I have consistently followed a regular aerobic fitness program (running, biking, swimming, etc.):

a) Not for over a year.      −2
b) Just started one.      0
c) Up to a year.      3
d) More than a year.      6     _____

8) I can come within the following distance of touching my toes with my legs straight:

a) More than 6 inches away.      1
b) Less than 6 inches away.      2
c) Can touch if I strain at it.      3
d) Can easily touch.      4     _____

9) I have sexual relations:

a) Fewer than 3 times per month.      1
b) 3 to 8 times per month.      2
c) 9 to 12 times per month.      3
d) 12 or more times per month.      4     _____

**TOTAL**     _____

EVALUATION:

| *Score:* | *You are:* |
|---|---|
| 2–18 | In poor physical condition—see your physician and begin exercising before it is too late. |
| 19–27 | In decent condition—make your program more vigorous and frequent. |
| 28–40 | Good to excellent condition—keep up the good work. |

## STRESS/DISTRESS

The following is a list of stressful events that bring distress if they occur in excess. Check the events that relate to your life within the last year and add up the points.

| LIFE EVENT | POINTS | SCORE |
|---|---|---|
| Death of a spouse. | 100 | ———— |
| Divorce. | 73 | ———— |
| Separation from marriage partner. | 65 | ———— |
| Detention in jail or other institution. | 63 | ———— |
| Death of a close family member. | 63 | ———— |
| Major personal injury or illness. | 53 | ———— |

| | | |
|---|---|---|
| Marriage. | 50 | _____ |
| Fired from work. | 47 | _____ |
| Marital reconciliation. | 45 | _____ |
| Retirement from work. | 45 | _____ |
| Major change in the health or behavior of a family member. | 44 | _____ |
| Pregnancy. | 40 | _____ |
| Sexual difficulties. | 39 | _____ |
| Gaining a new family member (birth, adoption, senior moving in). | 39 | _____ |
| Major business readjustment (merger, reorganization, bankruptcy). | 39 | _____ |
| Major change in financial status (worse or better). | 38 | _____ |
| Death of a close friend. | 37 | _____ |
| Changing to a different line of work. | 36 | _____ |
| Major change in number of arguments with spouse (more or fewer than usual). | 35 | _____ |
| Taking on a mortgage greater than $10,000 (purchasing a home, business). | 31 | _____ |

| | | |
|---|---|---|
| Foreclosure on a mortgage or loan. | 30 | ——— |
| Major change in responsibilities at work (promotion, demotion, transfer). | 29 | ——— |
| Son or daughter leaving home (marriage, attending college). | 29 | ——— |
| In-law troubles. | 29 | ——— |
| Outstanding personal achievement. | 28 | ——— |
| Spouse getting or quitting job outside the home. | 26 | ——— |
| Beginning or ceasing formal schooling. | 26 | ——— |
| Major change in living conditions (building home, remodeling, deterioration of home or neighborhood). | 25 | ——— |
| Revision of personal habits (dress, manners, associations). | 24 | ——— |
| Trouble with boss. | 23 | ——— |
| Major change in working hours or conditions. | 20 | ——— |
| Change in residence. | 20 | ——— |
| Change to a new school. | 20 | ——— |
| Major change in usual type and/or amount of recreation. | 19 | ——— |

| | | |
|---|---|---|
| Major change in church activities (attending more or less than usual). | 19 | _____ |
| Major change in social activities (clubs, dancing, movies, visiting). | 18 | _____ |
| Taking on a mortgage or loan of less than $10,000 (purchasing car, TV). | 17 | _____ |
| Major change in sleeping habits (more or less sleep, or change in time of sleep). | 16 | _____ |
| Major change in number of family get-togethers (more or fewer than usual). | 15 | _____ |
| Major change in eating habits (eating more or less food, change in meal hours or surroundings). | 15 | _____ |
| Vacation. | 13 | _____ |
| Christmas. | 12 | _____ |
| Minor violations of the law (traffic tickets, jaywalking). | 11 | _____ |
| TOTAL | | _____ |

EVALUATION:

These stressors are cumulative and can build to damaging proportions. Compare your total points with the following:

| Score: | You are: |
|---|---|
| Less than 150 | Considered safe. |
| 150– 199 | You have a 35 percent chance of moderately serious illness within the next two years. |
| 200– 299 | You have a 50–50 chance of illness within the next few months. |
| 300+ | You are in a high risk category with an 80–95 percent chance of a serious illness. |

(*Source:* T.H. Holmes and R.H. Rahe in the *Journal of Psychosomatic Research*, 1967.)

## ATTITUDE

|  | POINTS | SCORE |
|---|---|---|
| 1) The number of social contacts I actively maintain are: | | |
| a) 0 to 3. | −2 | |
| b) 4 to 6. | 0 | |
| c) 7 to 10. | 3 | |
| d) 11 or more. | 6 | _____ |
| 2) I consider myself to be: | | |
| a) Tense and impatient. | 1 | |
| b) Volatile but usually reasonable to others. | 2 | |

   c) Usually pleasant, rarely
      upset.                        3

   d) Expressive of my emotions
      in a tactful manner, usually
      calm and easygoing.       4        _____

3) The pace of life I set for
myself is:

   a) Very busy, always on the
      run.                      1

   b) Usually busy, oftentimes
      overbooked.            2

   c) Sometimes hectic, and I
      like it that way.       3

   d) Sometimes busy, but always
      at a pace that I enjoy.    4        _____

4) My enjoyment of art, crafts,
and music is:

   a) Very little.           1

   b) Sporadic.             2

   c) Sometimes.           3

   d) Often.               4        _____

5) I would consider my sense of
humor to be:

   a) What do you mean by
      "sense of humor"?     1

   b) Dull or rarely used.    2

   c) Strong but not used often.     3

   d) Sharp and frequently used.    4     _____

6) The following applies to my situation:

   a) There are several people I hate and I am going to get even with.    1

   b) People irritate me, but I can sometimes ignore them.    2

   c) I usually forgive and forget.    3

   d) I forgive easily and enjoy most people.    4     _____

7) My attitude toward myself would best be described as:

   a) I'm no good.    1

   b) I try but I just don't measure up.    2

   c) Most of the time I'm a pretty good person.    3

   d) I like myself and forgive myself easily.    4     _____

8) My goals in life are:

   a) Vague; no direction.    1

   b) Sometimes I think about that.    2

   c) General directions.    3

d) Specifically defined, realistic but challenging to achieve.                                    4        \_\_\_\_\_

9) I experience depression:

   a) Often and severely.                1
   b) Occasionally.                       2
   c) Sometimes.                          3
   d) Rarely.                             4        \_\_\_\_\_

10) When faced with emotions, I usually:

   a) Ignore them; adults don't cry.                                  1
   b) Wait until they build up and explode at someone.               2
   c) Express them most of the time.                              3
   d) Express them—cry it, write it, say it, but get it out in a tactful manner if possible.    4        \_\_\_\_\_

11) My opinion of life is:

   a) It stinks.                          1
   b) It's more trouble than it's worth.                               2
   c) Sometimes enjoy it.                 3
   d) Make the best of every situation, enjoying as much as possible.                          4        \_\_\_\_\_

12) My education level is:

   a) Elementary school.          1
   b) Some high school.           2
   c) College graduate.           3
   d) Graduate degree.            4        _____

13) My dreams are:

   a) Usually scarey.             1
   b) Violent and disruptive of
      my sleep.                   2
   c) Usually pleasant, some
      nightmares.                 3
   d) Usually entertaining and
      pleasant, few nightmares.   4        _____

14) My job is:

   a) Dull drudgery, unfulfilling.   −2
   b) Tedious with rare moments
      of gratification.              0
   c) Usually pleasant.              3
   d) Rewarding, challenging,
      satisfying.                    6     _____

15) My confidence level would
    best be described as:

   a) Very low.                   1
   b) Low, many fears.            2
   c) Moderate, some fears.       3

d) High, usually rational caution rather than fear.      4     _____

16) I would consider my relationship with my Creator to be:

a) What Creator?      1
b) Lukewarm.      2
c) Fairly strong.      3
d) Very close, on a daily
basis.      4     _____

17) With respect to a lifetime
mate:

a) I have none, nor anything
close.      1
b) I have a mate, but not a
close relationship.      2
c) My mate and I are fairly
close.      3
d) My mate and I are a
"mutual admiration soci-
ety."      4     _____

TOTAL     _____

## EVALUATION:

*Score:*     *You are:*

11–34     At high risk for psychogenic diseases and early death—revise your attitudes.

35–51     At moderate to low risk for mind-related ailments.

52–72    At low to very low risk for mind-related ailments and psychologically stand a good chance of living longer than normal.

## PHYSICAL ENVIRONMENT

|  | POINTS | SCORE |
|---|---|---|

1) I live:

a) In a downtown area of a big city.  1
b) Very close to a big city.  2
c) In the suburbs of a city.  3
d) In the remote countryside.  4  _____

2) My drinking water is:

a) City water with poor taste.  1
b) City water that is reported to be pure.  2
c) Bottled water.  3
d) Filtered and cleansed thoroughly through my own very effective water purifier.  4  _____

3) Nuclear power stations or nuclear waste treatment sites are:

a) Within 10 miles of where I
   live or work.                       1
b) Within 30 miles of where I
   live or work.                       2
c) Within 60 miles.                    3
d) Nowhere near.                       4          _____

4) The amount of canned food I
   consume is:

a) Considerable, daily.               1
b) Some on a daily basis.             2
c) Some on a weekly basis.            3
d) Very little, very rarely.          4          _____

5) Pesticides are sprayed:

a) Near my home on a regular
   basis.                             1
b) Near my home occasionally.         2
c) Near my home infrequently.         3
d) Nowhere near my home.              4          _____

6) I drive:

a) More than 1,000 miles each
   month and don't wear a seat
   belt.                              1
b) More than 1,000 miles each
   month and do wear a seat
   belt.                              2

c) Fewer than 1,000 miles
each month with a seat belt,
around town.                              3

d) Fewer than 1,000 miles
each month with a seat belt,
mostly on the highway.                    4          _____

7) My sunlight exposure would
best be described as:

a) Heavy doses on weekends
in the summer, am fair-
skinned.                                  1

b) Short periods daily throughout the summer, am fair-
skinned.                                  2

c) Short periods daily throughout the year, often with
sunscreen; am fair-skinned.               3

d) Short periods throughout
the year, with sunscreen;
am darker-skinned.                        4          _____

8) My exposure to major airport
flight patterns is:

a) Considerable; I live or work
in the flight pattern.                    1

b) Some; I live or work near
the flight pattern.                       2

c) A little; an airport is nearby.        3

d) Rare; I live in the country.           4          _____

9) My exposure to working or playing around heights (more than 10 feet) is:

   a) Considerable.     1
   b) Some.     2
   c) Some, with safety precautions taken.     3
   d) Very little, always with major safety precautions taken.     4     _____

10) I:

   a) Smoke tobacco products daily.     -4
   b) Work around heavy tobacco smoke.     -2
   c) Occasionally am around tobacco smoke.     0
   d) Am rarely in an enclosed area with tobacco smoke.     4     _____

11) The following products are found frequently in my home or workplace:

   a) Pesticides, exhaust fumes, plastics, formaldehyde, asbestos.     1
   b) Plastics, particle board, synthetic items.     2

   c) Some synthetics, mostly
      cotton, wool, leather, wood.     3

   d) Mostly cotton, wool,
      leather, wood, steel, glass,
      etc.     4      \_\_\_\_\_

**TOTAL**      \_\_\_\_\_

**EVALUATION:**

*Score:*    *You are:*

6–22     At high risk for a harmful physical environment.

23–33    At moderate to low risk for meeting accident or death from your environment.

34–44    At very low risk in this category.

## GENETIC ASSESSMENT

| | POINTS | SCORE |
|---|---|---|
| 1) Obesity is found in my close family (parents, grandparents, siblings): | | |
| a) Often: marked obesity. | 1 | |
| b) In some. | 2 | |
| c) In one or two. | 3 | |
| d) In none. | 4 | \_\_\_\_\_ |

2) Heart disease is found in my
   close family:

   a) More than twice.            1
   b) Once or twice.              2
   c) Only once.                  3
   d) Never.                      4        _____

3) High blood pressure is found
   in my close family:

   a) More than twice.            1
   b) Once or twice.              2
   c) Only once.                  3
   d) Never.                      4        _____

4) Cancer is found in my close
   family:

   a) More than twice.            1
   b) Once or twice.              2
   c) Only once.                  3
   d) Never.                      4        _____

5) Diabetes is found in my close
   family:

   a) More than twice.            1
   b) Once or twice.              2
   c) Only once.                  3
   d) Never.                      4        _____

6) The lifespan of parents, grandparents, uncles, and aunts
would be described as:

|   |   |   |
|---|---|---|
| a) None has lived past 60. | −4 | |
| b) Only a few have lived past 70. | 0 | |
| c) Many have lived past 70. | 3 | |
| d) Many have lived into their 80s. | 8 | _____ |

TOTAL _____

EVALUATION:

| Score: | You are: |
|--------|----------|
| 1–12 | At high risk genetically—you must make a sincere effort to optimize your lifestyle to counteract this. |
| 13–18 | At moderate to low risk for having your genetic background cause severe disease or early death. |
| 19–28 | At low to very low risk for genetically based diseases or early death. |

## BODY MAINTENANCE

| | POINTS | SCORE |
|---|---|---|

1) The best description of my feet
is:

a) Painful, have frequent trouble with them.     1
b) Have some trouble with them.     2
c) Very few problems; wear comfortable shoes and walk much.     3
d) No trouble; wear comfortable shoes and walk often.     4     _____

2) The best description of my back is:

a) Aching often; have had medical treatment.     1
b) Some discomfort.     2
c) Few problems; sit upright usually.     3
d) No problems; don't sit for long periods, and do exercises to keep back in shape.     4     _____

3) The best description of my teeth is:

a) Gone.     1
b) Mostly present, with numerous fillings.     2
c) Have some fillings or caps.     3
d) Have very few problems.     4     _____

4) My eyes would best be described as:

    a) Often tired and bloodshot; need corrective lenses.    1

    b) Sometimes strained; read often in marginal lighting.    2

    c) Fairly healthy.    3

    d) Healthy; I "sun" them and exercise them regularly and read only in proper lighting; I use sunglasses in glare situations.    4    _____

5) My gastro-intestinal tract would best be described as:

    a) A nuisance, frequent heartburn, indigestion, or constipation.    1

    b) Gives me some trouble.    2

    c) Fairly healthy.    3

    d) No trouble at all; regular soft bowel movements.    4    _____

6) My ears' exposure to noise is: (work or recreation)

    a) Considerable: no protection used.    1

    b) Considerable: some protection used.    2

    c) A little: no protection used.    3

d) Very little; protection worn
   when exposed to it.                    4          \_\_\_\_\_

TOTAL                                                \_\_\_\_\_

EVALUATION:

*Score:*    *You are:*

6–12        At high risk for having some or many bodily parts
            not working well in your old age.

13–18       At moderate to low risk for having missing or
            defective bodily parts in your old age.

19–24       At low to very low risk for having problems with
            your bodily parts in old age.

# WHAT ARE YOUR CHANCES OF LIVING TO 100?

On the following list, combine the scores you have received
from the various tests. Some are more important than others;
for that reason they are multiplied by a factor before entering
the final score. The scores of the stress and the body maintenance tests do not apply in this evaluation.

                                                     SCORE

1) Your score from the dietary evaluation.          \_\_\_\_\_

2) Your score from the physical fitness evaluation
   \_\_\_\_ . Multiply that number by 2, and enter.     \_\_\_\_\_

3) Your score from the attitude assessment. _____

4) Your score from the physical environment assessment. _____

5) Your score from the genetic assessment _____ Multiply that number by 2, and enter. _____

TOTAL _____

EVALUATION:

| Score: | Your Chances of Living Past the Normal Life-span are: |
|---|---|
| 296–324 | 90 percent or better |
| 268–295 | 80 percent |
| 240–267 | 70 percent |
| 212–239 | 60 percent |
| 184–211 | 50 percent |
| 156–183 | 40 percent |
| 128–155 | 30 percent |
| 100–127 | 20 percent |
| 72–99 | 10 percent |
| Less than 72 | 5 percent or less |

# 4

## Genetics

"I chose my parents wisely."
—BERTRAND RUSSELL

[• Comparing genetics to games of chance • The difference between nature and nurture • Is there a genetic predisposition for overweight? • How does aging occur? • The DNA blueprint and its part in aging • What are free radicals?]

Human genetics can be compared to games of chance. To see how genetics operates, take twenty-three sets of dice. On half of them mark the various physical and mental characteristics of your mother and her side of the family—color of hair and eyes, stature, weight tendencies, I.Q., tendency for allergies or diseases, and so on. Mark on the other half the physical and mental characteristics of your father and his side of the family.

Now toss them onto a table. The results may or may not

describe you or one of your brothers or sisters. If you kept tossing them, eventually you would get a rather accurate description of yourself. There are enough variables in genetics to make each person distinctly unique and different from every other person, even though some very strong traits may exist in all members of one family. By the law of averages, with the billions of possible combinations, it is unlikely that two exactly identical people have ever existed on earth. Each baby is unique, the result of a blueprint developed by chance, based upon the traits or characteristics of the parents.

There is nothing you can do to change your genes. If you have such health-related traits as overweight, tendency to alcoholism, high blood pressure, diabetes, or heart disease, you are stuck with them. However you do not have to consider yourself a victim of them. If you can become aware of the traits and characteristics you have inherited, you can plan to make the best of what you have been given.

Continuing the gambling analogy, think of your genes as cards dealt you in a game. The fact that you are alive and healthy enough to read this book indicates that you have at least decent cards, and possibly very good ones. You have already experienced the luck necessary in the game of life. Whether you can win with the cards you have been dealt depends upon your knowledge of these cards and your skill at playing them. Often a championship player with marginal cards can beat a novice with very good cards.

We propose to show you how to play your cards for the very best results, no matter what kind of hand you were dealt.

Think of your cards as your "nature." The way you play these cards is your "nurture." Nurture can improve on nature.

Some inherited traits, such as skin color and eye color, are firmly set. Others are more flexible. They may be considered as ranges or predispositions, which can be swayed for better or worse by your lifestyle.

We have pointed out earlier that one can develop an intelligence beyond that of the parents through ideal diet, education, and emotional stimulation. One other example that is visibly apparent is the taller stature developed by second-and-third generation orientals after exposure to western diets.

Disease resistance appears to be a relatively flexible genetic characteristic. Although cancer, diabetes, heart disease, and a number of other ailments have been shown to run in families, this does not mean that children of parents who have suffered one of these diseases will automatically be victims of the same. There is enough variability within genetics to give you a fighting chance.

It is advisable, however, for anyone with a family tendency toward heart disease to pay particular attention to our advice concerning that ailment. Those who have a family history of alcoholism should employ abstinence toward alcohol rather than the usual social moderation recommended. People with a family tendency toward overweight should be very cautious of a creeping waistline. By wisely being alert to these matters, you can direct your genetic tendencies in your favor.

CASE HISTORY: Dr. M.B. is a long-time friend of Dr. Philip Smith. They attended college together over sixty years ago. At that time, M.B. confided to Smith his concern about the lack of longevity in his family. M.B.'s father had died at the age of 46 of a massive coronary occlusion. Three others in his family—two uncles and a grandfather—had died before the age of 50. All had a tendency toward overweight and suffered from heart disease.

M.B. was a brilliant student, and his concern about longevity prompted him to pursue genetics for his undergraduate degree. He became convinced that, although his own genetic traits were marginal, they could be maximized to give him a longer and more productive life than his ancestors had enjoyed. He went on to medical school, specializing in internal medicine. Twelve years later, he became department chairman in a major medical school.

During the time M.B. was a student, there was little knowledge about the heart-disease risk factors that he had to beware of, so he formed his own postulates. They proved to be amazingly accurate. He took excellent care of himself, avoiding tobacco and alcohol products. He became a distance runner and a tennis player. He ate sparingly and kept his hands away from the salt shaker. He also reduced his consumption of fat to less than half what the average person eats.

Dr. M.B.'s keen insight and his staunch adherence to his program paid off well. Now almost 80, he has already outlived his ancestors by three decades. He still bikes many miles each day. He is alert, active, and happy—not just surviving.

The story of Dr. M.B. should offer hope and promise to those who see early death or fatal disease as an unavoidable family inheritance. Dr. M.B.'s research and effort proved beneficial to himself, but they also proved to be of great benefit to society. You should not think of your own pursuit of longevity as a selfish effort; by adding years to your life you are also increasing your potential for productivity and usefulness to others.

## Nature and Nurture

Science still has a great deal to learn about the influences that genes and environment exert on the individual. Much has already been revealed to us, but much more has yet to be uncovered. We do know that a child of normal-sized parents (i.e., not overweight) has only an eight percent chance of becoming an overweight adult. A child of one overweight parent and one normal-sized parent has a forty percent chance of being overweight. And a child of parents who are both overweight has an eighty percent chance of being overweight.

There does appear to be a genetic predisposition toward overweight in some families. However, it is not yet clear how much of that tendency is genetic and how much stems from nurture. In obese families, eating patterns may prove to be as much to blame as genetic cards. Too much food, the wrong kinds of food, speed-eating, or sedentary habits may be a part of child-rearing. There has long been a belief that a fat baby is a healthy baby, so parents sometimes tend to overfeed, not realizing that fat cells developed in childhood can make weight control as an adult extremely difficult.

It is important, then, to get to know your body, to discover what is your nature, those genetic cards you were born with, and to assess your past as well as your present environmental influences so that you can nurture those advantages you possess.

## How Does Aging Occur?

Imagine that you have built yourself a fine house that you are very proud of and want to keep in good repair. In order to do this you keep the original blueprints in a safe place. When something needs repair, you pull out the plans and check them to avoid making mistakes on your wiring, plumbing, rafters, whatever. However, with time, the original blueprints become faded and difficult to read. From time to time you may have a photocopy made, but each successive copy has less definition than the last. Eventually the plans become difficult to read; the original blueprints are gone; and it becomes impossible to avoid making mistakes in the repair and maintenance of your house.

This analogy describes what happens to your body in aging. Our bodies have blueprints for making repairs. At the center of the human cell is a long molecule that looks something like a spiral staircase, wrapped back and forth inside the cell nucleus. This is the DNA molecule; it is found within each cell in your body, and it contains the blueprints of your genetic code. All daily repair and new cell construction is done from the plans contained on the DNA blueprints. Eventually, the body builds and repairs with less efficiency; the exact time when this occurs depends upon each person's individual biological clockwork. When the blueprints are no longer copied with precision, problems with mind and body are compounded, and physical deterioration occurs.

No one has been able to halt the process of DNA blueprint deterioration. Nor have scientists discovered how to fix damaged DNA as yet. However there are some suggestions that can be made to slow it, by keeping the DNA blueprint as clear and as readable as possible.

To preserve the blueprint, the DNA molecule has to be protected from the destructive effects of something called "free radicals." Deterioration of DNA is caused by free radicals, which are incredibly reactive chemicals that possess an electrical charge from a free electron. (They have also been called the great white sharks of the biochemical sea of life.) They do not last very long in your body, but while they are there and operating they have an incredible ability to oxidize and destroy tissue.

A great deal has been learned about aging through the study of a rare disease known as progeria, a bizarre condition in which the biological clockwork goes awry, aging a person at ten or more times the normal rate. A child of six years old may look like a person of eighty or ninety, and is literally dying of old age.

What exactly are these free radicals and how do we recognize them? Technically, most free radicals appear in the form of a super-activated oxygen molecule with a free electron whirling about it. But that's somewhat technical for the average person to understand. Looking about you in your everyday life, you can see that iron and some other metals rust. They do this because oxygen can change the molecular structure of the metal, a process that is a mild form of free radical destruction. Similarly, the reason hydrogen peroxide is such an effective disinfectant is because it performs free radical destruction on bacteria.

Another example of free radicals can be seen in your kitchen. You may have two different kinds of cooking fats, one of which has to be refrigerated while the other can be left out in your cupboard. The latter, called saturated fats, are normally hard at room temperature and are almost invulnerable to free radicals such as oxygen. These are convenient for the grocer to sell and for you to store because they will not deteriorate. (These include naturally saturated fats such as lard and synthetically saturated fats such as hydrogenated vegetable oils.)

Unsaturated fats are very vulnerable to free radical destruction. This is why safflower and soybean oils will become rancid if left at room temperature too long. Refrigerating them will slow down the lipid rancidity, or deterioration, of the fats that results from free radical destruction.

To carry this concept to the human body, imagine a room stuffed with balloons that are filled with water. This would be a vastly enlarged three-dimensional picture of a tiny section of your body's tissue. Each balloon in this room represents a cell, the water inside each containing various organelles of cell function, and the balloon being the cell wall. (You have around sixty trillion cells in your body.) The walls of the cells are composed of molecules that are protein and unsaturated fat in nature. The unsaturated fats in the cell wall are vulnerable to the actions of free radicals, just like the rusting iron in the rain or the safflower oil left out on the kitchen counter.

When free radicals attack the cell wall (or balloon), the cell must repair itself or die. In the attack on the unsaturated fats by the free radicals, lipid peroxides—or "bad fats"—are produced. These bad fats decompose to form aldehydes, and the aldehydes can cause harm to proteins and DNA, as well as to the remaining unsaturated fats. These aldehydes are capable of rearranging the structure of proteins and DNA, crippling its ability to perform the needed repairs.

Once a cell is destroyed by free radical action, the products of decomposition may proceed to attack and destroy other cells and molecules. The cells' protection against free radicals exists in something called antioxidants, which the body produces through proper nutrition. Although free radical destruction seems to be an inevitable consequence of living, it can be slowed down by these antioxidants. Scientific data suggest that it can be slowed down considerably.

In death, the body no longer produces antioxidants, so the free radicals have free run of the body. It is their action that causes rigor mortis. By turning the unsaturated fats of the cells into saturated fats, the body becomes stiff very quickly, since saturated fats are hard at room temperature.

In the process of aging, the actions of the aldehydes produced in free radical destruction are significant. Through what is called "cross-linkage," the aldehydes rearrange the cell structure so that the cell cannot function properly or repair itself because of the damaged DNA. The result, ultimately, is the sagging skin, dull mind, and poor digestion of old age.

As aging progresses through free radical destruction of DNA, many things happen. Errors in the growth and repair of tissue occur with increasing frequency. The skin becomes less resilient. It takes longer to get adjusted to waking up in the morning. Bruises, cuts, and breaks heal more slowly. The functioning of the mind becomes foggy. Digestion and absorption are not as efficient as they once were.

In normal people these signs and symptoms begin after age thirty and accelerate after age fifty. It is possible to defy the norm and delay these processes by several decades. Your resistance to free radical destruction depends on your body's internal chemical environment—as maintained by your genetic code, nutrition, exercise, and attitude—combined with those things you expose your body to in the physical environment—such as radiation or cigarette smoke or smog—and taking into consideration the impurities in your food—such as nitrates and ethylene dibromide (EDB).

But this all begins with your genetic cards. The time may come when doctors and scientists can exchange a few of the cards you were dealt. The science of genetics has been on an ever accelerating pace since the 1970s, when the technique of gene-splicing was introduced. Genetic engineers are now able to reach inside the cell's DNA, remove a section, and implant it into the DNA of another cell. Geneticists have found the area on the gene's blueprint in humans that makes insulin, have removed it, and—by placing it in a rapidly productive tiny organism—have been able to make bacteria manufacture human insulin, an essential substance for diabetics.

Gene mapping and electron microscopes have given scientists the ability to take a few of your cells and determine what genetic diseases you may be carrying. Through this process, they can tell you if Tay-Sachs disease, sickle cell anemia, cystic fibrosis, or other genetic disorders may occur in your family, thereby helping to prevent the heartache of giving birth to an afflicted child.

We do not recommend, however, that you sit and wait for genetic scientists to make the discoveries that will resolve your health problems. You will be further ahead in the game if you begin now to set your life on a healthy course. Do your own bit of genetic research by looking around at your immediate family members, your parents and their parents. From these genetically similar people, you can gather a reasonable idea of the advantages and disadvantages that exist in your genetic cards. If there are any diseases that appear more than once in your immediate family, make note of them. There are also very likely to be advantages—perhaps longevity or intelligence—in your genetic inheritance as well. Make note of them too.

Consider both advantages and disadvantages as you plan your strategy to take charge of your life and lifestyle.

---

**R$_X$**

- Carefully scrutinize your family members for their genetic traits—physical, intellectual, emotional, disease resistance, and longevity. Based upon this, draw up a list of genetic pitfalls you intend to avoid through the prescriptions that are provided in the following chapters.

- Do not become overly confident or pessimistic from your appraisal of your genetic inheritance. You must consider these as general guidelines and not guaranteed traits. Your lifestyle will affect your genetic parameters in a positive or negative direction.

# 5
## Attitude

"A man is not old until regrets take the place of dreams."
—JOHN BARRYMORE

[• The relationship between mind and body • Behavior, health, and disease • How stress increases susceptibility to disease • Altruistic egotism—treating yourself and others with love and respect • The racehorse vs. the turtle— finding your own pace • What emotional burdens are you carrying? • The importance of social contacts • Are you fulfilling a poor self-image? • The right brain and the left brain—encouraging your full potential • The effects of artificial illumination and color • What is the right sleep pattern for you? • The importance of setting goals and achieving goals]

W hy do some people find exercise stimulating and enjoyable while others loathe the idea of physical activity? Why do some people overeat or choose the wrong foods even though they know better? Why do some people knowingly abuse or neglect their bodies? What is the all-important key in your program for improving your chances of living a long and productive life?

The answer to all these questions exists in one word— attitude.

There is a close relationship between mind and body. Philosophers, theologians, scientists, physicians, and others have long attempted to define the spark of life that lies within the human being, calling it variously "psyche," "ego," "soul," "subconscious," or one of many other names. Whatever one chooses to call it, there is undeniably an energy within human beings that has an awesome potential.

If an individual's energy is encouraged and nourished, that person is likely to be healthy, happy, and long-lived. An individual whose energy is stunted, maligned, and discouraged will have a difficult time finding ideal health, developing creative talents, being happy, and living to a robust old age.

Studies have discovered that most of those who have lived beyond the average 75-year lifespan are people who are happy and positive in nature. In societies where people commonly live to ages of eighty or ninety, it is traditional to venerate and pay tribute to the aged for their accumulated knowledge and wisdom. These elders work hard, play often, and enjoy their people's festive celebrations with gusto.

Conversely, where older people are not cherished or respected, the mortality rate increases. It is common in our society for older citizens not to survive long after such difficult events as retirement from work or loss of a spouse. After these stressful events, the feeling of usefulness seems to pass. We have all heard people speak of such cases, saying "He (or she) simply lost the will to live."

The remarkable powers of hypnosis, of meditation in eastern

religions, and of miracle cures in Christianity have long been documented. The Christian Bible, the Hindu Bhagavad Gita, the Buddhist Dhammapada, and the Moslem Koran all make references to the relationship between spiritual and physical health. The mystical eastern cults have shown the mind's ability to control the heartbeat, tolerate pain, affect breathing, and accomplish other phenomenal physical "miracles." Even the old country doctor believed in the effectiveness of prescribing a placebo for ailments he could not otherwise treat.

It is only in recent years that mental attitude has come under scientific scrutiny, however, and with each passing year of research its role in health and longevity is becoming more focused. Biofeedback techniques have documented the connection between mind and body; and there have been several excellent studies indicating that certain personality types have an inclination toward heart disease (notably the hard-driving, impatient, and intense personalities), while others seem to be at a higher risk for cancer.

Dr. Hans Selye, Canadian physician and pioneer researcher of stress theories, has done much to document biological responses to the mind's postive and negative attitudes. In 1974, Drs. Friedman and Rosenman published the book *Type A Behavior and Your Heart*, providing scientific evidence that cardiovascular ailments could be encouraged or discouraged by attitude. A layman—editor and writer Norman Cousins— has provided accounts of personal illnesses, detailing the interaction of his mind, emotions, and body in the healing process.

In the first of his books on the subject, *Anatomy of an Illness*, Cousins reported on his experience with an untreatable collagen disease. He set himself on a program to alter his lifestyle and outlook on life, a program that included spending an hour each day laughing at his favorite comedy team on film. In time, his untreatable condition disappeared. Later, after experiencing a heart attack, Cousins wrote about his mental and emotional responses in *The Healing Heart*, pointing out the dangers of the panic and fear that engulfed him. Indeed, the fear and resultant biochemical changes that take place from the body's production of the stress hormones are the greatest risk in heart attacks, because they seriously overload an ailing heart.

The introduction to *The Healing Heart* was written by Dr. Bernard Lown of Harvard University, a renowned cardiologist. In it he recounts two interesting cases of his own, in both of which the patients were influenced by overheard comments. In one a dying man misunderstood a reference to his heart having a "wholesome gallop," which is indicative of a failing heart; he took it as encouragement and recovered. In another, a woman with only a mild heart condition misunderstood a chance remark by someone other than Dr. Lown, interpreted it negatively, and died.

It may be possible for the mind to write a prescription for almost anything the body needs. There is some indication that the concept of the mind as apothecary may be more than theory. The human mind produces substances called "endorphins" that have pain-killing and euphoric abilities. Produced through extensive exercise, after childbirth, during meditation, and by means of other stimulation, endorphins are incredibly effective at sedating pain and producing a natural "high."

In many—if not all—situations in life, it is not what is happening that counts, but how you perceive it. And how you perceive yourself and others. The human mind is truly the last frontier. Your brain, less than two quarts of gelatinous gray matter within your skull, is an incredible organ, whose potential has only begun to be realized.

## Stress

In recent years, it has been fashionable for people to blame all their physical woes on their "stress level." There is considerable misunderstanding of stress; it is not entirely a negative condition. By definition in kinetics, stress is a force exerted by one body part against another. In psychology, it is a condition that causes tension in body, mind, or both.

We wish to make a semantic differentiation between "stress" and "distress." Stress is not necessarily a bad thing; in many ways it is good. It is vital to the wondrous accomplishments that set mankind apart from the rest of the animal kingdom. Stress forces you to make plans for tomorrow; it gives you a reason to get up in the morning; and it provides the impetus to make your life productive.

On the other hand, distress is excessive—or harmful—stress. Dr. Hans Selye compared stress to a violin string. Only when the string is tightened to a precise degree does it produce a beautiful melodious sound. When the string is limp, without enough tension, the sound is either dull or nonexistent. When it is tightened beyond its ideal tension point, it produces shrill sounds or it breaks.

This is precisely what happens with stress and your mind and body. The correct degree of stress keeps you productive and happy with your accomplishments and goals. Not enough leaves you listless and useless. Too much can break you.

Stress and distress are significant factors in the way humans have had to adapt to modern society. Nature designed our bodily system with stress hormones, called catecholamines, which include epinephrine, dopamine, and norepinephrine. These give us what is called a "flight or fight" reaction to stress. This system was designed to be used only occasionally and for brief periods of time. When the reaction is set off, changes occur in blood pressure, pulse rate, blood sugar, and blood fat, which create a serious burden on the circulatory system.

It worked very well for the caveman. When he saw a predatory animal, his brain signaled alarm to his entire body. Only a split second passed before the chemical changes occurred, preparing him to fight the predator or to turn and run. It is possible to see the effects of this same system in other animals. When confronted with danger, dogs and cats react with the hair on their backs standing up as if charged with electricity, which presents a larger, more formidable appearance to their foes. The "goose pimples" we get in reaction to stress, cold, or fear are vestiges of the same process. They occur in response to the stress hormones, as does the urge—in extreme fright— to void ourselves of urine and feces, a reaction that rids us of anything that might slow us down in escaping. As a part of this, the male's genitals will contract close to the body so that there will be less obstruction in running.

A racing heart, an elevated blood pressure, rushes of insulin, and the resulting availability of fuel to burn were all essential for the caveman.

The problem is that these same chemicals flow through the human system at great frequency in modern life, unless they are checked by some means. We are no longer cavemen but office workers, who feel stifled by our sedentary lives, or are pushed too hard for decisions, or feel afraid of our bosses or our environment. These mental states, along with many others—such as the loss of a loved one or a conflict between conscience and practicality—can create the catecholamines that were meant to protect us from physical threats. On rare occasions, the stress hormones may perform their original purpose as vital survival tools, but flowing too often through our systems they become silent killers.

In one of his early studies in the field of stress, Dr. Selye tied rats to a laboratory table so they could not move, then measured the biochemical changes that took place in them. He found that the stress hormones affected their stomach secretions so severely that the rats developed ulcers within 24 hours. There is some comparison between the restricted rats and our modern confined workday lives.

Having successfully measured the biological result of distress, Dr. Selye saw a need for philosophical and psychological remedies to the problem. He found one solution in exercise. In an experiment using two groups of rats, he subjected one group to electrical shocks, flashing lights, and loud noises to prevent them from sleeping. He did the same with the other group, but prepared them first with a thorough conditioning program on a treadmill, getting them exercised into good physical shape, and allowing them to run the treadmill between torture sessions.

The first group of rats developed definite stress symptoms and soon died. The second group, amazingly, did not. Dr. Selye concluded that exercise is an essential survival tool for modern humans, subjected to a world filled with stress.

## Altruistic Egotism

Dr. Selye also developed some impressive theories about lifestyles that can help to avoid distress. One very important theory involved the concept of the "altruistic egotist." These two terms may have opposite meanings, but when joined together they help us adapt to the complexity of modern life. The dictionary defines altruism as "unselfish concern for the welfare of others," while egotism (or egoism) is defined as "self-centered, only interested in one's own good."

The pure altruist is a rather saintly person, perhaps highly impractical in the congested, impersonal environment of the modern urbanite. The egotist looks out for number one. He may be able to survive the impersonal world, but without friends or love to nurture him. Today's survivor must be hybridized between the two opposing persons, and it is a hybrid that must be delicately balanced. This concept has a basis in most of the religions of the world, but it is best summed up in the Biblical quotation, "Love thy neighbor as thyself."

Others have done research in this field and have added considerable understanding to the subject. Dr. George Vaillant, a psychiatrist, directed a forty-year study of Harvard graduates, which revealed that altruism was one of the principal qualities that assisted even the most poorly adjusted men to deal successfully with the stresses of life. Dr. Linda Nilson, a sociologist at the University of California at Los Angeles, studied over one hundred disasters to examine the altruistic tendencies among the disaster victims. She found that, though these people's lives had been seriously disrupted, they almost invariably assisted their neighbors who were suffering with them.

Many of us can identify with this. Victims of blizzards, floods, earthquakes, and blackouts can recall from their own experience. The Chicago blizzard of 1967 and the great New York blackout proved that, even in the most impersonal urban area, people could band together for survival. Dr. Nilson interpreted that the victims of these disasters were thrust back to a primitive tribal cohesiveness, when it was instinctive to band together for the common good, knowing that one's survival was allied to the survival of all. Perhaps most significant, Dr. Nilson also found that the survivors reported experiencing an exhilarating sense of well-being with themselves and their neighbors.

There have been studies of self-centeredness and loneliness as well. Dr. Dean Ornish, author of *Stress, Diet and Your Heart*, has found that self-centeredness creates a sense of isolation, and isolation breeds loneliness, which in turn kills. James Lynch, Ph.D., a researcher in psychosomatic medicine at the University of Maryland School of Medicine and author of *The Broken Heart*, has shown that lonely people—those who are divorced, widowed, or elderly—are much more likely to die from heart disease than are other people.

All of these efforts are carrying us closer to proving Dr. Selye's theory, and giving us insight into the sociological and psychological aspects of our physical health. For our survival we must learn to care for our neighbors and for ourselves on an equal basis. By helping others we can improve our own view of ourselves. This has been confirmed by a study conducted by Dr. Lowell Levin of Yale University and by another done by the California Department of Mental Health, which found that people cared for themselves more when they had a high self-esteem and a high regard for others.

It is entirely dependent on attitude. Life is a team sport. The only way one can survive is for all to survive. It is similar to a mother and child: the mother cannot effectively nurse a baby if she is not herself in good health, well-fed, and rested. And it is important to take care of others without waiting for immediate gratification, without saying, "What do I get out of this?" If you give only to get, you have negated the potential benefits of altruism. Help others for the sheer joy of it. You will reap as you sow.

## The Racehorse vs. the Turtle

Another of Dr. Selye's important theories concerns the means by which one assesses one's proper place in life. Are you a racehorse or a turtle? In his studies, Dr. Selye found that many people suffered distress because they were living at a pace that did not fit with their natures. Some were "racehorses" operating on a slow schedule; others were "turtles" trying to function at a fast schedule. Both suffered ill effects.

Dr. Selye's theory postulates that we each have an internal pace that is a combination of our nature and our nurture. We are born with a tendency to take life either fast or slow, and this is altered to some degree by our upbringing. He believes that we should live our lives according to this internal pace, neither faster nor slower. Some of us—the racehorses—should stay busy with only occasional rests amidst our crammed schedules. Others—the turtles—should not be forced to do this. Those of us who are turtles should be allowed to follow an unhurried pace through life.

"Go with the flow" is an apt motto.

* * *

CASE HISTORY: C.B. was a competent attorney, but her health was growing increasingly undependable. When we talked with her one night after a nutrition lecture at La Costa, we learned that she was actually artistic by nature. Her true loves in life were sculpting and watercolor painting.

We asked her why she did not pursue these talents rather than law, and she confessed that it had been her father who had wanted her to pursue a legal career.

She was not happy with the hectic pace of her life. Her days seemed to be an endless stream of hassles and arguments, which were distressful to her. As a child she had been easygoing and adaptable; the pace of her legal career went against her nature.

Living a pace that was alien to her internal clockwork—doing what she did not like and not doing what she loved—made C.B. frequently tired, overweight, often sick, and sometimes very ill. She was a turtle trying to be a racehorse, and this was taking its toll on her health and her enjoyment of life.

We have a favorite axiom: "Find something you would do for free, then find a way to be paid to do it." We suggested this to C.B., and she listened.

Two years later we received a letter from her, along with a photo of her, her new husband, and her new baby. She appeared to have lost twenty-five pounds and had a happy smile that surely could have lit up her hometown. She had given up her law practice. She wasn't getting rich from the sale of her artwork, but she was happier than she had ever imagined was possible.

## Emotional Burdens

Many of us allow our feelings to lie suppressed inside, unable or unwilling to express them because of societal pressures. It is important to find ways to release our emotions. There is a parable that illustrates this.

Two monks were walking down a country road and came to a flooded area. On the other side was a young woman pondering how to get across without soiling her clothes.

Without hesitation, one of the monks crossed the muddy waters, picked up the young woman, and carried her across.

After the two monks had gone on their way in silence for several miles, the other monk finally exploded. "You know our rules about contact with women! How could you carry that young woman?"

The first monk looked at him calmly and replied, "I only carried her across the puddle. You have been carrying her for the last two miles."

Who—or what—are you carrying? Do you take on all the problems of parents, children, siblings, or neighbors, even though there is nothing you can do about their situations? Do you hold grudges or resentments? Do you hold anger or hatred secretly and silently inside?

These are all heavy burdens, and unless you can release them they can do you harm.

CASE HISTORY: R.W. had aged considerably in the three years since we had last seen him at La Costa. Although he was less than fifty years old, he complained of various symptoms of aging. He confessed that he had been sick often in the past two years with flu, pneumonia, peptic ulcer, and other afflictions. His diet was "normal" (which is slightly better than atrocious), and he exercised minimally.

On the second day of this stay at La Costa, R.W. met Dr. Smith on the golf course, and they played together. As the afternoon sun caressed the greens, Dr. Smith learned R.W.'s woeful story. Some years before, he had entered into a handshake business venture with an old college friend. Their first few years had been grueling, but their persistence had eventually paid off with a comfortable income. Then trouble had crept in. R.W.'s partner had slowly been stealing the business, as well as R.W.'s wife. Unwilling to admit that a decade of sixteen-hour workdays had been wasted, he still went to his office and endured in silence. But his mind was occupied with feelings of hurt and loneliness, and a desire for revenge.

He lacked the confidence to believe he could do anything else, and he vacillated between thoughts of killing his partner and his ex-wife and killing himself. Of course neither of these acts of vengeance would solve his problems. Short of an expensive—and probably unsuccessful—lawsuit, there seemed to be nothing he could do to salvage his long, hard work.

By his own admission, R.W.'s marriage had always been a superficial relationship. Dr. Smith recommended a clean break, with total forgiveness for both the partner and the ex-wife. After some discussion, R.W. agreed to take the advice, feeling he had nothing to lose.

R.W. moved to another city and began a new business. His talent for business returned with renewed vigor, and he prospered financially beyond his highest goals. He met and married a woman who had two children from an earlier marriage, and this newfound family gave him great pleasure. He improved his diet and exercise, following the routines he had learned at La Costa.

The next time Dr. Smith saw R.W. four years later, he looked fifteen years younger.

Distress, hate, loss of confidence, loneliness, vengefulness, and hoplessness were among the intangibles that had been destroying R.W.'s mind and body. His change in attitude allowed him to realize that, and he was able to again perform at peak capacity.

## Social Contacts

Of the various psychological parameters that influence longevity, one has been well documented—social contacts. Loners die sooner than people who have close ties with others. A large-scale study conducted in the San Francisco area has revealed this very clearly. Over a long period of time, the researchers followed the lifestyles and social connections of thousands of people. As a result, they were able to document an extraordinary relationship between number of social contacts—friends, family, and pets—and longevity. The loners died early, while those with regular companionship lived much longer.

It is easy to become socially isolated in today's society. After retirement, many people move to a distant location away from family and old friends and have difficulty establishing new relationships. The same is true of some elderly people after their old friends die; they cannot bear to form new friendships that might end in the same heartache.

Even when you are absorbed in your own affairs, it is

important to maintain lively social contacts. When you are feeling depressed, or if you are overly shy, endeavor not to hide from others. Maintain an extensive support group of friends, family, and pets. They help you to live longer, and you help them.

## Self-Image

In the early 1960s, Dr. Maxwell Maltz introduced some startling facets of the human mind in his book, *Psycho-Cybernetics*. His work in plastic surgery had revealed to him that people who had minor cosmetic defects considered their problems to be enormous, and as a result acted truly as if they were ugly. He also found that some people who were quite attractive physically maintained a self-image of ugliness.

He proceeded to investigate other personality types and discovered that people tended to fulfill their self-images—whether smart, brave, stupid, timid, or whatever. Some people with great talent or potential may develop—through parental or peer abuse—a self-image of being "lowlife" at a young age, then spend the rest of their lives proving this to be true.

It is possible to change your self-image. If your self-image can be improved—and it can—then your outer problems can be resolved quickly. Studies have shown that many people who are obese, anorectic, or bulimic have disturbed self-images. Before they can adjust their weight to its proper level, it is necessary for them to envision themselves as thinner, heavier, or healthier.

Ask yourself what you want to be, then try to visualize yourself as that—happy, lithe, intelligent, brave, wealthy, or whatever. If you can truly believe in the self you envision, you have an excellent chance of making that self-image a reality. To change a poor self-image takes time, just as breaking any other bad habit does, but it is worth it. People with a positive self-image are generally happier, more productive, and longer-lived than their selfdestructive peers, for they take care of themselves beter than do those with a negative self-image.

## Powers of Mind
### Right Brain, Left Brain

The human brain is divided into two parts. There has been considerable study in recent years directed toward the functioning of the two halves—right brain and left brain. (See Figure 5.1.) Each performs distinctly different functions. The left side is the rational, logical, intellectual side, controlling your capacities for logic, mathematics, science, language, and writing. Western society has placed great emphasis on the development of the left-brain activities. The right side is the aesthetic and creative side, dealing with the appreciation of arts, music, dance, and nature. Far too many of us neglect the development of our right brain.

Infants and young children are permitted, even encouraged, to develop both sides equally. The left side is developed through learning to speak, to work puzzles, and to read and write. The right side is encouraged through allowing them to play, to fantasize, and to create with sand, clay, paper, and crayons.

But after a few years, right-brain activity is discouraged among a high percentage of the population, because of the misconception that it is a waste of time. However, this asym-

## FIGURE 5.1
## LEFT AND RIGHT FUNCTIONS OF THE BRAIN

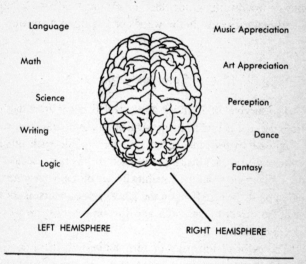

Language

Music Appreciation

Math

Art Appreciation

Science

Perception

Writing

Dance

Logic

Fantasy

LEFT HEMISPHERE                RIGHT HEMISPHERE

metrical development can lead to problems in learning, behavior, health, and ultimately in the length of life. It is mentally comparable to physically tying one of your legs behind you at a young age and telling you that you must move about with only one. Of course you would eventually adapt to using only one leg, and that limb would become highly developed. But your development would have been asymmetrical. If after a number of years the second leg were freed, it would require a great effort to develop it to the degree of the other, and you would probably forever have an uncoordinated walk.

There is evidence to suggest that truly happy people are

well developed in both hemispheres of the brain. They don't all paint or sculpt or play musical instruments, but they have some way of enjoying nature and being creative. For some it may be woodworking, for others crocheting, and for still others merely taking walks in the woods or fishing in a stream.

## Color and Light

The survival of all living things is dependent upon the light from the sun. A bird's navigational ability to migrate thousands of miles is dependent on the sun. Bees guide each other to nectar by using it. Bears know when to hibernate because of the sun's angle. And the breeding cycles of many creatures are based on the sun's effect on the pineal gland, which is located near the center of the brain and encourages or depresses the sex hormones.

The color of light and of surroundings is also important. Zoo biologists have discovered that it is important for them to reproduce the native environmental colors in order for captive animals to breed.

As humans, we may prefer to believe we are not as affected by these instinctive responses as are the lower animals, but we are no different. We have pineal glands, and we need at least some exposure to sunlight each day. Sunlight on human skin allows us to make our own vitamin D. Though there are considerable advantages to artificial light, it is not quite the same as sunlight, which is composed of many colors and wavelengths. Artificial lighting—especially fluorescent—does not possess all of the colors that are involved in making the pure white light of the sun.

The colors missing from artificial illumination affect the pineal gland and the brain as well. According to Dr. John Ott, a photobiologist who has researched the subject of malillumination, inadequate exposure to pure white light can create serious behavioral problems. In one ninety-day study at an experimental elementary school, time-lapse photography was used to record the effects on students when full-spectrum light was introduced. It was visibly clear that there was a significant reduction in hyperactivity among some of the students. One child improved dramatically, gaining a full year in his reading skills during the ninetyday period of the study.

Dr. Ott's photobiology experiments have also found that certain colors have the ability to excite humans, while others sedate. Several correctional institutions—including the Santa Clara County Jail, San Jose, California; the San Bernardino County Probation Department's Youth Center; and the Veteran's Administration Medical Center in Los Angeles—have tried the color theories he has developed with impressive results. In March 1979, the United States Naval Correctional Center in Seattle, Washington, tested Dr. Ott's theories. They had one cell that seemed to be plagued with continual violent behavior; as the initial holding tank, it was the major trouble spot in the center. After painting the cell pink, they recorded 156 days with no outbreaks of erratic or hostile behavior by the inmates.

It is important for you to consider the kinds of light and color that surround you in your daily life. It does have its effect upon you. Do you spend much of your time in fluorescent lighting, surrounded by drab gray walls? Do your surroundings stimulate or depress you? Do you find yourself longing for blue sky and sunlight? If so, you need to do something to alter the light and color of your surroundings.

R
 X

- Allow yourself full-spectrum lighting for as much of the day as possible. This can be indirect sunlight or fullspectrum interior lighting.

- Allow yourself fifteen to thirty minutes of sunlight exposure on your skin each day, unless your physician recommends against it.

- For one hour each day remove your glasses or sunglasses to enable the eyes (and thus the pineal gland) to absorb the full spectrum of indirect sunlight.

- Be aware of the colors around you and of their influence on your behavior, health, and moods. If you can alter the colors of your surroundings, choose colors that will enhance your attitude and your health.

## Sleep and Rest

The need for sleep is universal among animals. Sleep recharges the mind and body. However, the amount and frequency of sleep needed may vary with different people. Some are polyphasic and do not need a long evening of sleep, but require several short naps throughout a 24-hour period. Thomas Edison was of this type, and he frequently found that breakthroughs on his inventions would follow a short nap. Most people are monophasic and require one long rest, usually at night. Some can adapt their patterns to sleep either days or nights; others find this impossible.

You have probably gone without sleep on some occasion,

so you may be aware of the effects of lack of sleep. For the sake of health and longevity, it is important for you to get adequate sleep and rest. Inadequate sleep over long periods of time can cause mental and physical problems. At the very least it will cause alterations in your attitude. For example, a disc jockey, who was attempting to break the world record for sleeplessness, managed to go for a week before the depression and hallucinations became unbearable. For six months afterward, he suffered from severe depression. During the Korean War, the morale of prisoners was broken down by keeping them awake before brainwashing.

Do you give your mind and body adequate sleep and rest? Do you have problems sleeping? If so, do you know the cause, and can you remedy it?

Lack of sleep affects your attitude and your health. Proper sleep improves your resistance to disease and assists in the recuperation from injuries.

Do you find you need rest during the day when you cannot possibly take a nap? If so, there is a short exercise that will take only five or ten minutes, by which you can refresh yourself. All it requires is a comfortable chair and a quiet, darkened room. Sit down, close your eyes, and envision your entire body relaxing—one part at a time. When you feel all your muscles have become limp, focus your mind on a pleasant place you have visited. Try to recall the smells, the colors, the sun, the breeze—whatever the sensory experience was—right down to the minute detail. After a few minutes, allow yourself to come out of the concentration. You will find yourself refreshed and ready to face the world again.

R x

- Make sure you have a comfortable mattress for sleeping.

- Go to sleep with pleasant thoughts.

- Do not drink just before going to bed. Alcohol affects your sleeping and breathing patterns.

- Do not eat much just before bed. A full stomach can bother sleeping.

- Avoid sleeping in excessive cold or heat.

- Avoid sleeping in tight clothes.

- Avoid sleeping in noisy surroundings.

## Faith

There is a common thread running through the numerous and diverse peoples of the world; virtually all have a religion that emphasizes that a close relationship with God is essential for a productive and happy life. A belief in a Creator is important for good mental and physical health. It helps you to place yourself in proper perspective with nature and with your neighbors. Perhaps it also permits you to believe in miracles. Certainly it enables you to believe in the miracle of life.

Consider the miracle of your body—sixty trillion cells working in harmony, yet each specializing: a heart muscle that will pump 55 million gallons of blood in a lifetime; a vascular network long enough to encircle the earth two and a half times; a brain that can outperform the most advanced computer. Consider nature—plants that perform chemical miracles in capturing the sun's energy to form food energy; small and seemingly fragile ocean creatures that can survive underwater pressures that would crush strong construction materials; birds that know how to migrate great distances, flying in complex aeronautical formations.

The belief that these things are not merely accidental, that there is some purpose in the universe, and that one is a part of it produces faith in life; and faith in life is all-important in the desire to go on living. While we do not wish to advocate one religion or belief over another, we do say that a belief is important to your health, and that it is important for you to have a means of communicating with your Creator on a daily basis. It is irreplaceable as a means of improving and maintaining a positive attitude.

Victor Frankl, a world-renowned psychotherapist and a survivor of a Nazi concentration camp, has spoken of humans as being "created with a God-shaped void." Fill that void for a more exuberant and lengthy life.

## Goals

Many people today suffer boredom and depression from lack of purpose. Without direction, they suffer both mentally and physically. It is helpful for people to know where they have been in life, and it is important to know where they are, but it is critical for people to know where they are going. A good, positive attitude in life is difficult, if not impossible, without some direction.

It is necessary to have a goal in order to reach a goal; it is necessary to have a direction to get where you want to go. Yet many people say they want something without actually setting goals. One would not set out on a lengthy automobile trip without taking along a map, nor would one go to a train or airline terminal and say, "Give me a ticket," without stating a destination. It is necessary to be specific in order to get whatever one wants.

Spend some time thinking about what you want out of life. Psychologists have suggested that writing down your goals every six months or so can be very helpful. By setting down your goals tangibly, you set in motion the mechanisms for achieving them. Your subconscious will help you to gather the energy and means for fulfillment.

To do this, divide your goals under several main headings, such as "emotional objectives," "tangible objectives," "intangibles," and so on. Be realistic in what you set, but don't hold back; be generous to yourself. Try to envision what you want your life to be like within six months, and consider all its aspects to include in your listing. As you go to bed each night, read over your list as though these goals have already been realized. And always be prepared to set new goals, once these are achieved.

## The Mind and Disease

Your mind plays an important role in the prevention of disease, and in your ability to recover when you become ill. This is true both of degenerative diseases and of infectious diseases. Through your attitude you can increase your immunity to a great many ailments, or—conversely—you can cause yourself to become much more susceptible to them.

It is no coincidence that many of the great epidemics have

occurred during or just after wartime. War creates psycholog-ical distress, which lowers disease resistance. When the psy-chological sufferers are exposed to germs and viruses, disease becomes widespread, whether it be the bubonic plague as in 1347, when there was a major war in Europe, or the influenza epidemic in 1918, at the end of World War I.

Have you ever noticed that you seem to catch a cold or the flu or some other ailment during or after a major crisis in your life? There is a physical as well as a mental reason for this.

Saliva contains various factors that help us to resist disease; they are called immunoglobins. Studies have shown that the levels of the immunoglobins in saliva vary with changes in our moods. When we are unhappy or depressed, we have a lower output of these substances. The same is true when we are under severe stress. With lower levels of immunoglobins, we are more susceptible to disease.

Maintaining a good and positive attitude toward life is the first step toward good health—and through it toward living a longer life.

---

**R<sub>X</sub>**

- *Live*. Get involved in life and people. Find work that you enjoy. Experience sunsets, flowers, food, people, and the other joys of a positive attitude.

- *Love*. Avoid hate and revenge. Encourage, help, and love other people. By loving others, you neutralize your own problems in life. Give thanks for what you have.

- *Laugh*. Humor gives you a balancing stick to walk the tightrope of life. Enjoy yourself and others.

continued

- *Learn*. Take a class. Read a book. Join a study club. Learning gives vigor to the mind and thus to the body. Learning enables you to look forward to the future, and looking forward to the future is a vital key to a youthful mind.

## ❦❦ 6 ❦❦

# Exercise

"You've reached middle age when all you exercise is caution."
—FRANKLIN P. JONES

[• Move it to lose it • How you have been conditioned not
to exercise • Exercise and aging—dis-ease is a result of dis-
use • Why exercise is the most practical and effective
longevity aid • Exercise and illness • Choosing an exercise
program for your needs • The four phases of an exercise
program—warm-up, strength, endurance, cool-down • Getting started on your exercise program • Determining your
level of fitness • Stretching exercises • Strength and toning
exercises • Face and neck exercises • The "I-don't-have-time-
for-exercise" program]

Use it or lose it!" That is what biologists have told us for
years, referring not only to muscles, but to intellect, sexual
activity, and other bodily functions as well. If not regularly
used, any part of your body can atrophy.

For effective weight loss, a slogan that is now becoming

popular is: "Move it or lose it!" And with good reason. Without exercise, dieting can actually be counter productive, because the dieter is likely to lose lean tissue through the calorie restrictions, and then gain fat tissue after returning to a "normal" diet. Weight reduction without exercise can be compared to an ocean voyage without a boat—you aren't going to get very far.

Humans evolved from highly active animals. Even our recent ancestors lived lives of constant movement and manual labor. However, as we have developed more and more technology to perform our work for us, we have become increasingly sedentary—and increasingly obese. The only other creatures on earth who experience obesity are the pets we keep over fed and under-active. Our sedentary lifestyle disrupts many of the normal functions of the body, increasing the likelihood of obesity, serious illness, poor mental functioning, and shorter life-spans.

Our conditioning to give up exercise takes place slowly as we approach adulthood. The baby in its mother's womb begins exercising months before birth. Infants and young children are naturally inclined to movement throughout all their waking hours, though television has altered this somewhat. The adjustment to sitting in classrooms is difficult for elementary school children; most look forward to recess, when they can go outside to play. By high school, any physical activity other than clearly regimented sports is frowned upon as immature, and by college only athletes can get exercise without being considered "childish." Adults, our society tells us, must be staid and dignified and sedentary. Isn't it curious how people say that life got serious and less enjoyable right around the time they hung up their tennis shoes for high heels and wing tips?

It may be more than coincidence that statistics show obesity in western society begins to become a problem once people reach age 25.

## Exercise and Aging

There is considerable evidence to support the theory that it is not the years but the sedentary lifestyle that makes us "old." The "dis-ease" of old age may well be nothing more than the results of "dis-use" of the body. Physical inactivity expended over a period of years has predictable results. Without exercise, the brain does not receive the oxygen and nutrients it needs, which can lead to premature senility. Calcium stores are lost from the bones, bringing on osteoporosis, a disease which hollows out the bones. Continuously sluggish blood allows fats to sediment along the blood-vessel walls, blocking blood flow, causing atherosclerosis. Erratic blood sugar regulation takes place, and high blood pressure occurs. There is a general softening of tissue, and lethargy, fatigue, and depression develop.

All of these conditions occur with continued lack of exercise. These are also the complaints that often occur with "old age."

There are numerous examples that confirm that long life is strongly linked to continuing exercise. On his eightieth birthday, bodybuilder Charles Atlas tore in half a large telephone book. On his sixty-ninth birthday, Jack LaLanne swam across San Francisco Bay with his hands tied. A San Francisco man, aged 107, was in the habit of running three miles each day through Golden Gate Park before going downtown to his job as a waiter. Arthur Reed, believed to have been 123 years old when he died, had a job tossing pig-iron when he was in his eighties and regularly rode his bike the 100-mile distance from Oakland to Fresno while in his nineties.

There are several remote societies in the world that are renowned for long life. They have very few things in common. The one notable universal thread is that they all live in hilly or mountainous terrain, which they must traverse in their daily activities. Walking steep inclines burns about three times the number of calories that walking on level ground does. The most celebrated of these long-lived peoples are the Hunzas of the Himalayas in Afghanistan. They may not live to be 130 or more as once thought, but they clearly live well beyond the "normal" range, and they clearly exercise in their nineties and hundreds.

One young author, researching these people, had great difficulty following an ancient goatherder as he was driving his flock up a mountain trail. The goatherder was a great-great-greatgrandfather.

Exercise is likely the most practical and effective longevity aid available today. It can:

- Allow you to eat as much as you want without getting overweight.
- Bring your appetite into alignment with bodily needs.
- Relax you while stimulating you to action.
- Tone your muscles and give you a sleeker look.
- Improve your complexion by flushing the pores of the skin, heightening the beauty of skin, hair, nails, and face.
- Sharpen your self-image and enhance your confidence.

- Enable you to enjoy sports and have the energy for after-workout activities.
- Improve your intellectual functions by increasing the circulation to the brain.
- Stimulate the production of endorphins for a natural "high."
- Allow you to fall asleep quickly and rest soundly.
- Increase oxygen-carrying capacity to all cells of the body.
- Considerably develop and strengthen the heart muscle.
- Lower blood pressure.
- Lower the resting pulse rate to reduce lifetime stress on the heart.
- Improve your sex life, both the quality and the quantity.
- Lower fats in the blood—both cholesterol and triglycerides.
- Increase disease resistance and improve all other bodily functions.
- Stabilize blood sugar levels, thus helping diabetics, hypoglycemics, and anyone with poor energy.
- Prevent or cure most common back ailments.
- Develop circulation in the heart muscle for greater chance of survival after heart attack.
- Delay, buffer, or prevent arthritis by maintaining joint mobility.
- Increase your lifespan, giving you both more years and more enjoyment of those years.

CASE HISTORY: M.N. came to La Costa after beginning an intense political campaign for elective office in Washington,

D.C. At 56 years of age, he considered himself "normal." His objective in coming to La Costa was merely a little rest and some "body tuning" to prepare himself for a grueling campaign. The condition of his health, however, was worse than he thought.

A medical examination revealed numerous problems. His weight and his percentage of body fat placed him in the obese category. His blood chemistry showed elevated fats and sugar, along with other matters of concern. His diet was clearly deplorable, and he had a family tendency toward overweight and heart disease.

M.N. was placed on a satisfying but low-calorie diet that was high in fiber and low in fat, salt, and sugar. An exercise program was developed for his specific needs, introducing him gradually and slowly to greater activity. He was encouraged to spend time with his wife, relaxing and reducing his stress level.

His political record was testimony that when M.N. put his mind to something he accomplished it. After attending a few of the evening lectures at La Costa, he understood fully what was at stake in his new health program, and he complied strictly with it. Three weeks later he left La Costa twenty pounds lighter, with an improved blood chemistry profile, a tan, and a winning smile. He went on to his political campaign and won his election.

Had M.N. not done something about his health at that point, he would have become one of the millions of semiambulatory people in their sixties waiting for an early demise. Perhaps more important than the political office he achieved by altering his routine is that M.N. earned himself a few extra decades of active life.

## Exercise and Illness

Lack of exercise is a major factor in many of the most serious disorders afflicting people in the developed nations, including the number one killer—heart disease—which has been rising dramatically in this century. Exercise is a part of the three-pronged attack doctors use to treat heart patients, the other two factors being diet and drugs. Diabetes, osteoporosis, and arthritis are all encouraged by lack of exercise, and programs of exercise can help to improve patients' conditions. Emotional disorders are reaching epidemic proportions in the West, and mental health experts are finding that in many cases exercise can be used as an effective therapy.

Exercise has been used as a major form of psychotherapy for people who complain of depression, anxiety, and even hyperactivity. People who exercise find themselves more positive, relaxed, and stimulated for work and relationships. By regulating blood sugar and improving oxygen flow to the brain, exercise helps to relieve many emotional problems. One psychiatrist we know has even used long-distance running to treat schizophrenic patients, with some success.

Even if your only mental problem is a "sluggish mind," exercise can benefit you.

CASE HISTORY: For her excellent work in medical school, V.B. was given a week at La Costa by her grandparents. They told her that it would do her good to get the rest before tackling the state medical board examination, which was to be a month away.

V.B. was an intelligent and pleasant young woman, but she was also rather anxious, perhaps because her many years of strenuous study were now focusing in on a single lengthy test that would determine whether or not she could reach her goal.

At first she resisted the relaxation of her week, intent upon studying. We told her of a study that had been done involving students taking an examination. This study divided the students into two groups. One group was allowed to do whatever they wished during their exam breaks—sit, smoke, eat, talk, whatever. The other group was led on an intensive stair-climbing program during the breaks. This latter group scored significantly higher on the examination.

V.B. was impressed with this revelation, and she combined her study at La Costa with plenty of rest, sunshine, exercise, and good food.

A few months later we received a letter from her, with a business card enclosed. On the business card, the letters "M.D." appeared after her name. She said in her letter that the stair-climbing lesson had helped in her exam. For her practice she had purposely taken an office on the fourth floor of a medical building so that she could get exercise going to and from work.

People who exercise regularly become ill much less frequently than their sedentary friends. There are reasons that go beyond the obvious ones:

- Vigorous exercise creates a mild fever that makes your body less hospitable to pathogenic organisms.
- By increasing the flow of all bodily functions, lymph moves more freely, rallying the defending white cells to action against invading organisms.
- By reducing psychological stress, exercise discourages

the common psychosomatically induced flus and infections.

- During exercise, the sinuses and upper respiratory tract increase mucous output, purging the system of visiting bacteria and viruses.

## Exercise and Weight Control

In western society, obesity has become a serious malnutritive condition, and not all obese people look or seem overweight. Some people may be overfat without being overweight. Exercise is critical for both types of people. Without it, overweight people are doomed to sort through the ever-increasing list of fad diets, with each failure increasing depression and lowering self-esteem. For those who are overfat without being overweight, exercise is the only answer. It can work miracles.

CASE HISTORY: C.J. was a model, and she had the kind of face that could launch a thousand ships. Over the course of her modeling years, that face earned her several million dollars. She was 29 years old and her career was floundering when she checked into the La Costa Spa. She was rapidly being overtaken by younger beauties who were anxious for her position of fame and fortune.

C.J. feared that she was over-the-hill for a top model. Her body was no longer what it had once been, and she had been struggling desperately to regain her firm slenderness. She was not technically overweight, but a medical examination revealed her to be surprisingly out of shape through her high percentage of body fat. Otherwise she had no major health problems.

She confessed that she had been trying every means possible

to keep her weight down so that she could continue her modeling career. She had employed diuretics, cathartics, and self-induced vomiting to maintain her weight. Indeed her teeth were beginning to show the darkening signs that can come from stomach acids in vomiting. C.J. had also tried all the over-the-counter diet drugs, as well as prescription drugs.

She was a victim of two common and dangerous myths: 1) that mild over-the-counter drugs like diuretics and laxatives are not harmful, even if taken for long periods of time, and 2) that eating and then vomiting is a convenient and harmless way to enjoy eating without gaining weight.

Her strange eating habits had created numerous subclinical vitamin and mineral deficiencies. Excessive fluid loss had dehydrated C.J.'s facial skin, creating premature wrinkling. Also, her continuous use of heavy makeup had caused her previously perfect complexion to deteriorate. Although her weight was good, her muscle tone was deplorable. Her hair and nails had lost their youthful sheen.

After talks with the La Costa staff—medical director, dieticians, and exercise coordinator—a program was worked out for C.J. She was given a 1200-calorie-per-day diet, high-potency vitamin supplements, and—most important—an exercise program. She had once enjoyed playing volleyball, and now she returned to it. After two weeks, she had worked herself into her routine well, and was making good progress. She continued her health-promoting program, joining a volleyball league and playing at every opportunity despite her busy schedule. She returned to La Costa ten months later and gave us a copy of her latest cover girl magazine photograph. She looked gorgeous, the perfect picture of health. Her body was firm and tanned, and her hair and nails had regained their luster. Most important, she had reduced her percentage of body fat.

Any weight-loss program you undertake without exercise will ultimately prove futile. It is ironic but understandable that overweight people who are out of shape are those who are least interested in exercise. It is far easier to accomplish weight loss and to make it permanent through exercise than through complicated fad diets. Once the overweight person understands this, the long succession of fad diets is over.

Exercise is vital to lifetime weight-control because it:

- Burns the stored fat.
- Elevates basal metabolism so you burn more calories even when sitting or sleeping.
- Allows you to eat properly while losing weight, thus avoiding the common nutritional deficiencies that afflict dieters.
- Lowers the body's set point. Your body has a weight that it would like to be. Based on genetics, the number of fat cells, and your lifestyle, this set point is difficult to argue with. Weight loss below your set point produces insatiable appetite and anxiety.

## Choosing Your Exercise Program

What sort of exercise program should you undertake? Just as there is no single perfect food with all the essential nutrients and no risk, there is no one perfect exercise. Almost any form of exercise is probably better than no exercise, however. The only possible exceptions would be the jogger sucking up lead fumes and carbon monoxide alongside a busy freeway, and the weekend athlete who plans a one-day total fitness program that may land him in the hospital.

Your exercise program should be planned specifically for your needs. We propose to offer you some guidelines, through which you can choose exercises, activities, or sports that will keep you healthy. If you have any concern about your ability to exercise, check with your physician to determine if your choices are right for you.

There are three general terms that must describe any exercise program: It must be fun, it must be vigorous, and it must be regular. You should choose a program that you will enjoy; if an exercise program is not fun for you, it is unlikely that you will adhere to it for long. Often, well-intentioned health-care professionals insist on certain exercises for an unrealistic period of time, and their patients grow weary of them, eventually acquiring an aversion to what may seem to them to be torture.

One word of warning is needed for those who are badly out of shape: it will take at least two weeks before any regular exercise program will be pleasurable. And remember exercise is for life, not just for a few brief weeks before you can return to your old habits.

Your program must be vigorous. If you don't get tired from it, then it isn't doing you any good. There are no machines— roller bars or vibrating belts—that can do the work for you. You must make the effort and do the sweating. And the best exercises give the entire body a good workout, not just the legs or arms.

Your exercise should be performed regularly, at least three times a week, more if possible. Those who try to cram all their exercise into a weekend every few months are asking for serious injury, especially as they grow older.

Your ideal exercise program also has three general objectives—flexibility, endurance (or cardiovascular fitness), and strength. Your workout should be planned to include exercises that will assist you in the development of each of these objectives, and it should be performed as an orderly routine that will introduce your body gradually to motion (as warm-up) before performing strength and endurance exercises, then gradually allow it to return to normal levels (as cool-down).

It should be planned in four phases:

1) *Warm-up*. This is composed of flexibility exercises, and it should last about five minutes. Without regular stretching, your muscles will become tighter each year as a natural result of aging. Older people are often still and tend to pull muscles easily because they have allowed the tightening to occur without using flexibility exercises to slow down this inevitable process. It is important to start these exercises slowly. If you feel pain at any point, stop exercising. If you feel mildly fatigued and relaxed afterward, consider your mission accomplished.

2) *Strength*. These exercises should last about fifteen to sixty minutes, depending on your condition and on how important strength is to you. You may choose isometrics, calisthenics, or weightlifting, depending upon whether you want minimal fitness or powerful muscles, or something in between. Calisthenics are an excellent general workout, and can be used by a wide range of people. They consist of such exercises as push-ups, sit-ups, dips, and jumping jacks. Isometric exercises can accomplish strength fitness, but they are not generaly recommended for the elderly and for people with high blood pressure. Weightlifting requires equipment and a separate room in your

home or membership in a gym; it is generally the choice of only serious athletes.

3) *Endurance*. These are exercises for the heart, blood vessels, and lungs, and they should last a minimum of about fifteen minutes. The objective is to reach your target heart rate. This rate is different for people of different ages, and it is a target to strive for once you are in good condition. Its purpose is to improve the efficiency of the heart, lungs, and circulatory system.

The specific breakdown times for a 45-minute workout program are shown in Table 6.1.

The following chart indicates the rate for people in good shape:

| AGE: | TARGET HEART RATE: |
|------|--------------------|
| 20 | 140 to 170 beats per minute |
| 30 | 130 to 160 beats per minute |
| 40 | 125 to 150 beats per minute |
| 50 | 115 to 140 beats per minute |
| 60 | 105 to 130 beats per minute |

You can determine this by taking your pulse rate after a few minutes of exercise. There are two ways of finding your pulse—on the bottom side of your wrist or at the neck just below the jawbone. To check your pulse at the wrist, turn one palm up and place the second, third, and fourth fingers of the other hand on the thumb side of your wrist until you feel a steady pulsation. To check your pulse at the neck, place the same three fingers at your neck about an inch below the curve of your jawbone. Practice finding your pulse a few times before

---

**FIGURE 6.1**

**TIME ALLOTMENTS FOR OPTIMAL EXERCISE ROUTINE**

**Forty-five Minutes Total Workout Time**

---

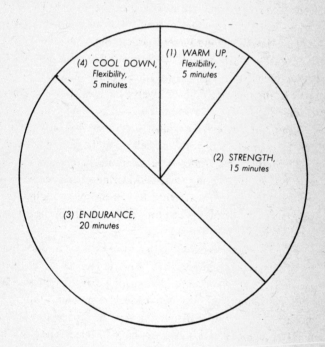

(4) COOL DOWN,
Flexibility,
5 minutes

(1) WARM UP,
Flexibility,
5 minutes

(2) STRENGTH,
15 minutes

(3) ENDURANCE,
20 minutes

beginning these exercises. When you are ready to determine your heart rate, you must take the pulse rate immediately after stopping exercises, for the heart rate drops off significantly as soon as you stop exercise to rest. You should take the pulse for fifteen seconds, and multiply the counted beats times four.

But we must advise you not to strive for this early in your fitness program. Depending on your present condition, you should allow two to four weeks of regular exercise before reaching your target heart rate.

There are various kinds of endurance exercises. Walking, biking, and swimming are excellent for beginners. There are various levels of endurance to seek. We assume you don't wish to enter Hawaii's Iron Man competion, but wish merely to be fit. To accomplish this we recommend that you aim for the twelve-minute run. The optimal fitness goal would be the capability of running two miles in twelve minutes. If you are able to achieve this, you are within range of becoming an athlete.

Again, we advise you against attempting this on your first day. Start slowly and work yourself up to the objective over a long period of time. Assess your condition carefully and honestly before undertaking this, considering your age, weight, and level of current inactivity. If you are overweight, over forty, and can't recall the last time you tried to run, begin this exercise by walking.

We recommend that you go to a local track or an open field for this exercise. Running near heavy traffic can be counterproductive, because you will be inhaling exhaust fumes. Also extensive running on pavement can cause problems with feet and legs. To begin, walk or run your best pace for twelve minutes, logging the distance you have traveled. The distance you can cover in that period will tell you a great deal about the health of your heart, lungs, circulatory system, and oxygen carrying capacity. If you finish one mile in the twelve-minute period, you are in average condition, which is to be interpreted as "poor."

4) *Cool-down.* This should last about five minutes and it consists of further flexibility exercises, starting out vigorously and tapering off. The objective is to slowly allow your body to return to normal.

You have many forms of exercise to choose from in planning your program. Make your selection by taking into consideration all of the various factors of your age, personal habits, motivation, lifestyle, and schedule. Your program must be practical for you to accomplish. Are you the kind of person who needs the motivation of a group of people all engaged in the same objective, or would you feel inhibited or self-conscious by a gym? Can you enjoy exercise for the sheer pleasure of it, or do you need to feel that you are accomplishing some chore or task in the process? Is there some sport you once enjoyed but have given up? Are there tasks that need to be performed around the house, but you've avoided because of the physical effort required?

Give some thought to these matters. It would be foolish for you to go out and spend money for membership in a gym if you will be unlikely to go more than once or twice. You won't last very long at jogging or playing volleyball if you don't consider these sports to be enjoyable.

There are some people who would feel completely out-of-place joining a basketball team, but will happily cut their own firewood. (Vigorous wood-chopping is a better aerobic fitness program than any other exercise.) Some people would refuse to consider a daily jogging routine, but would have no objection to walking many miles each day in performing their daily chores. Some would be satisfied to pedal a stationary bicycle at a fitness club, while others would prefer to bicycle to a destination—to work or to a scenic weekend location.

Although we will be offering calisthenic exercises that we recommend, it is important for you to realize that this form of strict routine is not the only way you can get the exercise you need. You can build your strength and endurance any way you choose. However, we do recommend you utilize the flexibility exercises for warm-ups.

In Table 6.2, we have evaluated various forms of exercise on a scale of one to ten, according to their values for flexibility, strength, and endurance, considering the degree or risk, the need for other people to accomplish them, and expense. There is no such thing as a "perfect ten" exercise, but some of the scores might surprise you. The greater the need for others in a sport, the lower its score. The greater the risk, the lower the score. And the greater the expense involved, the lower the score.

We don't advise incurring a great expense at the outset of your new fitness routine. Spend only the money you absolutely have to in the beginning; wait until you are sure you like the activity before investing heavily. Two things are very important for any exercise program, and we do advise obtaining them—an exercise bra for women and an athletic supporter for men, plus a good pair of shoes suitable for your sport. Beyond that it's up to you.

Some people do have a tendency, however, to get more excited about buying equipment for exercising than they do about the sport itself. They decide to take up jogging, go out and buy the finest designer label baby-blue jogging suit with the most expensive running shoes. For good measure they buy a portable stereo with headset so they won't be bored running

## TABLE 6.2
### LOOKING FOR THE "10"

| Event | Flexi-bility | Strength | Endur-ance | Risk | Need Others | Cost | Over-all |
|---|---|---|---|---|---|---|---|
| Baseball | 6 | 7 | 4 | 4 | 2 | 5 | 4.6 |
| Basketball | 7 | 7 | 9 | 5 | 3 | 7 | 6.3 |
| Boxing | 7 | 9 | 9 | 1 | 4 | 6 | 6.0 |
| Dancing | 7 | 6 | 7 | 8 | 4 | 7 | 6.5 |
| Fencing | 6 | 7 | 7 | 4 | 4 | 6 | 5.7 |
| Football | 6 | 9 | 7 | 2 | 3 | 4 | 5.2 |
| Gymnastics | 9 | 8 | 6 | 5 | 8 | 6 | 7.0 |
| Ice Hockey | 6 | 7 | 8 | 3 | 3 | 4 | 5.2 |
| Jazzercise | 8 | 6 | 8 | 8 | 6 | 5 | 6.8 |
| Jumping Rope | 6 | 7 | 9 | 9 | 10 | 9 | 8.3 |
| Martial Arts | 9 | 9 | 10 | 5 | 7 | 6 | 7.7 |
| Rugby | 7 | 8 | 8 | 3 | 3 | 8 | 6.2 |
| Running | 5 | 5 | 10 | 8 | 10 | 9 | 7.8 |
| Running Stairs | 3 | 7 | 10 | 8 | 10 | 10 | 8.0 |
| Rowing | 6 | 8 | 8 | 8 | 10 | 5 | 7.5 |
| Scuba Diving | 7 | 6 | 6 | 5 | 8 | 2 | 5.7 |
| Snow Skiing | 4 | 7 | 7 | 2 | 9 | 2 | 5.2 |
| Soccer | 5 | 5 | 9 | 5 | 3 | 9 | 6.0 |
| Surfing | 7 | 7 | 6 | 5 | 10 | 6 | 6.8 |
| Swimming | 7 | 7 | 7 | 9 | 10 | 6 | 7.7 |
| Tennis | 5 | 6 | 6 | 8 | 4 | 6 | 5.2 |
| Volleyball | 6 | 6 | 7 | 8 | 3 | 8 | 6.3 |
| Walking | 6 | 5 | 6 | 9 | 10 | 10 | 7.7 |
| Weight-lifting | 4 | 10 | 6 | 6 | 8 | 6 | 6.7 |
| Wood Chopping | 6 | 9 | 10 | 6 | 10 | 8 | 8.2 |
| Wrestling | 6 | 9 | 8 | 4 | 4 | 8 | 6.5 |

up and down. After this great expense, they feel they must get their money's worth on the first day. Suffering painfully sore muscles, they give up after one try. The expensive equipment rests in the closet until a charity drive comes asking for anything they want to throw out.

On one occasion, we met two extremely disgruntled scuba divers who had invested considerable time and money in getting certified and buying the best equipment. They had hoped to come up with enough lobster or abalone to cover the cost of the gear. Their first day of scouring the ocean bottom turned up nothing. Then, along came a young boy with a chewed-up diving mask, who proceeded to bring up the biggest pink abalone they had ever seen.

Your success is not dependent on your equipment or on the money you spend. We knew one young man who was spending his summer as an exchange student in Brazil. He wanted to stay in shape for football practice in the fall, but there were no gyms available. With ingenuity he came up with a solution. He spent the summer lifting rocks. (We must admit that he earned a reputation for strangeness among the rural Brazilian population, however.)

Wait until you see if you like a sport before investing a large amount of money. Buy only what you need in the beginning. Of course, some sports will require a few essentials. Certainly you should invests in good shoes. In some sports, such as handball, racquetball, or basketball, eye injuries can occur, so it would be worthwhile to buy protective goggles. Naturally for basketball, you'll need a basketball, and for skiing you'll need skis. But, shop wisely.

## Getting Started On Your Program

Before you begin your fitness program, determine your level of fitness to avoid taking on too much too soon. If you are even slightly unsure about your fitness level, see your physician for advice before starting. The following test can help you to decide on your level, whether beginner, intermediate, or advanced. For each item, circle the answer that applies to you, and insert the accompanying number in the score column at the right.

|  | POINTS | SCORE |
|---|---|---|
| A. My age is: | | |
| Up to 25 years. | 1 | |
| 26 to 45 years. | 2 | |
| 45 years or more. | 3 | _____ |
| B. My skin pinch at the belly button is: | | |
| Less than one inch. | 1 | |
| One to two inches. | 2 | |
| Two or more inches. | 3 | _____ |
| C. My health problems are: | | |
| None. | 1 | |
| Some. | 2 | |
| Many. | 3 | _____ |

D. Smoking.

|  |  |  |
|---|---|---|
| Never have. | 1 | |
| Used to, but quit. | 2 | |
| Still do. | 3 | _____ |

E. The last time I seriously exercised was:

|  |  |  |
|---|---|---|
| Less than a year ago. | 1 | |
| One to two years ago. | 2 | |
| More than two years ago. | 3 | _____ |

F. My resting pulse, beats per minute is:

|  |  |  |
|---|---|---|
| 45 to 55. | 1 | |
| 56 to 70. | 2 | |
| 71 or more. | 3 | _____ |

TOTAL _____

EVALUATION.

| *Score:* | *You are:* |
|---|---|
| 6–9 points. | Advanced. |
| 10–13 points. | Intermediate. |
| 14–18 points. | Beginner |

Depending on your level of fitness—beginner, intermediate, or advanced—you should determine your starting level for all forms of exercise—flexibility, strength, and endurance. With the flexibility and strength exercises, all levels may perform the same routines, but the less advanced you are the fewer you should do with less initial expectations. For flexibility, stretch slowly and only to the point that mild discomfort begins. It should not hurt. As you advance, the angle or stretch can increase. Do fewer repetitions in the beginning. For strength exercises, do fewer repetitions and perform less movement; if you are using weights, start with less weight and increase gradually.

For the endurance exercises, we recommend different types of exercise for the different levels. For beginners, we suggest walking, fast walking, swimming, or biking. For intermediates, we suggest all of the above, plus jogging, biking rapidly, walking stairs, engaging in martial arts, playing volleyball, dancing, jazzercising, playing soccer, surfing, or snow shoveling. Advanced exercisers can do any of the above, plus running, stair running, jumping rope, rowing, playing basketball, playing ice hockey, chopping wood, or performing gymnastics.

Although most of these exercises can be performed by both men and women, we feel some differences in expectations should be pointed out. Women will generally do better at flexibility exercises, while men will generally have greater success at the strength and endurance routines. If you are performing your exercises with someone of the opposite sex, don't attempt to compete. Go for your own fitness needs.

We have one last bit of advice before getting started. Learn to breathe properly. You may think you know how to breathe, since you've been doing it all your life, but both men and women frequently do it incorrectly.

The most common mistake women make in breathing is to inhale by raising or lifting the rib cage, thinking incorrectly that this will prevent a protruding belly. What it does is ventilate only the top of the lungs, creating too much tension in the muscles of the shoulders, neck, and throat, causing the rib cage to become rigid.

The most common mistake of men in breathing is that they contract the diaphragm while expanding the lungs, forcing the abdominal wall forward. Since the abdominal wall is not tightened with each exhalation, they soon develop a pot belly.

When you breathe correctly, your ribs spread with each breath and your abdominal wall contracts with each exhalation. To learn to breathe correctly, try the following exercise:

Cup your hands over your lower ribs so that your fingertips meet. Inhale slowly as if you were smelling a flower. As you inhale, gently press your hands against the lower ribs, directing them apart and to the sides like an accordion. As you inhale, count to eight or ten. As you exhale, again counting to eight or ten, open your mouth and breathe out with an audible sigh. You should be able to feel your abdominal muscles tightening while you are exhaling.

Many volumes have been written on the subject of exercise. Our objective is not to guide you in the specific program you should adopt, but merely to convince you that your long life depends on some form of exercise. However, we can offer you a few basic routines for flexibility and strength that you can use to begin your program. We hope that you will eventually go on to other more extensive exercises.

## Stretching Exercises

### THE LEGS

*Hamstrings.* Sit on the floor with your right leg stretched out in front of you and your left leg folded so that the bottom of the left shoe touches your right thigh. With both arms, reach for the right foot, as illustrated in Photo 1. Do not bounce back and forth. Do not continue to stretch once pain is encountered. Hold for a count of ten, then sit back. Repeat the procedure. Change positions to stretch out your left leg with your right folded, and repeat the exercise.

PHOTO 1

*Thigh and Groin.* Sit on the floor with your right leg stretched out in front of you and your left leg folded out to the side or behind you, as illustrated in Photo 2. Allow your upper trunk to drop backward, reaching backwards with your arms to brace against sudden falling. When you have stretched back as far as you can, hold for a count of ten. Change positions to stretch out your left leg with your right folded back and repeat the exercise.

PHOTO 2

*Calves.* Stand upright an arm's length or more away from a solid wall. Keeping your feet flat on the ground, lean forward toward the wall, bracing yourself against the wall with your arms bent at the elbows. Allow your body to slowly lean into the wall until your calf muscles feel they are being stretched. Hold for ten seconds, then return to standing position.

*Towel-Stretch for Calves.* Sit on the floor with your legs extended straight before you. Grip the ends of a bath towel, one end in each hand, and loop the towel around your toes, as illustrated in Photo 3. Slowly pull back on the upper part of your feet with the towel to stretch the calf muscles. Hold the position for ten seconds, then release. Repeat the exercise twice for a total of three sets. (This is a particularly helpful exercise for women accustomed to wearing high-heeled shoes.)

PHOTO 3

*Inner Thigh Stretch.* Sit on the floor with your legs in front of you, but bent outward slightly so that the soles of your feet meet. Place your arms behind you, with palms flat on the floor to support the weight of your upper body as you lift your hips in the manner shown in Photo 4. Allow the movement and the force of gravity to stretch the inner thighs. Hold for ten seconds, then return buttocks to the floor. Repeat the exercise twice for a total of three sets.

PHOTO 4

*Karate Blade*. Lie on the floor on your left side, with your left arm supporting your head as indicated in Photo 5. Lift your right leg straight upward at the same time you raise your arm to point toward the ceiling. Then, move your leg forward, while your arm moves behind you. Follow this by the opposite motion—moving your leg behind you, while your arm moves forward. Repeat ten times, then return to your resting position. Repeat the entire exercise two or more times for a total set of three.

PHOTO 5

## THE SPINE

*Neck Rotation.* Stand upright with your hands relaxed at your side. Bending your neck as far as is comfortable, rotate your head slowly a full 360 degrees twice in one direction, then twice in the other direction, as shown in Photo 6. Repeat.

**PHOTO 6**

*Upper Trunk Rotation.* Stand erect with your hands on your hips. Bending at the waist as far as is comfortable, rotate your upper trunk a full 360 degrees twice in one direction, then twice in the other direction, as shown in Photo 7. Bend to each direction as much as you can without inducing pain or losing your balance. To avoid harming the lower back, bend your legs slightly at the knees. Repeat.

**PHOTO 7**

*Side Stretch*. Stand erect with one hand on your hip and the other above your head. Bend from side to side, as shown in Photo 8, continuing for about thirty seconds. Then change arms and repeat for another thirty seconds. (This is not only good for stretching, but also for toning the muscles on the sides of your stomach, giving you a leaner waistline.)

**PHOTO 8**

*Rock and Roll.* Lie down on your back and bring your knees up to your chest, securing them there by wrapping your arms around them. Raise your head off the floor so that you are resting on the small of your back and your tailbone. Rock back and forth as far as possible without losing the correct position. Beginners should repeat five to ten times; intermediates repeat ten to fifteen times.

## Strength and Toning Exercises

### UPPER BODY

*Chair dips.* Stand erect between two sturdy straight-backed chairs. Supporting yourself with your hands on the tops of the chair backs, lower your body, keeping your feet off the floor, as shown in Photo 9.

PHOTO 9

Then lift your body back up, straightening your arms. Repeat five times. Beginners should do two sets of five repetitions; advanced should do three sets of ten repetitions. (This exercise is very good for your shoulders, chest, and triceps.)

*Men's Push-Ups.* Push-ups are still a classic exercise for developing strength of your upper body. Lie on the floor on your stomach, placing your hands out to the side at shoulder level with palms flat on the floor. Raise yourself up on your hands and toes, keeping your body straight from shoulders to toes. If you are not in good shape, it is advisable to bend slightly, lifting your buttocks, to avoid damaging your lower back. Slowly lower your body until your chin touches the floor; then raise your body back up again. Repeat five times. Beginners should do two sets of five each. Advanced can do one of the more difficult variations: (1) Do the push-ups with clenched fists. (2) Between lifting and falling to the floor, clap your hands briskly. (3) Do the push-ups with your hands on the floor and your feet on a chair, as shown in photo 10.

*Women's Push-Ups.* Perform your push-ups with your knees and feet resting on the floor, as shown in Photo 11. Bend your arms at the elbows to lower your body to the floor, then bring your body up slowly, all the while keeping your body in a straight line from shoulders to knees. Repeat five times. Beginners should do two sets of five repetitions, and intermediates should do two sets of ten repetitions. (This helps to build the muscles under the breasts and may improve your bustline.)

PHOTO 10

PHOTO 11

*Towel Stretch for Arms.* Sit on the floor with your legs folded in front of you. Grasp a large bath towel with one hand at each end, holding it behind your neck. Attempt to stretch the towel outward, as shown in Photo 12, for about ten seconds. Repeat twice for a total of three sets. (This exercise helps to prevent flabby arms.)

PHOTO 12

*The Can-Can.* This exercise requires two unopened cans of tomato sauce or other produce can of comparable size and volume to use as weights. Grasp one can in each hand, gripping firmly. Standing erect, alternately extend one arm up (at the two-o'clock position) while bending the other behind your head, as shown in Photo 13. Develop a smooth motion of both arms moving simultaneously. Beginners should do three sets of ten repetitions. (This helps to prevent flabby arms by toning the forearm.)

PHOTO 13

## THE SPINE

*Yoga Cobra*. Lie face down on the floor, placing your hands at shoulder level, palms flat on the floor. Slowly raise your upper trunk with your arms, leaving your hips and legs on the floor, as shown in Photo 14. Then arch your back and neck as if pointing your head toward your buttocks. Slowly lower your body to its original position. Beginners should do this five times; intermediates should do ten times.

PHOTO 14

*Reverse Leg Lifts*. Place two plain straight-backed chairs side to side. (The chairs must not have arm-rests.) Rest your upper trunk on the seats of the chairs face down. Raise both legs until they are in alignment with the rest of the body, as shown in Photo 15. Then lower your legs slowly, but do not allow them to reach the floor. Beginners should repeat this three times. Advanced should do three sets of ten repetitions.

PHOTO 15

## LEGS

*Groucho Walk*. Starting in an erect standing position, bend your knees to a low crouch, as shown in Photo 16. In this position, walk around your yard or room. Beginners should do this for about one minute; advanced should do three minutes.

PHOTO 16

*Skier Squat.* Brace your back against a sturdy wall and lower yourself to a position in which your thighs are at a right angle to your back and lower legs, and parallel to the floor. Beginners should hold themselves in this position for thirty seconds; advanced should hold for four minutes.

*Towel Stretch.* Sit on the floor with your legs extended in front of you, knees slightly bent. Grasp a large bath towel, one end in each hand, and loop it over your feet. Lift your feet into the air, pulling on the towel with your arms while pushing away with your legs, as shown in Photo 17. Do this for ten seconds. Repeat for a total of three sets. (This is an excellent exercise for arm and leg fitness and toning.)

PHOTO 17

## STOMACH

*Stomach Crunchers.* Lie on the floor on your back, with your hands clasped behind your head and your knees bent. Using the muscles of your stomach and legs, bring your knees up to meet your elbows, as shown in Photo 18, then return to the resting position. Do not pull on your head with your hands.

PHOTO 18

PHOTO 19

Beginners should do two sets of five repetitions; advanced should do three sets of twenty. To improve muscle tone and tightness on your sides, you can vary this exercise by turning as you raise up to bring your left knee to your right elbow, then doing the standard of both elbows to both knees, and following with the right knee to the left elbow. (See Photo 19.) This variation helps to trim the "love handles" at the waist.

*Leg Lifts.* Lie on the floor on your back, with your hands at your sides. Press your lower back toward the floor, then raise your legs, keeping them straight, as shown in Photo 20. Once your legs have reached an angle of 45 degrees from the floor, slowly lower them, but do not allow them to return to the floor. Raise them again, repeating the action. Beginners should do two sets of five repetitions; advanced should do three sets of twenty repetitions. (This is good for the lower back as well as the stomach.)

PHOTO 20

*Sit-Ups.* Lie on the floor on your back, with your knees bent and your arms outstretched at your sides. Raise your upper trunk into a sitting position, at the same time bringing your outstretched arms into a folded position in front of your chest, as indicated in Photo 21. Return to your lying position with arms outstretched. If your feet tend to lift from the floor as you sit up, you may need someone to hold them for you, or you can brace them under a chair or couch. Beginners should do two sets of five sit-ups; advanced should do three sets of twenty.

PHOTO 21

## FACE AND NECK

*Lion's Roar.* To help smooth the cheek area of your face and bring blood circulation to your throat, open your mouth wide and stick out your tongue, holding his expression for ten seconds. To achieve the right expression, it may help to roar like a lion. Repeat this three times.

*Chin Firmer.* Lie on the floor on your back, with your arms at your sides. Lift your head and shoulders off the floor to look at your feet, as indicated in Photo 22. Do not return to the original position, but—keeping your shoulders off the floor—move your head backward to look at the wall behind you. Before allowing your head to return to rest on the floor, beginners should do five repetitions, and intermediates should do ten. Both should do two sets of this exercise. (This helps to firm the rarely used chin muscles to avoid sagging facial lines and an indistinct chin.)

PHOTO 22

## The "I-Don't-Have-Time-For-Exercise" Program

Many sedentary people know they need exercise, but avoid it because they can't seem to find the time in their busy schedules. They go on day after day, year after year, thinking one day they'll have the chance to correct the poor habits of a lifetime. Ideally, your exercise program should be at least 45 minutes performed three times a week. However, it is better to get some exercise than none at all. If you can find twenty minutes three times a week, we have a special program especially for you. Because your time is limited, your effort will have to be concentrated into the following procedures:

*Warm-Up.* To prepare yourself, perform the stretching exercises we have suggested for the legs and spine—Hamstrings, Thigh and Groin, Calves, Towel Stretch for Calves, Karate Blade, Neck Rotation, and Upper Trunk Rotation. This should take you only two to three minutes.

*Aerobics.* Spend twelve minutes moving on a set of stairs. If you are a beginner, start by walking slowly up and down the stairs, with occasional rests if necessary. As you continue this program, your pace on the stairs should quicken with each week. When you are able to sustain a brisk, running pace on the stairs for the entire twelve minutes, you can consider yourself advanced.

*Cool-Down.* To unwind from this effort, walk around for about two minutes, shaking your arms lazily, rolling your head, and bending your upper trunk.

*Strength and Muscle Tone.* For a special concentrated exercise program, we have a special La Costa combination exercise that you can do for strength and muscle tone. You begin by lying on the floor on your back, placing your hands behind your head and forcing your lower back to the floor.

*Step 1:* Raise your legs to a 45-degree angle as shown in Photo 20 (the illustration for the Leg Lifts). As you raise and lower your legs, however, you will be doing isometrics with your arms and neck. Continue raising and lowering your legs throughout the following steps.

*Step 2:* Attempt to press your head downward, while your hands and arms resist by pressing against the neck.

*Step 3:* Continue Step 2, but alternate between left and right arms to resist the downward pressure of the head.

*Step 4:* Attempt to move your head to the left, while resisting with your left arm, then move your head to the right, resisting with your right arm. (This exercise takes only a few minutes, but it gives the thighs, stomach, lower back, neck, arms, and buttocks a good workout.) Develop a rhythm in this exercise in which you do five leg lifts or more for each direction of the neck and arm isometrics.

With these few exercises, which can be performed in twenty minutes, you have a minimal routine that enables you to exercise and stretch most areas of your body. No matter how busy you are, you no longer have an excuse for staying soft and flabby. No special equipment is needed, just you and your body.

We have offered you the basics here, merely as an introduction to get you in the habit of exercise. Once you have begun to get your body in shape, many of you will want to go further than the exercises we have outlined. You have numerous alternatives available to you, a great many of them involving equipment that helps build your body. Equipment is not necessary for developing a lean, muscular physique, but most serious athletes do use free weights, such as dumbbells or barbells, spring devices, or variable resistance devices, such as the stationary Nautilus and the portable bullworkers. The major reasons for using equipment are: (1) it helps to regulate your progress; and (2) it can produce faster results if what you desire is muscle-building.

You must decide for yourself what level of fitness or muscularity you want. You may also consider the matter of cost and time. For some, simple exercises done in the privacy of home are best. For others, an investment of money in equipment is worth it. And for others, who may like the camaraderie of friends intent on the same objectives, joining a gym may be the solution. What is important is to retain your good physical health by exercising.

R
 X

- As a minimum, walk a half hour each day and spend five minutes in flexibility exercises before and after you walk.

- As an optimum, establish an exercise program for yourself incorporating routines for flexibility, strength, and endurance.

- Set fitness goals for yourself, whether minimum, optimum, or somewhere between. Once you achieve your goals, set higher ones.

- If you are overweight, have a health problem, are older than age 40, or have been relatively inactive for more than a few months, consult your doctor before beginning an exercise program.

## ❀❀❀ 7 ❀❀❀

# Nutrition

"Let thy food by thy medicine and thy
medicine be thy food."

—HIPPOCRATES

[• Nutritional intake affects health and longevity • Excess,
deficiency, and imbalance are serious forms of malnutrition
in the developed world • How technology produces foods
that fool us • New lifestyles create new nutritional needs •
The food you eat affects learning and behavior • Food allergies • Choosing the right foods • What is the proper percentage of carbohydrates, fat, and protein? • Guidelines for
good nutrition • Nutrient density and the relative values of
food • Risk vs. benefit of foods • Changing your attitude
toward food • The new exchange system—dairy, fat, fruits,
vegetables, bread/grains, meat/protein]

Your body is an organized gathering of 60 trillion cells working in harmony. It is an amazingly complex system of organs
that permit you to be aware of your surroundings. Your body

can adapt to a wide range of external environmental conditions while maintaining a stable internal environment. It is a system that requires building materials for growth and repairs, fueling to produce energy, and a wide range of nutrients to perform these tasks. This amazing "machine" that is your body is built from and maintained by the foods you have consumed over your lifetime. Based upon the way your body looks and functions, would you say that the food you have been giving it is top quality?

Since earliest recorded time, shamans, medicine men, priests, and other healers have relied on foods, herbs, and potions for cures against disease. Hippocrates, who lived to an age of ninety at a time when thirty was an old age, taught food as a basic of the healing art to his medical students. The connection between food and illness was sometimes obvious: gout, a disease of protein metabolism that causes painful joints, has always been known as "the rich man's disease," for its victims were invariably overweight middle-aged men who consumed high-fat and -sugar diets.

The first firmly established proof of a relationship between diet and health took place when it was shown that limes cure scurvy.

Today we have clear scientific evidence that nutritional intake—both the quality and the quantity—seriously affects health and longevity. The primary killers of the twentieth century are heart disease, hypertension, diabetes, and cancer; the primary cripplers are osteoporosis, arthritis, obesity, and infections. All are closely related to diet, though diet is not the only factor involved. In some cases, however, it is a key factor.

## Malnutrition in an Age of Plenty

Near the end of the eighteenth century, based upon the rate of population growth at the time, Thomas Malthus predicted unavoidable mass starvation within the next century. This prophecy was based entirely on mathematical calculations, and it did not take into account the incredible developments of agricultural technology that would take place in the nineteenth and twentieth centuries. We live in an age of abundant food supplies, at least in the West. The United States, Europe, Canada, and Australia have become veritable food factories.

Yet, in a sense, Malthus has been right. With an abundance of food, the people of the western nations are suffering from malnutrition.

When one speaks of "malnutrition," most people picture an emaciated baby from a third world nation, starving for want of food. Deficiency, however, is only one form of malnutrition: the other two are excess and imbalance, and they can be just as life-threatening as deficiency. Obesity is the most prevalent form of malnutrition in the developed world.

Considering only the United States, without the rest of the western world, the statistics are staggering. Though comprising only five percent of the world's population, the United States consumes nearly 50 percent of the world's red meat. At least half of the population consumes too much food, while shipping enough food abroad to stem the tide of a trade imbalance, and throwing away each day enough food to feed another fifty million people. The average American consumes over 120 pounds of sugar per year, some of it from the more than 300 cans of soda pop he drinks; he also consumes twelve gallons of liquor and five pounds of food additives. Pastries, candy, sugared breakfast cereals, and refined flour are also a large part of the American diet.

The United States Department of Agriculture recently surveyed 37,000 people, finding that over half were low in their intake of vitamin B-6, that 39 percent were low in magnesium, and nearly one-fourth were low in vitamins C and A, with lower rates of deficiencies of folate, vitamin E, and zinc.

How could this be? There are numerous reasons for the changes in western diet, some of them technological, some caused by change in lifestyle. Table 7.1 outlines some of the causes and effects in our nutritional health.

Some of the factors shown cause almost imperceptible effects, while others ought to be quite clear to us. Most people are taught some of the basics of nutrition and have at least a general idea of the values they should be getting from the food they eat. However, technology has helped to create foods that can fool us. In processing, many foods are stripped of their nutrient value, while having salt, fat, sugar, and additives mixed into the final products to satisfy the taste buds. Also, most people are not aware that our new lifestyle has increased our bodies' needs for certain nutrients, while diminishing needs for calories. Psychological stress, smoking, alcohol consumption, drug usage, fasting, fad-dieting—all present the body with nutritional needs it did not have in less complex times.

There is also a traditional view that "a fat baby means a healthy baby," which is hard to rid ourselves of. It lingers from an era when food was not as abundant as it is now, passed on from generation to generation. Few people have not heard the admonishment of a parent: "Clean your plate; think of the

## TABLE 7.1

| Cause | Effect |
| --- | --- |
| Rural to urban migration. | Consumption of less fresh food, more refined foods, with more supermarket temptations. |
| Sedentary lifestyle, with technology assuming work. | Fewer calories are burned; obesity and heart disease increase. |
| Women taking jobs, no longer in the home. | Consumption of fewer home-cooked meals, with less nutritional supervision of children. |
| Increased income. | Increase in restaurant eating, fast foods, expensive meats, and snack foods. |
| Advances in food technology. | Increase in fabricated convenience foods, more processing, with increased nutrient loss. |
| Increase in single people, living alone. | Lowered appetite, with meals missed or substandard meals, frequently convenience prepared foods. |
| Increased stresses in life. | Increased nutrient needs, accelerated nutrient loss, with radical changes in eating patterns. |
| Increased drug usage, both prescription and non-prescription. | Elevated nutrient needs. |
| Rise in teen pregnancy. | Very high nutrient needs, with generally poor nutrient intake. |
| Increased alcohol use. | Elevated nutrient needs, with reduced nutrient intake. |

continued

| Tobacco use. | Elevated need for certain nutrients. |
| Fad dieting or fasting. | Unbalanced or no nutrient intake. |
| Increased environmental pollutants. | Increased nutrient needs to overcome. |

starving children in..." (Depending on your generation, you can fill in the last word, using "China," "India," or "Africa.")

CASE HISTORY: J.A. came to La Costa with serious weight and health problems. She was at least 55 pounds overweight, and although she was only 42 years old, she had already undergone removal of her gall bladder and her ovaries.

J.A.'s weight problems stemmed in a large degree from her upbringing. Her parents had grown up in poverty in eastern Europe, with rarely enough to eat. After immigrating to the United States, they started a family and became more affluent. Their family affairs and their expressions of family love centered around food. The children were constantly admonished to clean their plates, with reminders about the "starving millions" in the world.

J.A. was an obedient child. She was an enthusiastic eater and understandably chubby from her earliest years. She ate large servings; she ate often; she ate rapidly; she ate for rewards ("Be a good girl and I'll buy you a soda pop"); she ate when she was elated; and she ate when she was frustrated.

As a result she suffered from physical ailments from malnutrition and obesity. Because she was weighted down with excess baggage, even her breathing was labored. To overcome her problem, she needed more than just the weight-reduction program of La Costa; she needed emotional support as well.

Her attitudinal training toward food had to be altered, and for that she needed a support group of others who suffered similarly.

We suggested that she join either Overeaters Anonymous or Weight Watchers. She also needed the help and support of her husband. (The divorce rate is higher than normal for couples in which only one undergoes a program of weight-loss.)

J.A. followed our advice. When she and her husband returned to La Costa nine months later, they had both lost weight. They were considerably healthier, and both looked terrific.

Attitude, stress, sedentary lifestyle, technology, and our use of drugs, alcohol, and tobacco—all contribute to our malnutrition. But perhaps it is the fast pace of our lives that keeps us from giving proper thought to what we eat. We patronize fast food establishments; we skip meals; we try bizarre weight-reduction diets; we drink and smoke to excess. And we dine out far too frequently.

Dining out should not be a hazardous affair, yet few people consider nutrition when they are selecting a restaurant. Most consider first the taste of the food and the atmosphere, with other factors such as service, cost, and view entering into the decision. What they are getting is far more calories, fat, salt, sugar, cholesterol, alcohol, and empty calories than they would have by eating at home.

It is all-important that we take a moment now and then to think about the real purpose of eating—to supply the body with the proper nutrients in the proper amounts that will optimize the chemical processes of life.

## Diet and Disease

Although obesity is the number one malnutritive condition in the developed nations, our poor nutrition also contributes to other killing diseases. Eating too much of the wrong kinds of foods, combined with not eating enough of the proper nutrients, has produced epidemics of heart disease, hypertension, diabetes, cancer, osteoporosis, arthritis, common infections, and mental illness.

These stem from the fact that we consume too much fat, salt, sugar, cholesterol, alcohol, red meat, and empty-calorie junk-food, while not eating enough whole grains, fish and poultry, fresh fruits and vegetables, legumes, and low- and nonfat dairy products.

Our diet has also contributed to the increase in emotional illness. To some extent, you truly are what you eat, for your brain functions through the nutrients delivered by your food supply. There have been studies that show that the diets of children can affect their learning ability and their behavior. The human mind has several requirements that must be supplied by the diet:

- Oxygen is delivered to the brain by the red blood cells, which are made from iron, protein, folic acid, vitamin B-6, and vitamin B-12.
- Fuel, preferably in the form of blood glucose, must be delivered to the brain on an even and constant basis.
- The brain must have nutrients to metabolize the blood glucose, including thiamine, niacin, riboflavin, pantothenic acid, and chromium.

- Raw materials (or precursors) are needed by the brain to build the chemicals that "jump" the distance between nerve cells. These vital neurochemical transmitters are made from tryptophan, tyrosine, choline, and other factors supplied by the diet. (Vitamins B-6 and C are involved in this.)
- The brain requires nutrients, including sodium, potassium, calcium, magnesium, and water, to form the "electrolyte soup" in which nerve impulses are conducted along the nerve cells.

Not only do people think better on a balanced diet, their emotions are more rational when the diet gives their brains all the ingredients they need.

There is one other dietary problem that has been on the increase in technological society—food allergies. While allergies may have various physical manifestations, they also can affect the brain, causing irrational behavior. When the large proteins from allergic foods are absorbed before digestive breakdown—as they should not be—the body reacts to the whole food protein as a foreign invader. The body's reaction can include a swelling of some portions of the brain. There is reason to believe that many of these allergic reactions stem from excess stress, chemical pollutants from our environment, and poor nutrition.

Despite all this, there are two aspects of western society that give us hope. The first is that we have abundant food and resources to correct our dietary deficiencies. The second is our willingness and ability to change our dietary habits when evidence is presented that change will be beneficial. When scientists broadcast (somewhat prematurely) in the 1970s that egg cholesterol was a major factor in heart disease, the poultry business suffered badly. When medical reports stated that polyunsaturated fats lowered fats in the blood, people began buying more vegetable oils.

We know you are both capable of and willing to improve your nutrition, once you know how.

## Choosing the Right Foods

In 1977, the nutrition of the American people became a concern of the United States government. The U.S. Senate Select Committee on Nutrition and Human Needs investigated the average American diet, with the help of scientific data and a gathering of renowned scientists. Their findings, along with their recommendations for changes, were published in 1977. The breakdown of the current diet and the suggested alterations are shown in Table 7.2.

While they found our level of protein consumption satisfactory, the animal protein sources contributed far too much fat and cholesterol. In the carbohydrate category, we consume far too much refined sugar and not enough complex and natural carbohydrates.

The specific changes recommended are as follows:

- Increase the consumption of fruits, vegetables, whole grains, and legumes.
- Decrease the consumption of refined sugars.
- Eat less fat and fatty foods.
- Of the fat consumed, choose less saturated and more unsaturated fats.

**TABLE 7.2**

**SENATE DIET GOALS**

| Nutrient | Daily Intake | |
| --- | --- | --- |
| | Current | Recommended |
| Fat | 45% of total calories<br>7% polyunsaturated<br>19% monounsaturated<br>16% saturated | 30% of total calories<br>10% polyunsaturated<br>10% monounsaturated<br>10% saturated |
| Carbohydrates | 46% of total calories<br>18% sugar<br>28% natural | 58% of total calories<br>10% sugar<br>48% natural |
| Protein | 12% of total calories | 12% of total calories (increase vegetable protein) |
| Cholesterol | 600 milligrams | 300 milligrams |
| Sodium | 6 to 18 grams salt | 5 grams salt or less |
| Fiber | Low intake | Increase intake substantially |
| Calories | Too much (resulting in overweight) | Balance calorie intake and output |

- Except for young children, consumption of dairy products should be low-fat or nonfat.
- Decrease the consumption of cholesterol (e.g., eggs, butterfat, organ meats, and red meat).
- Eat less salt and fewer salty foods.
- Consume only enough calories to maintain ideal body weight.

Those are all excellent guidelines to follow. However, it is not easy to remember all of them when you go to the grocery store or into a restaurant for dinner. We have four general concepts that may help to instill in you a deeper understanding of nutrition so that eventually you may be able to make your choices without effort. The four concepts we propose are:

1. *Nutrient Density.* The term "nutrient density" refers to the amount of vitamins, minerals, fiber, and protein per hundred calories of food. This concept helps you to avoid the usual "dos" and "don'ts" of diets. No food is all good or all bad. By considering nutrient density, you can choose between foods, determining in each situation which food is better for you than another. For example, peanuts provide a respectable amount of protein and niacin, but they are also high in fat (75 percent of their calories) and high in total calories (about 840 calories per cupful). If you have a choice between peanuts and popcorn for snack food, by nutrient density popcorn would be better. Popcorn is high in fiber and complex carbohydrates and is sixteen percent protein. With only 25 calories per cupful, popcorn provides more nutrients per calorie than peanuts. Following this example, broccoli is more nutrient dense than steak, and oranges are more nutrient dense than soda pop.

2. *Relative Values of Food.* Once you have accustomed yourself to the concept of nutrient density, you can easily adapt your attitude to the relative value of various foods.

The nutritional rainbow (see Table 7.3) offers the advantages of graphic simplicity, while permitting you a rationale for your choices. Based on risk vs. benefit and nutrient density, it is devised to rank a wide variety of foods according to relative value. Generally, if most of the foods you eat are from the higher bands of the rainbow, they will very likely help to lengthen your lifespan. If most of your food selections are from

## TABLE 7.3

## THE LA COSTA NUTRITIONAL RAINBOW

- Eat small, frequent meals, beginning with a large breakfast and tapering off in meal size during the day.
- Consume a minimum of Salt, Fat, Sugar, Cholesterol, Alcohol, Refined Foods, and Processed Meats.

- Eat a variety of unprocessed foods.
- Consume a maximum of Whole Grains, Fresh Fruits and Vegetables, Legumes, Low and Non Fat Dairy Products, Low Fat Fish and Poultry, and Clean Water.

Rainbow arcs (outer to inner):

BROWN RICE · BARLEY · WHEAT · OCTOPUS · SOLE · AMARANTH · GARLIC · OATS · CARROTS · HADDOCK · COD · MILLET · RYE · WHOLE GRAIN BREAD · SPINACH · BASS · HALIBUT · BLACK-EYED PEAS · SALMON · GREEN PEPPERS · SOYBEANS · LIVER · SWORDFISH · BROCCOLI · ONION · NAVY BEANS · TURKEY · TROUT · ABALONE · CABBAGE · KALE · GARBANZO BEANS · CHICKEN · EGGS · TUNA · CLAMS · OYSTER · LOBSTER · ENDIVE · SPROUTS · PINTO BEANS · KIDNEY · HEART · SHRIMP · CAULIFLOWER · WHEAT GERM · PARMESAN CHEESE · BEET GREENS · BRUSSEL SPROUTS · CHARD · ASPARAGUS · TOMATO

BREWERS YEAST · LOW-FAT CHEESE · WHOLE WHEAT & FRESH FRUIT PIE · HIGH-FAT BEEF, PORK, VEAL, LAMB · HOME-MADE LOW-FAT GRANOLA · PEAS · LOW-FAT MILK · LIMA BEANS · CORN · POPCORN · SPIRULINA · LOW-FAT BEEF, PORK, VEAL, LAMB · HOME-MADE PIZZA, WHOLE WHEAT CRUST · VINEGAR · WHOLE MILK · ALMONDS · PECANS · PEANUTS · WALNUTS · BEETS · CELERY · DANDELION GREENS · LETTUCE

NON-FAT MILK · YOGURT · PEAR · APPLE · COMMERCIAL GRANOLA · AVOCADO · CRACKERS · CREAMED VEGETABLES · WHITE FLOUR · WHITE NOODLES · CAKE · BUTTER · SUNFLOWER SEEDS · ZUCCHINI · RADISHES · PUMPKIN · WINTER SQUASH

BUTTERMILK · TOFU · ICE CREAM · SWEETENED CONDENSED MILK · WHITE RICE · GELATIN DESSERTS · COMMERCIAL PIES · MAYONNAISE · KETCHUP · TOBASCO · SPICES · SOY OIL · SAFFLOWER OIL · SUNFLOWER OIL · PUMPKIN SEEDS · GRITS · SWEET POTATOES

PAPAYA · APRICOT · PINEAPPLE · DUCK · CHEDDAR CHEESE · MOST CHEESES · COMMERCIAL PIZZA · WAFFLES · PANCAKES · TEA · COFFEE · DIET SOFT DRINKS · CORN CHIPS · PICKLES · OLIVES · SYRUP · BUTTER · COCONUT OIL · STICK MARGARINE · OLIVE OIL · SESAME SEEDS · CORN · VEGETABLE JUICE

ORANGES · WATER-MELON · MELON · FRUIT JUICE · DATES · FIGS · CANNED FRUIT · BEER · WINE · SUGAR GUM · SOFT DRINKS · SALT · MSG · DISTILLED SPIRITS · PRETZELS · HYDROGENATED FAT · LARD · SUGARED OIL & VINEGAR · BLEU CHEESE DRESSING · BREAKFAST CEREALS · MARGARINE · CORN TORTILLA · TURNIP GREENS

TANGERINE · LIMES · HONEYDEW · BANANA · GRAPES · RAISINS · PRUNES · DRIED FRUIT · BOLOGNA · SALAMI · BACON · HOT DOG · SAUSAGE · DOUGH-NUTS · POTATO CHIPS · SOUP MIXES · PASTRIES · MOLASSES · HONEY

STRAW-BERRIES · BLUE-BERRIES · PLUMS · CHERRIES · RHUBARB · GUAVA · CANTA-LOUPE

Center: Rx: EAT HIGH ON THE RAINBOW

161

the lower bands, your diet may possibly shorten your lifespan.

Depending on certain conditions, some foods may move up or down in value in your particular diet. For example, if you have heart disease, then you would place liver and eggs one band lower on the rainbow. An active, growing child would place liver and whole milk one band higher.

If you display this nutritional rainbow prominently in your kitchen, eventually you will be able to recall the precise placement of each food, so that you can develop your own sense of nutritional judgment.

3. *Risk vs. Benefit of Foods*. A natural progression from the nutritional rainbow concept is your ability to weigh the relative benefits of various foods against their risks. There is always some risk involved in life; your ability to survive depends upon your minimizing your risks and balancing them against what you gain by taking them. When you leave your home to go to work, you risk accidents, but that risk is minor considering the benefits of earned income and the sense of accomplishment.

A similar attitude is necessary in your choices of food. Even the worst junk-food provides you with calories and water that your body can utilize, though you are taking a great risk by consuming them, especially if you do so on a regular basis. Some people avoid eggs and liver because of the cholesterol they contain, and certainly those who are at risk for heart disease should do so. But they are nutrient-dense foods, and their benefits can outweigh the risks for those people who are living a healthy lifestyle. Similarly, steak is high in fat and cholesterol, but it provides a good source of niacin, iron, vitamin B-12, and zinc.

You must learn to make these judgments in order to take charge of your life. No one else can do it for you.

4. *Occasional vs. Regular Indulgences.* We have no desire to turn you into a "puranoid." You know what this is; in recent years almost everyone has come to know at least one. It's a cross between a "purist" and a "paranoid," and it can be a highly obnoxious creature. Puranoids would never let a potato chip cross their lips, and they deliver a lengthy lecture when they observe someone else eating one.

It is just as foolish to live in fear of foods as it is not to think of food values at all. We want you to learn to choose foods wisely, not to become a slave to rigid rules that will hamper your enjoyment of life. Unless you have a serious health problem, an occasional indulgence in a hot dog and beer at the baseball game won't hurt you. It is when you have a regular pattern of hot dogs and beer that you will insult your body, and it will rebel.

The wise and sensible person will know that empty calories will have to be worked off in exercise, and will act accordingly. (Even the best of diets will do you no good if you persist in getting no exercise.)

## Changing Your Attitude Toward Food

Nutritionists have long searched for a way to translate the complex biochemical makeup of food into something easy for the average person to understand. An early attempt at this was the breakdown of the four food groups:

| GROUP | KEY NUTRIENT CONTRIBUTIONS |
|---|---|
| Dairy | calcium, phosphorous, water, protein, niacin, vitamin D, riboflavin, lactose |
| Meat | protein, iron, vitamin B-6, vitamin B-12, niacin, zinc |
| Fruits & Vegetables | folate, water, fiber, vitamin C, vitamin A, complex carbohydrates, simple carbohydrates |
| Breads & Cereals | thiamine, niacin, complex carbohydrates, fiber, iron, protein |

There were several problems with this method of categorizing foods. Two of the four categories are high in animal protein, fat, and cholesterol. Fruits and vegetables are combined into one group, while they actually have major differences in their nutrient contributions. Vegetarians had no way of following this breakdown, and when one ate butter or fried foods, the calories from fat were not counted.

For these reasons a new breakdown into six categories has been devised, as follows:

| GROUP | KEY NUTRIENT CONTRIBUTIONS |
|---|---|
| Dairy | calcium, phosphorous, water, protein, niacin, vitamin D, riboflavin, lactose. |
| Fat | linoleic acid, vitamin E, calories |

| Fruits | vitamin C, fiber, water, simple carbohydrates, bioflavonoids |
| Vegetables | folate, water, fiber, complex carbohydrates, vitamin A |
| Bread/Grains | thiamin, niacin, complex carbohydrates, fiber, iron, protein |
| Meat/Protein less (low, medium, and high fat) | protein, iron, vitamin B-6, vitamin B-12, zinc |

By using this new exchange system (approved by all major health organizations in America) to select your foods and plan your meals, it is possible to calculate both your calories and your nutrients more accurately. Your body requires some of each of the six categories, but the foods should be kept in balance.

To understand this balance, study the breakdown recommended by the U.S. Senate Select Committee on Nutrition and Human Needs. By eating a wide variety of foods and by consuming them as close to their natural condition as possible (i.e., not overly refined or processed), you have a good chance of having a well-balanced diet.

There are those who will protest that they have heard these things before, but can't follow the recommendations because "nutritious foods don't taste good." For these people, some adjustment will be necessary. Their sense of taste has become distorted by conditioning to sucrose (white sugar), salt, fat, monosodium glutamate, and other condiments of the food processor. Their need for salty, sweet, or fatty foods is an acquired one, and their taste buds—once reconditioned—will appreciate the natural, nutritional flavors far more.

The earthy, gutsy flavor of whole grains can become addictive after you have refrained from the refined equivalents for awhile. Your palate will prefer fresh steamed vegetables once it has forgotten the creamed, canned by-products. You will find that fresh fruits taste far better than frozen desserts after a time.

We do not deny that there will be an initial shock when you give up the nonnutritional condiments, but if you can let go of them for a month, your palate will not want to return to them. You will actually begin to enjoy the natural flavors of foods. This is one thing that guests at La Costa frequently comment on—how different real food tastes. Once accustomed to these flavors, they come to look upon the artificial flavors of highly refined foods as cloying.

And you dessert lovers do not have to give up your favorite course of the meal. Such natural sweets as pumpkin pie, made from fresh pumpkin with whole wheat crust and sweetened with honey, is both nutritional and delicious.

You do not have to give up enjoyment to be healthy. You merely have to rid yourself of the societal conditioning that tells you anything healthy can't be fun. If there was truth in that, the human race would not have survived this long.

**R<sub>X</sub>**

- Eat foods as close as possible to their natural state. Refining usually removes valuable nutrients, adds questionable agents, and increases food costs.

- Eat a wide variety of foods in order to avoid ingesting excess toxins of both natural and synthetic origin and also to possibly include unknown but essential nutrients.

- Eat small frequent meals, beginning with a large breakfast, gradually reducing the size of the meals as the day progresses.

- Let the bulk of your diet be whole grains, fresh fruits and vegetables, and legumes, with smaller amounts of low-fat dairy products, fish and poultry, and meat more as a supplement than as a staple.

- Minimize your intake of salt, fat, sugar, alcohol, and junk-food.

- Drink plenty of clean water (five to ten cups) each day.

- Theoretically, it should be possible to get all nutrients "with a fork and spoon." Realistically, the typical western lifestyle may require you to adopt a daily rational supplement program consisting of:
    - (a) A broad spectrum low-potency multiple vitamin-mineral supplement
    - (b) Five hundred to one thousand milligrams daily of vitamin C.
    - (c) One hundred to two hundred international units daily of vitamin E.
    - (d) Calcium and magnesium in a two-to-one ratio (250 and 125 milligrams respectively, or more if your diet is low in dairy products).

## ✖»➤ 8 ✖«✖

# Nutritional Good Guys

"And the earth brought forth vegetation,
plants yielding seed after their kind, and trees
bearing fruit, with seed in them, after their kind;
and God saw that it was good."

—GENESIS 1:12

[• Foods can be both nutritional and delicious • You can
consume too much protein • Learning to eat the right kind
of protein in the right amount • Carbohydrates are important
in your diet • The dangers of refined sugars • Fiber performs
important functions • Regular water intake is essential • Vitamins and minerals in a proper balance are vital to life • Some
important questions and answers about vitamins and minerals
• Choose your cookware and pottery carefully—it can affect
what you eat • Learning to eat by grazing rather than gorging]

To recondition yourself to accept nutritional foods requires a
better understanding of what is good and bad in diet. This is
especially true if you were bribed as a child with statements
like, "If you eat your vegetables, you can have a nice piece

of chocolate cake." Parents who make such statements don't fully realize the harm they are doing to their children. It is not so much the bribe that does harm, but the underlying assumption that vegetables taste bad and chocolate cake tastes good. The obvious conclusion for children is that nutritious and delicious cannot exist in the same food.

This is a mistaken conclusion from a mistaken assumption. Foods that are good for you do taste good, and they are the rewards you give your body, not the chocolate cake.

However, this is not the only aspect of our food attitudes that needs clarification. A great many myths and misunderstandings have grown up surrounding everything from proteins to vitamins. We hope to be able to clarify many of these so that you can set out on a better course of healthy nutrition and longer life.

## Protein

A great many people misunderstand the significance and importance of proteins in diet. The word "protein" is derived from a Greek word meaning "prime" or "chief." When the excited Dutch chemist Mulder wrote about his newly discovered substance, he stated, "unquestionably the most important of all known substances in the organic kingdom." Indeed, this impressive statement is relatively true, since well over 50,000 people around the world die each day from insufficient calories and protein. Even in the western world, one out of six people is deficient in protein intake.

However, this generalized view has led to a myth that the more one eats of protein the healthier one is. This is not true.

Unfortunately the majority of people in the West eat too much protein, and their health suffers from it.

CASE HISTORY: B.W. came to La Costa to get himself into shape after failing a physical exam for a new life insurance policy. Until taking that exam he had thought himself in fairly decent condition for a slightly overweight executive of age 58, but his doctors had told him otherwise. He was more than just 25 pounds overweight; by percent body fat measurements, he was actually obese. With his cholesterol level, he was at a high risk for a myocardial infarction (heart attack).

The doctor's probing of B.W.'s heart and blood vessels revealed that numerous arteries were nearly blocked.

A computer diet analysis at La Costa showed excess protein, phosphorus, fat, cholesterol, and calories. His dietary deficiencies included fiber, ascorbic acid, folic acid, vitamin A, and zinc.

B.W.'s problems had started with the protein myth. When he was a young man, his high school football coach had told him that he should eat as much protein as possible because protein built muscles and manhood. Even though he had long ago stopped playing football, B.W. continued to follow that advice. He continued to indulge regularly in red meat.

B.W.'s lifestyle was typical of the successful businessman who has spent thirty years climbing to the top. His habits were sedentary; he ate out a great deal; and he endured a high level of stress. His diet was high in red meat, and high in fat.

At La Costa, he was placed on a dietary program of 600 calories per day, which was low in fat and high in fluid and fiber. He was given an exercise program that started with light activity but built to two hours a day by the end of two weeks.

After a month at La Costa, he was able to return home, retake his physical exam, and pass.

B.W. had suffered from a common myth: "Since protein is essential for life, then the more the better." He had to learn the hard way that ideal nutrition is a question of balance.

Protein *is* vital to life: we do not want you to make a mistake about that. Although some plants can manufacture their own protein from carbohydrates and free nitrogen, humans have to consume theirs. About eighteen percent of a healthy adult's body weight is protein. It performs a myriad of functions, from building body structure (bones, tendons, muscles) to creating the tiny molecules that keep your chemical system running (such as enzymes, hemoglobin, and immunoglobins).

Proteins are composed of *amino acids*, which form the "alphabet" of life. Like the alphabet of language, which can form almost limitless words with only 26 letters, the 22 amino acids (nine of which are essential to life) manage to create millions of different proteins. By arranging them differently, Nature can create a newt, a gnat, a human, or a redwood tree.

Your diet needs the nine essential amino acids that cannot be manufactured by your body, and it needs them in the proper ratio. Since animals are closer to humans than are plants, meat protein is generally higher in the ratio of essential amino acids than plant protein. (See Figure 8.1.) However, meat is high in fat and cholesterol, as well, and it is possible to obtain the essential amino acids from vegetables through a process known as protein matching. (See Figure 8.2.)

Meat contains the essential amino acids in the proper ratio. Corn has more methionine than it needs, but is seriously low in tryptophan and lysine. Pinto beans are low in methionine,

**TABLE 8.1**

**CATEGORIES OF PROTEIN**

| Protein Quality | PROTEIN QUANTITY | |
| --- | --- | --- |
| | *High* | *Low* |
| *High* | Meat, Fish, Poultry, Eggs, Yeast, Wheat Germ, Spirulina. | Brown Rice, Bacon. |
| *Low* | Legumes. | Fruits, Leafy Vegetables. |

but have extra lysine and tryptophan. By combining corn and pinto beans in the same meal in reasonably equal portions, you achieve a combination that is similar in protein quality to a steak. The deficit of one protein is compensated for by the excess of another.

For example, you can combine grains—such as corn, wheat, rye, barley, rice, oats, or millet—with legumes—such as lentils, soybeans, kidney beans, pinto beans, white beans, garbanzo beans, or split peas—to produce high-quality protein meals such as the following:

beans and tortillas
tofu (soybean curd) and brown rice
barley and lentil soup
cornbread and chili
peanut butter sandwiches

Or you can match high-quality proteins—such as beef, fish, dairy products, eggs, poultry, cheese, pork, brewer's yeast, wheat germ, spirulina—with medium-quality proteins—such as grains, legumes, and nuts—to produce the following meals:

## FIGURE 8.2
### COMPLEMENTARY PROTEINS

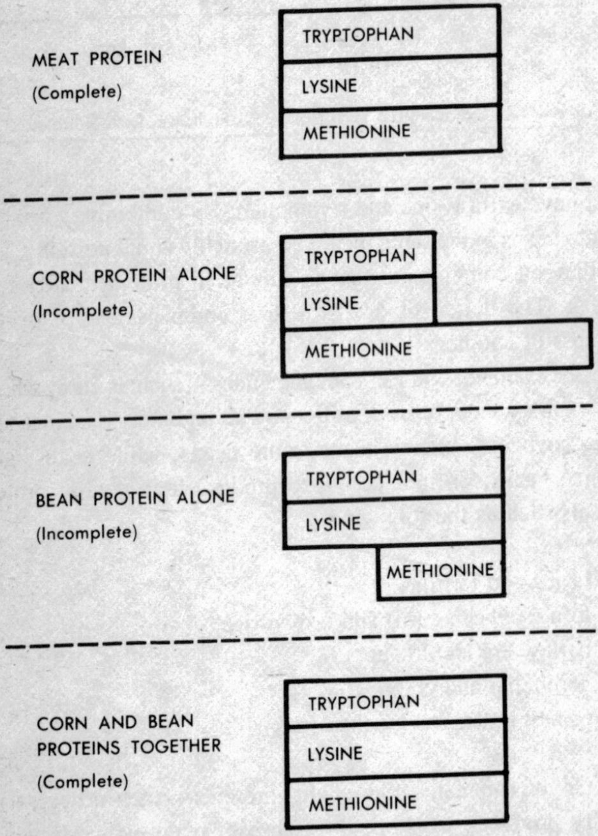

MEAT PROTEIN
(Complete)

| TRYPTOPHAN |
| LYSINE |
| METHIONINE |

CORN PROTEIN ALONE
(Incomplete)

| TRYPTOPHAN |
| LYSINE |
| METHIONINE |

BEAN PROTEIN ALONE
(Incomplete)

| TRYPTOPHAN |
| LYSINE |
| METHIONINE |

CORN AND BEAN
PROTEINS TOGETHER
(Complete)

| TRYPTOPHAN |
| LYSINE |
| METHIONINE |

milk on cereal
meat sauce on spaghetti (pasta is made from durum wheat)
quiche (eggs, cheese, wheat crust)
ham and split pea soup
wheat germ and garbanzo bean casserole

These are just a few of the possibilities. Menus for more imaginative meals with detailed recipes can be found in the Appendix.

It is important that you realize that several of the plant proteins are of high quality themselves. These include rice, wheat germ, brewer's yeast, and spirulina. This last is a tiny ocean organism that—when dried—is about seventy percent protein. When obtained in bulk, spirulina looks like green flour. It can be mixed in casseroles and soup without creating any offensive flavor while considerably improving nutritional value.

What we recommend is that you use animal proteins as the supplement in your diet rather than as the staple, relying primarily on plant proteins. The advantages of plant proteins are:

- They are cheaper; steak is 42 times the cost of soybeans.
- They are lower in fat and have no cholesterol.
- They are higher in polyunsaturated fats and linoleic acid.
- They are high in fiber and complex carbohydrates.
- They are lower in phosphorus.
- They are higher in potassium.
- They are less bulky and easier to store; they have long shelf life.

- They are very tasty when properly prepared.
- They increase your chances for longer life.

Precisely how you acquire your protein requirements is up to you. You control your health and the length of your life. It is most important, however, that you keep your protein intake balanced.

Be aware of the problems that can be caused by protein excess as well as protein deficiency. The symptoms of protein deficiency are: Stunted growth, problems in pregnancy, retarded brain development, loss of hair and nails, weakening of other structural proteins, edema and bloating, confusion and inability to concentrate, loss of digestive functions, and poor wound healing, with lowered resistance to disease.

An excess of dietary protein can cause: overweight, with its many accompanying hazards; kidney and liver stress, since these organs must process excess protein; loss of calcium from the body, which may lead to osteoporosis; high risk of heart disease and cancer, because animal proteins carry considerable fat and cholesterol; shortened lifespan.

How can you know precisely how much protein each individual needs?

There is a simple formula, based upon your age and weight. Protein needs are highest during stages of rapid growth such as among small children and expectant mothers. To figure your specific protein requirement, first determine your weight in kilograms. (To obtain this, divide your weight in pounds by 2.2.) Next, select the factor from the following list that best describes you:

Adult................................................. 0.8
Adolescent .......................................... 1.0
Older child .......................................... 1.5
Younger child ....................................... 1.8
Infant................................................ 2.2

Multiply your weight in kilograms by the factor to obtain the number of grams of protein you need each day. If you are pregnant, add thirty extra grams per day; if you are a lactating mother, add twenty extra grams.

For example, a 150-pound adult (68.2 kilograms) would need 55 grams of protein (68.2 × 0.8 = 54.5).

The average adult in the developed nations consumes more than ninety grams of protein each day or about 35 grams of extra protein that must be burned or stored as fat. These are 35 grams of extra protein, with its accompanying fat and cholesterol, that may eventually cause you health problems—if they are not already doing so.

---

**R**$_\text{X}$

- When you eat animal protein (meat, cheese, eggs, dairy products), endeavor to use it as a supplement rather than a staple. Soups, casseroles, and Asian cuisines help to achieve this balance.

- Do not eat burned proteins, such as well-done meat. These have been shown to cause cancer. Avoid smoked and salted meats.

- Seriously restrict your consumption of the fatty protein foods, such as prime rib, luncheon meats, bacon, duck, and hamburger.

continued

- Eat your calculated protein allotment within the reasonable and safe limits.
- Combine the recommended plant proteins for nutritious and delicious life-extending protein sources.

## Carbohydrates

Carbohydrates have earned an undeserved ugly reputation. Your body needs complex carbohydrates as a high percentage of the total food you consume. Its preferential fuel is glucose, which is carbohydrate. Your brain, the lens of your eye, and your kidneys function almost exclusively on blood sugar.

So why have carbohydrates gotten such a bad reputation? It is because there are two different kinds of carbohydrates— natural and refined—and two basic categories—simple (most sugars) and complex (starches). Table 8.3 may help you to differentiate. It is the refined carbohydrates—both simple and complex—that have created the greatest misunderstanding for this highly important food group. Your body needs the naturally occurring simple and complex carbohydrates, and it can use the refined ones, though they are far less nourishing.

Refining of foods frequently removes nutrients and fiber while leaving the calories. In the case of carbohydrates, the naturally occurring foods have considerable fiber that helps slow down their digestion and absorption by the body, helping you to avoid problems with blood sugar levels. Whole grains can be an excellent source of vitamin E and protein; their refined counterparts have little or none. Whole grains also contain sufficient chromium to metabolize their carbohydrates;

their refined versions have almost no chromium left. Pantothenic acid, vitamin B-6, and other valuable nutrients are also casualties of the refining process.

Diabetes and hypoglycemia are diseases of poorly regulated blood glucose, though they are—in a sense—opposite sides of the same coin. Diabetes is linked to a high blood glucose level, while hypoglycemia is of concern when the level falls below sixty milligrams percent. (Early symptoms of hypoglycemia are shakiness, clouded thought, depression, blurred vision, and weakness.)

---

**TABLE 8.3**

**CATEGORIES OF CARBOHYDRATES**

| Carbo-hydrates | *Naturally Occurring* | *Refined* |
| --- | --- | --- |
| Simple | Fruits, Honey, Milk, Sugar | Table Sugar, Corn Syrup |
| Complex | Whole Wheat, Rice, Oats, Barley, Legumes, Some Vegetables | White Flour, Potato Chips, White Pasta |

---

The blood glucose curves are illustrated in Table 8.4. The more gradual the curve, the more constant and predictable your energy level. A diet that is high in complex carbohydrates can assist your body in maintaining a much more regulated blood glucose curve.

CASE HISTORY: L.S. came to La Costa upon her doctor's recommendation. She had fought the battle of the bulge since giving birth to her first child. Most of her diets were high-protein regimens, which denied her carbohydrates. With her energy dwindling and her emotions volatile, she rarely got past the second day of any diet.

At La Costa she was placed on an 800-calorie per day diet, with multiple vitamin and mineral supplements. At first she refused to believe she would lose weight on this regimen; she

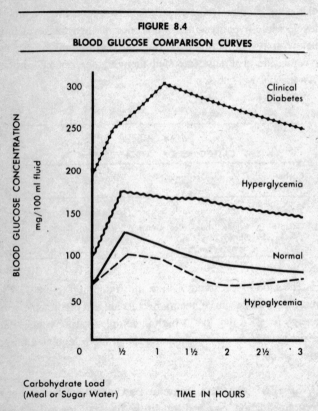

**FIGURE 8.4**
**BLOOD GLUCOSE COMPARISON CURVES**

Note the peaks and valleys in the chart. The more even and smooth the curves, the more dependable your energy levels.

was certain that we were giving her too much food. On several occasions she challenged the dieticians for giving her carbohydrates.

She was surprised when she began to lose weight eating a diet high in complex carbohydrates. She was also surprised at the energy she had while losing weight rapidly. Coupled with an extensive but gradual exercise program and classes to help her restyle her home habits, the 800-calorie diet enabled her to lose 28 pounds in one month.

CASE HISTORY: In her 61 years on earth, A.B. had become a connoisseur of sugar and its many offspring in the food industry. She checked into La Costa with numerous health problems—muscular weakness and occasional heart palpitations, borderline diabetes with obesity, constipation, and regular bouts of depression.

We approached her condition cautiously, reluctant to diagnose all of her problems as stemming from her diet. Most of her food intake seemed average—except for simple carbohydrates. (The average westerner consumes over 120 pounds of sugar a year, far too much for good health; A.B. consumed closer to 140 pounds a year.) Her exercise program was almost nonexistent, and her overall lifestyle pattern was atrocious. Before calling in a psychological counselor, we decided to give her a week on a different diet and exercise program to see if there would be improvements.

The diet she was given was 1200 calories a day, with high-potency vitamin and mineral supplements. Her high-sugar diet would have depleted her stores of thiamin and chromium. An exercise program was designed, beginning with swimming and stationary bicycling to work her slowly and gradually into activity.

Within four days, A.B. told us that she had noticed an improvement in her moods and daily elimination process. Within the trial week there was sufficient progress for us to realize that the improvements in diet and exercise were all she needed. At the conclusion of her three-week stay, she confessed her dietary history, confiding that she had been a refined sugar addict since her earliest years. Her mother had loved to bake, and had used this means of expressing her affection for her children. Reared on sugar-flavored baby food, she had had no trouble adapting to sugar-flavored breakfast cereals, pastries, candies, and soda pop.

A.B. had heard experts say that refined sugar was bad, but other experts had contradicted this. She had seen no need to give up her sweets until the experts could agree.

We explained to her that refined sugar provides the body with calories that are quickly absorbed, but that it does not provide the nutrients needed to burn the sugar. We compared it to filling up the gas tank in her automobile and then removing the spark plugs: there is fuel to burn, but not enough spark to burn it with. Without the thiamin, niacin, riboflavin, panto-thenic acid, and chromium required to metabolize sugar, her body had experienced problems with the muscular and nervous systems. Poor muscle tone in the intestines led to regular con-stipation; poor muscle tone in the extremities negated the chances of exercising to lose some of the abundant calories she con-sumed; missing energy nutrients in the heart region could have contributed to the palpitations she felt. The few calories she burned caused obesity, which promoted diabetes. Thiamin, niacin, and chromium shortages had created nervous problems that were manifested in her depressions.

It was nearly ten months later that we received a postcard from A.B. She had battled her sugar-educated taste buds for a month after returning from La Costa, but had finally won. She no longer craved high-sugar foods, and her health improved considerably. She had lost her excess weight and had gained a robust new shape from her exercise program. Her last statement summed it all up: "Never felt better."

## Fiber

Only a few decades ago, scientists saw little value in fiber in the human diet, perceiving it only as indigestible food matter. Because of this lack of understanding, we now have white bread, potato chips, peeled fruits, and other fiber-stripped food products, with the resultant epidemic levels of numerous diseases. In the 1950s, there were health faddists who advocated eating whole foods, but they were the only ones, and they were looked upon with a degree of scorn. Now much of the scientific community concurs.

Although it is not absorbed by the body, fiber does many favors for us during its brief stay in the digestive tract. Its principal function is to provide bulk without calories and to absorb water, fat, and toxic elements. The benefits of a high-fiber diet are:

- Less chance of overweight. High-fiber foods will fill you without giving you extra calories.

- Better-regulated blood glucose. Fiber slows down the absorption of carbohydrates, so there is a more gradual infusion of simple carbohydrates into the blood.
- Lowered fat and cholesterol absorption. Fiber binds these and carries them out of the system with feces. (Also, since high-fiber foods contain very little fat, there is less chance of heart disease.)
- Less chance of having problems in the intestinal tract, such as hemorrhoids, cancer of the colon, diverticulae. Fiber gently cleanses the intestines daily.

### TABLE 8.5
### FOODS HIGH IN NATURAL CARBOHYDRATES AND FIBER

| Grains | Legumes | Fruits | Vegetables |
|--------|---------|--------|------------|
| Rice | Soybeans | Apples | Broccoli |
| Barley | Black-eyed Peas | Cherries | Tomatoes |
| Whole Wheat | Garbanzo Beans | Bananas | Potatoes |
| Millet | Navy Beans | Peaches | Cauliflower |
| Rye | Lentils | Citrus | Pumpkin |
| Corn | Pinto Beans | Melons | Onions |
| Oats | Kidney Beans | Berries | Squash |

- Less toxin exposure. Fiber binds to toxic substances to carry them out of the system.

To help you identify those foods that are high in fiber, it is helpful to know that they are generally the same foods that are high in naturally occurring carbohydrates. All are also high in fiber.

Again, we must stress the concept of balance. We do not want you to go overboard in your consumption of fiber. Just as it is possible to have too little fiber in your diet, it is also possible to have too much. In addition to binding to toxic elements in your body, it also binds to certain essential elements such as zinc and calcium. If your fiber intake becomes too high, deficiencies of these nutrients can occur. Excess fiber intake can also cause diarrhea and fluid loss. Your fiber intake should be just right when you have soft and regular bowel movements.

Remember, the advantages of a diet that is high in naturally occurring carbohydrates are the following:

- You will be less likely to suffer from overweight, heart disease, diabetes, and intestinal problems.
- You will have more consistent and higher levels of emotional and physical energy.
- These foods are much cheaper than their refined counterparts, and cheaper than dairy and meat products.
- In their natural dry state, grains and legumes take up little space and require no special storage equipment, though we do recommend using tightly sealed containers.
- You will live longer and better.

---

$R_X$

- Minimize intake of starches such as white bread, crackers, and pastries.
- Minimize intake of refined sugars such as soft drinks, pastries, and candy.

continued

---

- One-half to two-thirds of your food intake should consist of whole grains, legumes, fresh vegetables and fruit.

- Consume fruit and vegetables in their whole form, not juiced or converted into desserts.

- For optimal blood glucose regulation, avoid alcohol, eat small and frequent meals (four to six per day), and exercise regularly.

## Water

There are people who have managed to survive for months without food. However, humans can exist only a few days without water. Our bodies are about two-thirds water, and it is an essential nutrient for life. Although we do have a thirst mechanism that tells us to consume fluids before dehydration becomes lifethreatening, a great many people do not consume enough fluids.

Regular water intake is essential to the human body, because it acts as a medium for chemical reactions, stores and disperses heat, and provides a means for transporting nutrients and toxins to their proper destinations.

CASE HISTORY: M.Y. was a regular visitor at La Costa, and her health was generally good. However, one day she shyly mentioned that she had periodic problems with urinary tract infections. A brief examination and diet history revealed that M.Y. was not a water drinker. To quench her thirst, she consumed a few cups of coffee during the day, and an alcoholic drink or two in the evening.

Caffeine and alcohol both acted as diuretics, causing M.Y.'s body to excrete more than normal amounts of urine, which was often deep yellow and strong smelling. She lived in a warm, dry climate. Without making a serious effort to consume fluids, she suffered from a general state of dehydration.

In a hot, dry climate an adult can lose up to ten quarts of fluid per day. The body uses water to cool the skin surface with sweat evaporation, with the result that less water is left inside to dilute the toxins found in the urine. If there is not a frequent and diluted flushing, bacteria can find their way up the urinary passage to cause infections. (Also, when the urine is diluted with large amounts of water, kidney stones are less likely to be formed.)

M.Y. assumed her usual vigorous exercise ritual while at La Costa, but she was encouraged to take regular breaks throughout the day to drink water and fruit juice. After a week, M.Y. had more frequent and less offensive urination. Her usually dry and flaky skin had also taken on a new look of smoothness. On her next visit to La Costa, six months later, she announced proudly that she had no more urinary tract infections. She was also more energetic, and her mind was much more alert when she got up in the morning. (The brain is highly reliant on proper fluid levels.)

We could all use regular water breaks during our daily routines. Not only should one make an effort to consume the right amount of water, but also water of a good quality. In recent years, because of industrial pollutants found in ground water, there have been questions about the purity and safety of city drinking water. If you have reason to question the quality of your water, we recommend that you buy reputable bottled water or obtain your own purifier.

Also, do not drink softened water, which is high in sodium and causes water retention. One visitor to La Costa came to Dr. Smith complaining of dizziness and severe imbalance. The culprit was the soft water she had been drinking, which produced water retention throughout her body and caused balance problems in her inner ear. Within a week of ceasing to drink softened water, her symptoms cleared.

- Drink five to ten cups per day of pure, clean water.

## Vitamins and Minerals

In the developed nations of the world, serious vitamin deficiencies are relatively rare. By "serious" deficiencies, we are referring to the kinds of problems the entire world knew in the past, and the third world nations still suffer from. Most of the 80,000 children each year who go blind from a deficiency of vitamin A are in the underdeveloped nations. However, surveys indicate that millions of people in the developed nations are consuming too little of various vitamins and minerals to maintain optimal health. These deficiencies are not so great as to cause scurvy, rickets, beri-beri, or blindness, but their cumulative long-term effect is to reduce the quality of overall health and probably to shorten lifespan.

A part of the cause of this low-level vitamin and mineral deficiency is the processing of our foods. We consume a highly refined diet with many indigenous nutrients cast aside in the processing.

Cancer has been shown to be related to lack of vitamins A, C, and E, and the mineral selenium. Heart disease has been shown to be related to insufficient levels of vitamins B-6 and C and of the minerals calcium and magnesium. Osteoporosis may be related to insufficient intake of calcium, magnesium, and vitamin D, with too much phosphorus, fat, and protein. Diabetes may be related to insufficient chromium.

And we suffer a host of other, less severe problems from the lack of proper vitamins and minerals.

CASE HISTORY: J.T. was young and attractive. However, when she checked into La Costa, she was irritable and lethargic, with a dry, cracked skin condition near her mouth and nose. When questioned during her medical examination, she confessed that she had tried several rather radical weight-reduction diets during the past six months. Some of the diets were high-protein, others involved no food at all.

J.T. was suffering the classical symptoms of thiamin deficiency.

High-protein diets, fasting, excessive alcohol intake, and high sugar consumption can all cause subclinical thiamin deficiency. Most cells of the body favor carbohydrates for fuel, and thiamin is required for burning carbohydrates. All cells will suffer from a thiamin deficiency, but nerve and muscle cells are the first affected, with the overt symptoms often occurring in the cells that the body may consider more expendable—those of the skin.

J.T. was given a multiple vitamin and mineral supplement, with high-potency thiamin (vitamin B-1) and a rational 1,000-calorie per day diet. Within a week, her symptoms cleared noticeably, and they were completely gone within two weeks.

J.T. was not just of average affluence; she would be considered wealthy. However, she was suffering from malnutrition because of her lifestyle of food abstinence, marginal diet when she did eat, and small but steady alcohol consumption.

CASE HISTORY: D.P. was a veteran smoker of many decades. She came to La Costa suffering from frequent bruising and general pain throughout her joints. Her hometown physician had diagnosed her condition as arthritis and had recommended that she attend a health spa in the southwest for heat treatments and dry air.

In her examination at La Costa, the excessive wrinkling of her upper lip presented a clue to a possible vitamin C deficiency. This was confirmed later by a computer diet analysis. Her intake of vitamin C was deficient even for a nonsmoker. Smokers require even higher amounts than normal.

We explained the condition to D.P., telling her that vitamin C is necessary for synthesis of collagen, a tough connective protein used throughout the body; that it is used to make infection resistance factors; and that it is essential in the manufacture of a vital brain chemical. Smoking renders vitamin C useless, so that—even if they have a decent amount of ascorbic acid in their diet—smokers are at a serious risk for subclinical deficiency symptoms.

Our advice is that smokers should quit their habit. Barring that option, they should take at least 500 milligrams of vitamin C a day.

D.P. listened very carefully to our explanation. However, what convinced her was our explanation that smoking prompts premature wrinkling of the skin, because collagen repair of the skin becomes ineffective without vitamin C.

"Poor health is one thing," she said, "but ugliness is another." She agreed to stop smoking.

She was put on a program to help her with her decision, and given high-potency vitamin and mineral supplements with 3,000 milligrams of ascorbic acid, along with an exercise program that would help her to purge her body more quickly of the long term effects of smoking. Two weeks later, her general aches in the joints had dramatically subsided.

CASE HISTORY: V.M. was depressed and desperate. When he checked into La Costa, he was 55 years old and had just had radical surgery to remove a cancerous area of his large intestines. The surgery was apparently successful, but his doctor had recommended that he alter his lifestyle to avoid further problems. Because it was clear V.M. could not do this on his own, the doctor suggested he go to a health institution to accomplish this.

V.M. was a tough case. He had been living a high-risk lifestyle, and it would be difficult to get him to change. He was a moody person, so counselors were brought in to listen to him and to teach him stress-reduction techniques and play-therapy. The director of the men's spa created an exercise program that V.M. thought he could stick to.

A computer diet analysis found many glaring excesses and deficiencies in his diet, including too little vitamin A, vitamin C, vitamin E, selenium, and fiber, with too much fat and well-done red meats. Low intake of certain vitamins known as "antioxidants" was probably a contributing factor in the causes of V.M.'s cancer.

If V.M. is able to stay on his high-potency supplements, balanced 1,800-calorie per day diet, exercise routine, stress reduction techniques, and positive attitude, he has a much improved chance of avoiding another bout with cancer.

Vitamins are required in small amounts, yet they are vital to life. They are needed to perform specific metabolic functions, and they usually become part of an enzyme system. If your body has one substance and wants to make another substance out of it, an enzyme system must be called in to make that change.

Table 8.6 outlines the functions and values of vitamins, minerals, and a few other substances that are vital to your good health. Study the table carefully to understand the specific needs and uses of each. This table also tells you the food sources for each, and the symptoms of deficiency or excess, along with the U.S. required daily amount and the amount that may be considered toxic.

Substances such as garlic and lecithin are not really vitamins or minerals, but they provide benefits for your bodily systems. Garlic has been shown to help reduce fat levels in the blood, assisting in lowering blood pressure while raising high-density lipoproteins (HDL). Lecithin is a phospholipid, which is a soap-like compound that can bind to both fat and water-soluble substances at the same time. This unique property allows lecithin to be of value in helping to lower cholesterol levels in the blood. Lecithin also provides choline, a raw material used in the manufacture of a valuable chemical the brain needs for emotional and intellectual functions.

Lecithin can be found in egg yolks and in soybeans. It can also be obtained in granular and tablet versions. We recommend a tablespoon of granular lecithin per day mixed with other foods.

Medical science is continually making new discoveries concerning the importance of minerals to the human body. Only twenty years ago, many scientists considered the trace elements selenium and chromium to be contaminants in the human body. Now they are regarded not only as vital to human health, but to be among those frequently in low supply in the typical western diet.

Of the sixty known minerals on earth, seventeen are now believed necessary to human nutrition, with another four being possibly essential, but our present knowledge of them is insufficient to be certain. Only recently have scientists been able to detect the tiny amounts of minerals in the body, for some exist in parts per billion or parts per trillion. To understand the difficulty of this, imagine dropping a pinch of sugar in an Olympic-sized swimming pool and then trying to find the sugar in the pool water.

Minerals usually serve one or both of two functions in your body. They may become part of the structural components, such as calcium and phosphorus in teeth and bones. They may also serve as an assistant in the various enzyme reactions. For example, zinc is involved in at least sixty different enzyme systems in your body.

Table 8.7 contains a listing of the minerals known to exist in the human body, along with the amounts considered to be essential to health. A few are known to be essential, but ony in trace amounts. Others may be important, and some others may possibly be toxins. If you are considering taking mineral

**TABLE 8.6**

| Nutrient | Functions | Food Source | Deficiency Symptoms |
|---|---|---|---|
| Vitamin A | Vision, mucous membranes cell division, skin maintenance, sperm production, egg development, growth, bone development, cancer prevention | Liver, green & orange vegetables and fruits (i.e., apricots, carrots), egg yolk | Poor vision, night blindness; keratosis (skin problems); low disease resistance, poor growth, pregnancy problems |
| Vitamin D | Calcium absorption, transport, deposition | Eggs, milk, butter, fish oil, fortified milk, sunshine on skin | Poor calcium metabolism, nerve & muscle impairment, bone demineralization |
| Vitamin E | Antioxidant; retards aging; energy metabolism; making DNA & RNA; heme synthesis; protects cell membranes; protects vitamin A | Wheat germ oil, corn, soy, cottonseed oil, mayonnaise, margarine | Widespread in animals, less obvious in humans; premature bursting of red blood cells, accelerated aging?; sterility; high risk of heart disease or cancer? |
| Vitamin K | Proper blood clotting | Green & yellow vegetables; synthesis by bacteria in intestines | Hemorrhaging; prolonged clotting time |
| Thiamin B-1 | Energy production, especially carbohydrates | Liver, pork, peas, nuts, fish, meat, whole grains, bran | Fatigue, anorexia, irritability, weakness, palpitations, numbness, beriberi (nerve & muscle disorders) |

## VITAMINS AND MINERALS

| Excess | Characteristics | USRDA | Supple-ment Levels | Toxic Levels |
|---|---|---|---|---|
| Headaches, orange skin & eyes, hair loss, diarrhea, nausea | Fat soluble; lost in oxygen, sunlight, or mineral oil; animal versions more potent than plant | 5000 I.U. | 5000–25000 I.U. | +50,000 I.U. for adults, less for child |
| Weight loss, nausea, increased risk of heart disease, failure to thrive | Fat soluble, lost in mineral oil, produced in skin by sunlight; lower toxic ranges may increase risk of heart disease | 400 I.U. | 400–1000 I.U. | 2000 I.U. + |
| Elevated blood pressure; inhibits vitamin A in liver; increases need for other fat soluble vitamins | Fat soluble; still poorly understood; supplements retard effects of pollution on lungs; easily destroyed; higher needs in premature infants | 30 I.U. | 100–1000 I.U. | ? 4000 I.U. |
| Unlikely | Destroyed by antibiotics & aspirin; related to health of intestines | None stated | 30 mcg + | ? 300 mcg |
| Unlikely; lost in urine | Water soluble; lost in heat & water; alcohol, stress & sugar increase needs | 1.5 mg | 2–100 mg | Unknown |

**TABLE 8.6 (Cont.)**

| Nutrient | Functions | Food Source | Deficiency Symptoms |
|---|---|---|---|
| Vitamin B-2 Riboflavin | Energy metabolism; make & break fats; deaminate proteins; major steps in energy production | Liver, milk products (not cheeses) | Skin, eye & tongue problems, cheilosis, dermatitis, glossitis, corneal vascularization |
| Vitamin B-3 Niacin | Energy metabolism; make & break fats; steroid synthesis; vasodilators; lowers blood fats | Liver, whole grain, peanuts, meat, egg, fish, milk | Muscle & nerve disorders; skin eruptions, poor memory, fatigue, pellagra |
| Vitamin B-6 Pyridoxine | Protein metabolism | Soybeans, liver, tuna, banana, lima beans, avocado, port, chicken, halibut | Nervous disorders, depression, skin problems, anemia, fewer lymphocytes, elevated risk for heart disease |
| Vitamin B-12 Cyanocobalamin | Cell growth, red blood cell growth, nerve maintenance, diverse functions | Liver, animal products | Sore tongue, fatigue, serious problems in growth stages (i.e., pregnancy |
| Folic Acid | New cell growth, red blood cell growth, protein synthesis | Liver, green leafy vegetables, salmon, whole grains | Anemia, growth problems, poor memory, sore tongue, digestive disturbances |
| Ascorbic Acid (Vitamin C) | Collagen synthesis (connective tissue); wound healing; maintains blood fats; antioxidant; iron absorption; serotonin & epinephrine production | Citrus, strawberries, broccoli, tomatoes, fruit, vegetables | Pain in joints; decreased wound healing; resistance to infection & bruising; bleeding gums; loose teeth, irritability; premature aging & wrinkling |

## VITAMINS AND MINERALS (Cont.)

| Excess | Characteristics | USRDA | Supplement Levels | Toxic Levels |
|---|---|---|---|---|
| Unlikely | Water soluble; increased need with sugar & alcohol consumption | 1.7 mg | 2–50 mg | Unknown |
| Unlikely | Water soluble; increased need with alcohol consumption, corn, sugar, liver problems | 20 mg | 20–1000 mg | Unknown |
| Unlikely | Water soluble; not replaced in white flour; oral contraceptives increase need | 2.0 mg | 2-100 mg | Unknown |
| Unlikely | Water soluble; difficult to absorb; older people have higher needs? | 60 mcg | 5–100 mcg | Unknown |
| Unlikely | Water soluble; increased need with many drugs, tobacco, alcohol, heat | 400 mcg | 400–800 mcg | Unknown, but must balance with B-12 |
| Rebound scurvy (can happen when intake changes from very high to normal low levels) | Water soluble; easily destroyed by light, heat, oxygen, time, smoking; protects against nitrites; RDAs have increased last 2 revisions | 60 mg | 100–5000 mg | Physiological adaptation at 5000 mg |

**TABLE 8.6 (Cont.)**

| Nutrient | Functions | Food Source | Deficiency Symptoms |
|---|---|---|---|
| Pantothenic Acid | Key factor in energy function | Liver, brewer's yeast, salmon, wheat germ, eggs, legumes | Susceptible to stress, muscle cramps, nervousness, mostly subclinical |
| Biotin | Energy metabolism, fat synthesis | Liver, peanuts, egg yolk, legumes, whole grain | Mostly subclinical; muscle & nerve impairment |
| Choline | Methyl carrier in many reactions; mobilizes fat away from liver, forms important brain chemical | Egg yolk, liver, soybeans, fish, cereal | Subclinical; erratic fat metabolism?; little known |
| Inositol | Little known; found in large amounts in the heart, brain, skeletal muscle | Fruit, meat, milk, nuts, vegetables, whole grains | Unknown |
| Rutin | Works with ascorbic acid & bioflavonoids to prevent capillary fragility | Buckwheat, white part of citrus fruit | Unclear; varicose veins?; hardening of arteries? |
| Calcium | Structural salts, teeth, bones; nerve & muscle function; blood clotting | Dairy products, canned fish, broccoli, beets, bone, turnip greens | Muscle cramps, palpitations, nerve problems, rickets, irritability, osteoporosis, tooth loss, fragile bones |
| Phosphorus | Energy metabolism; absorption & transport of nutrients; bones, teeth, pH balance | Meat, fish, poultry, eggs, protein foods, soda pop, most foods | Unlikely; bone demineralization, fatigue, loss of appetite |

## VITAMINS AND MINERALS (Cont.)

| Excess | Characteristics | USRDA | Supplement Levels | Toxic Levels |
|---|---|---|---|---|
| Unlikely | Water soluble; lost in food refining (i.e., white flour); aids in stress tolerance | 10 mg | 10–100 mg | Unknown |
| Unlikely | Water soluble; raw egg whites, alcohol, antibiotics, stress increase needs; most expensive vitamin | 300 mcg | 300–500 mcg | Unknown |
| Unlikely | Found in fatty foods; formed in body with certain substances | None stated | 500–1000 mg | Unknown |
| Unlikely | Diabetics have higher needs; all humans produce some | None stated | 100–1000 mg | Unknown |
| Unlikely | Water soluble | None stated | 100 mg + | Unknown |
| May be possible above 2000 mg per day | Higher needs in stress, sedentary life, high fat/protein diet, high phosphorus intake | 1000 mg | 200–1500 mg | ? + 2000 mg |
| Creates calcium imbalance; can be serious, may be common | Balance with calcium critical; processed foods high. | 1000 mg | Unwise; 200–1000 mg | Imbalance with calcium likely |

## TABLE 8.6 (Cont.)

| Nutrient | Functions | Food Source | Deficiency Symptoms |
|---|---|---|---|
| Magnesium | Catalyst in many reactions (i.e., energy, protein synthesis); nerve & muscle function; adaptation to cold | Nuts, soybeans, whole grains, clams, cornmeal, spinach | Nerve & muscle disorders, weakness, loss of appetite, irritability, poor calcium usage |
| Iron | Oxygen transport; convert Vitamin A; lower blood fats; antibody formation | Liver, red meat, eggs, poultry, dried apricots, raisins, spinach, broccoli | Anemia, fatigue, poor disease resistance, irritability |
| Zinc | Catalyst in many reactions; DNA & protein synthesis; fertility; skin growth; healing; taste buds | Oysters, wheat germ, beans, nuts, whole wheat, steak, lobsters | Lower disease resistance & wound healing; sterility, fatigue, taste loss, growth stunting |
| Iodine | Key element in basal metabolism; regulates body energy usage | Salt water food, high iodine soil, iodized salt | Fatigue, coldness, gained weight, cretinism, retarded growth & intellect |
| Copper | Works with iron; absorption, heme synthesis, oxygen release; nerve wrappings; energy metabolism | Widely distributed; shellfish, liver, cherries, mushrooms, whole grain cereals, gelatin | Collagen (connective tissue) breakdown, anemia, nerve disorders |
| Chromium | Glucose into the cells; therefore affects energy levels, fats in the blood & conditions which afflict diabetics | Brewer's yeast, whole grain, peas, clams, corn oil | Erratic energy levels; prediabetic; elevated blood fats; anxiety, fatigue, circulatory disorders |

## VITAMINS AND MINERALS (Cont.)

| Excess | Characteristics | USRDA | Supplement Levels | Toxic Levels |
|---|---|---|---|---|
| Unlikely; can create imbalance | Elevated need with alcohol, stress, drugs, disease; must be in 2 to 1 ratio with calcium | 400 mg | 100–700 mg | Imbalance with calcium more likely |
| Unlikely; possible in males | Heme (liver) source better absorbed; aspirin increases need; many women & child anemic | 18 mg | 10–300 mg | More likely in men +30 mg |
| Unlikely | High needs with alcohol, oral contraceptives, high fiber diet | 15 mg | 10–100 mg | Unknown |
| Unlikely | Raw cabbage, radishes & other foods increase needs | 150 mcg | 100–1000 mcg | Unknown |
| Can create mineral imbalance | Copper water pipes provide source; avoid excessive levels | 2 mg | 2–5 mg | 40 mg; and imbalance likely |
| Unlikely | Yeast is most potent source as GTF; higher needs in high sugar & soda pop diets; common deficiency in U.S. | Range 50–200 mcg | 100–1000 mcg | Unknown |

**TABLE 8.6 (Cont.)**

| Nutrient | Functions | Food Source | Deficiency Symptoms |
|---|---|---|---|
| Selenium | Prevent lipid peroxidation (rusting of fats); protect red blood cells; anticancer?; protect against toxic metals | Tuna, wheat, meat, brown rice, foods grown on selenium rich soil (varies with region) | Premature aging?; toxicity from pollutants; higher risk for cancer and heart disease |
| Manganese | Formation of connective tissue; synthesis of cholesterol & fatty acids; urea formation; lipids out of liver; energy | Green vegetables, whole grain cereals, tea, legumes, nuts | Unknown; diverse in nature |
| Molybdenum | Protein metabolism, uric acid formation; mobilize liver iron stores; aldehyde production; dental caries resistance | Legumes (peas & beans), meat | Unknown |
| Garlic | Provides selenium; helps lower blood pressure and serum lipids; reputed longevity food | Garlic | Unknown |
| Lecithin | Provides raw materials (choline) for brain chemicals; aids in lowering serum cholesterol | Soy (best); egg yolk (saturated type is of questionable value) | Unknown |
| Lactobacillus Acidophilus | Live active bacteria culture aids in intestinal functions (vitamin production, lowers pathogen levels) | Live yogurt, lactobacillus milk, actual live cultures | Unknown |

## VITAMINS AND MINERALS (Cont.)

| Excess | Characteristics | USRDA | Supplement Levels | Toxic Levels |
|--------|-----------------|-------|-------------------|--------------|
| Very toxic; 500 mcg; neurological disorders or cancer incidence | Works with vitamin E; should be taken together; least abundant and most toxic of all elements | Range 50– 200 mcg | 50– 200 mcg | 500 mcg |
| Weakness, nerve & muscle disorders | Alcohol increases needs; excessive calcium absorption | Range 2.5–5 mg | 2–50 mg | From industrial contamination |
| Diarrhea, slowed growth, anemia | Highest body levels found in liver, kidney adrenals, blood cells; in ratio with copper | Range 150– 500 mcg | 150– 1000 mcg | Unknown; imbalance possible |
| Unlikely | A valuable food substance infrequently found in U.S. diets | None | 200 mg + | Unlikely at reasonable intake |
| Unlikely | Soya lecithin may aid mental functions and help lower serum cholesterol | None | 500 mg + | Unlikely at high levels; provides Kcal |
| Unlikely | Beneficial bacteria for intestinal & bodily functions | None | ½ million bacteria and up | Unlikely |

supplements, please note that some minerals are probably toxic in more than trace amounts. Remember our continual warning that you should strive for balance. Excess can cause just as many problems as deficiencies.

Some relationships between minerals and diseases have been proven; others are merely suspected. The relationship between goiter and iodine deficiency is one that most people are aware of. There are still about 200 million people in the world suffering from goiter, though it is now very rare in the developed nations because iodine is added to table salt.

A few of the other suspected or proven relationships between minerals and diseases are as follows:

- Calcium and osteoporosis.
- Selenium and cancer, heart disease, and aging.
- Zinc and disease-resistance, wound-healing, and sexual dysfunctions.
- Aluminum and Alzheimer's disease.
- Calcium and magnesium and heart disease.
- Chromium and diabetes, hypoglycemia, and heart disease.
- Potassium and weakness or cramps.
- Iron and anemia.
- Fluoride and dental cavities.
- Lead and general toxicity.
- Sodium and hypertension.

CASE HISTORY: Film star R.K. arrived at La Costa with a subtle gray pallor on his ruggedly handsome face. He had come for a rest before going on location for a movie he was to star in. Normally, he was a healthy man with a good lifestyle. At age 42, he exercised more than his Beverly Hills neighbors, and he tried to eat a balanced diet. He was even a regular blood donor.

However, he was suffering from fatigue, shortness of breath, and irritability. (This latter had prompted his wife to suggest that he take this trip alone.) He suffered repeated bouts of colds and minor illnesses, along with chronic headaches, which he attributed to the stress of acting and marital problems.

He had been treating his headaches with six to eight aspirins a day.

His medical tests revealed a surprise: he was low in folic acid and iron. Nearly half of the women and children in the United States are iron anemic, but we were not expecting it in a middle-aged male who had made a decent effort to follow good nutritional standards.

R.K. suffered iron loss from two sources: his blood donations and his excessive aspirin consumption. (Aspirin causes tiny amounts of blood loss in the intestines, which can become significant or cumulative over a long period of time.)

R.K. was put on an 1,800-calorie per day diet that emphasized iron-rich foods such as meat, fish, poultry, and liver. He was given multiple vitamin and mineral supplements with extra iron and folic acid. Daily vigorous exercise was recommended.

It usually requires more than a month for an anemic person to manufacture sufficient red blood cells to feel noticeably better. R.K. had to leave to make his picture before that, and we did not see him until six months later, when he returned to La Costa. Then he told us he had more energy than he had possessed in years.

His wife smiled in agreement.

\* \* \*

**TABLE 8.7**

## MINERALS IN HUMAN NUTRITION

| Mineral | Amount Found in a 70 Kilogram Adult Body | Importance |
|---------|------------------------------------------|------------|
| Calcium | 1160 g. | Known to be essential and found in relatively large amounts in humans. |
| Phosphorus | 670 g. | |
| Potassium | 150 g. | |
| Sulfur | 112 g. | |
| Sodium | 63 g. | |
| Chlorine | 85 g. | |
| Magnesium | 21 g. | |
| Iron * | 1 g. | Known to be essential and found in relatively small amounts in humans. |
| Manganese | 0.015 g. | |
| Copper * | 0.080 g. | |
| Iodine | 0.024 g. | |
| Chromium | Trace | Known to be essential, and found in relatively small amounts in humans. |
| Cobalt | Trace | |
| Fluoride | Trace | |
| Molybdenum | Trace | |
| Selenium * | Trace | |
| Zinc | Trace | |
| Nickel | Trace | Possibly essential; are essential in animals, but little is known about human needs. |
| Silicon | Trace | |
| Tin | Trace | |
| Vanadium | Trace | |
| Cadmium * | Trace | Found in the body, but no known functions; could be toxins or could serve functions. |
| Aluminum * | Trace | |
| Arsenic * | Trace | |
| Barium | Trace | |
| Boron | Trace | |
| Bromine | Trace | |
| Gold | Trace | |
| Lead * | Trace | |
| Mercury * | Trace | |
| Strontium * | Trace | |

* Probably toxic in anything more than trace amounts.

We are asked numerous questions about vitamins and minerals. At this stage of scientific study, some can be answered and some cannot. A few may be of benefit to you.

*Do you need vitamin and mineral supplements to stay healthy?*

No. If you were to eat large amounts of high-quality foods and to exercise your nutrients into a well-toned body, avoiding tobacco, drugs, alcohol, high stress, pollution, and empty-calorie junk-food, you would probably need no supplements. Unfortunately, this kind of pure lifestyle is rarely found in the developed nations. Therefore, supplements are usually of value.

*Can you eat whatever you want if you take supplements?*

No. Foods contain many nutrients that are not found in any vitamin and mineral supplements. Foods also contain substances that may be essential to health, the value of which is not yet known. Vitamin and mineral supplements should be considered insurance that you are receiving near-optimal levels of some of the micronutrients. Good foods should always be the foundation of any nutrition program.

*Is there a difference between organic and synthetic vitamins?*

No. A vitamin is a vitamin because of its chemical structure, whether from a food substance or a chemical laboratory. Both work identically in humans as well as in laboratory animals. However, studies show that often the natural source of the mineral (i.e., iron from liver, calcium from dairy products) is better absorbed by the body. Also, certain auxiliary factors, such as bioflavonoids in citrus fruit, may aid in the workings of vitamins, such as Vitamin C. This does not mean that you should pay the exorbitant price for allegedly "natural" vitamins, but rather should continually emphasize foods as your main source of nutrients.

## What will supplements do for you?

If you are leading the typical western lifestyle, you should be able to notice several improvements in your health after you begin taking vitamin and mineral supplements. Also, you stand a better chance of avoiding some of the leading degenerative—and deadly—diseases. Drug-nutrient interactions, increased nutrient needs for alcohol, nutrient demands from excessive stress, fasting, smoking and regular intake of nutrient-poor foods—all can lead to suboptimal nutritional status. With supplements to help correct this, you should find increased energy levels, improved resistance to infection, improved healing rate, better outlook on life, improved appearance, and—ultimately—a longer and better life.

## Shouldn't the Recommended Daily Allowance (RDA) for any nutrient be enough?

Maybe. Occasionally, the RDAs have been revised upward to reflect the results of new studies into the importance of vitamins and minerals. Although these guidelines are established by prestigious scientists based on dozens of valid studies, there are some weaknesses to the RDAs. They cannot take into consideration the vast diversity of human needs based upon biochemical individuality. Insufficient data exist on the nutritional requirements of the very young, the older adult, the superactive individual, and the sick person. Very little is yet known about trace elements such as selenium, vanadium, and molybdenum. There is no RDA for linoleic acid, fiber, or complex carbohydrates, though it is generally agreed that these are essential to the diet. The RDA is to be considered a general guideline, and it is an excellent one. It is not to be carved in stone.

---

R<sub>X</sub>

- Get your nutrients with a fork and spoon if at all possible. Vitamins from food may contain auxiliary factors that aid in the functioning of that vitamin. Minerals from food are often better absorbed than those from pills. A varied diet will contain all of the vitamins and minerals while pills contain only a select few.

- The lifestyle of western society has created elevated nutrient demands, and many foods consumed have lost nutrients through processing. For that reason, supplements are vital for some people, and possibly helpful for others.

- If you do not regularly eat soy products, take one or two tablespoons each day of soya lecithin.

- If you do not regularly eat fresh garlic, take 1,000 milligrams or more of garlic extract with parsley (to dilute its infamous fragrance).

- Drink fluoridated water; pregnant women and young children should take fluoride tablets.

- Take your vitamin and mineral supplements with food, at mealtime, and in divided dosages to provide for maximum absorption with minimal chance of gastric disturbance.

- Do not overuse or abuse vitamin and mineral supplements. Taken in excess, such nutrients as vitamin A, vitamin D, and selenium can be toxic. If you feel you need more than the USRDA of any nutrient, consult your doctor.

---

## Food Containers

It is not only important what you eat, how much, and when, but also what you eat out of. Some cookware and pottery can affect the food you eat. Lead, aluminum, and copper can cause problems when ingested in large amounts. Though the problem is less serious than it once was, many pottery shops—especially those in underdeveloped nations—use lead-based glazes for their products. By eating off lead-glazed ceramic dishes over a long period of time, one can develop lead toxicity without ever suspecting the cause.

Some canned foods can present a similar problem from lead. While the canning of food helps to resolve problems of storage, there is some concern about cans sealed with a lead seam or plug. Certainly foods should not be stored in the cans after opening, because the tin leaches into the food once exposed to the air. This is especially true of fruit juices. Pewter contains lead and should not be used as regular cookware.

Aluminum cookware should be used with discretion. Alzheimer's disease has been associated with excess aluminum in the brain. Do not use aluminum for acid foods such as tomatoes or pineapple, nor is it advisable to expose hot foods to aluminum for a long time, e.g., by inserting aluminum "nails" into potatoes to help them bake faster.

Copper distributes heat nicely, but there is a delicate balance in your body between copper and zinc. Using copper water pipes or copper cooking vessels can disturb that balance. There is plenty of copper in food to take care of your nutritional needs.

The modern chemist has produced nonstick polymer surfaces for cookware. These pans are certainly convenient to use, since they allow you to cook with very little fat. If you use nonstick cookware, we recommend using high-quality products that do not scrape or scratch easily, so that you do not consume this nonstick substance.

---

- Use steel, iron, glass, high-quality nonstick pots, and unleaded ceramic for cooking and eating food. The good old-fashioned iron cookware has the added advantage of contributing some iron to your diet.

---

## Periodicity

"You eat like a bird," is an accusation frequently leveled at people who eat slowly in small amounts. This should not be considered an insult but a compliment. The birdlike eaters tend to live longer than others who gorge themselves, just as birds in the wild are among the longer-lived creatures.

Humans once were grazing creatures, eating small amounts many times a day as their tribes moved through the bush or forest. Sometimes there would be a sparse food supply, followed by occasional gorging on a killed animal or at the time of harvest. For this reason, evolution permitted us to store fat for the sparse seasons.

When food supplies are regular and abundant, fat storage is relatively unnecessary. When the supplies are less dependable, the body must adapt to accommodate the situation so that it can survive. These adaptations include an expanded capacity of the gastro-intestinal tract, enhanced efficiency of nutrient absorption, and the enzyme systems adapting for fat storage.

Studies have proved that "grazers" have a better chance of living longer than their "gorging" counterparts. Eating small and frequent meals helps your digestive tract, waistline, heart, circulatory system, energy level, and pancreas. By fasting, on the other hand, dieters gear the body's enzyme system for fat storage, which is exactly the opposite of what they want. Fasting can also lower thyroid output, which makes the body less likely to lose its precious stores of fat.

For best health, we recommend that—as the day progresses—you consume meals that are gradually smaller in size and calorie level. A big breakfast has a better chance of being burned before the day is over than a big dinner, which is likely to be deposited as fat along the walls of blood vessels while you sleep. There is an old adage: "Breakfast like a king, lunch like a prince, and sup like a pauper." This makes good sense.

Everyone—athletes, dieters, diabetics, hypoglycemics, heart attack victims, elderly, business people, housewives—can benefit from the grazing approach to eating.

---

$R_X$

- Eat small and frequent meals, consuming the same number of calories you need, but spaced out over four to six meals a day rather than the standard three.
- Start your day with a large and nutritious breakfast, and let your meal sizes taper down through the day. Soup and salad make an ideal dinner, with a small snack like popcorn before bedtime.

## ꩜꩜꩜ 9 ꩜꩜꩜

# Nutritional Bad Guys

"More people have been killed with a fork
and spoon than all other weapons combined."
—R. PHILIP SMITH, M.D.

[• The attraction and the danger of Junk Food Road • Western
society is consuming salt in excessive amounts • High blood
pressure and salt, calcium, and potassium • The differences
between natural complex sugar and simple refined sugar •
Learning to balance your fat intake to avoid atherosclerosis
• Understanding cholesterol—the value and the danger •
The abuses of food refining—removal of valuable nutrients,
addition of questionable items, higher prices, wasted energy
• Blessings and curses of caffeine • The abuse of alcohol—a
serious health issue]

In almost every major city in the developed world there is a
Junk Food Road. You've been there; you know what it looks
and smells like. Wafting odors of cooking oil, bright neon
signs, and pilgrims lined up for a fast meal of hamburgers, hot

dogs, doughnuts, pizza, french fries, pies, and fish 'n, chips. These places are all interspersed with liquor and candy stores and ice cream parlors.

Junk Food Road's major contribution to the diet of the West is excess fat, salt, sugar, cholesterol, and empty calories. If visits to these fast food establishments were an occasional treat, there would be no harm for healthy adults, but many people follow a regular diet of junk-food. Then they will follow this with a happy-hour session at their favorite bar, which will go into overtime at home. Many also consume excess soda pop and coffee.

Each of these nutritional bad guys is relatively harmless in reasonable quantities—at least when essential nutrients are obtained elsewhere and a reasonable program of exercise is followed. But we consume them in unreasonable quantities. One major hamburger chain has finally had to give up posting the number of hamburgers sold because they have reached into the uncountable billions.

We can't ask you to avoid Junk Food Road; that would be unrealistic. What we recommend is that you keep your visits to a minimum and make a conscious effort to reduce your overall intake of the nutritional bad guys as much as possible. Salt, sugar, fat, cholesterol, refined foods, caffeine, and alcohol, in large amounts—which unfortunately today is the normal amount—can cause serious harm to your health, cutting short your lifespan.

## Salt and Sodium

Of the four taste buds—sour, sweet, salt, bitter—there is one devoted especially to salty foods. Because of these taste buds, your body does seek out salty foods; it has a need for sodium. Your blood is as salty as the ocean, out of which life evolved. In the circumstances of extreme heat, where there is excessive perspiration, heat prostration or even death can occur without adequate salt. This was a problem in coal mines at the turn of the century. In India, where vegetarian diets and tropical heat make salt consumption essential, Mahatma Ghandi used a salt strike to get the attention of the British rulers. Centuries ago, salt was such a valuable commodity that our word "salary" is derived from the practice of paying for work in salt.

But there is no scarcity of salt today. Quite the contrary is true. One out of eight people in western society suffers from high blood pressure—a serious ailment that can be brought on by excessive salt intake. Table salt, chemically known as sodium chloride, contains about forty percent sodium. (Thus, ten grams of salt contains four grams of sodium.) It is the sodium that causes water retention in some people.

It has been shown that a healthy adult can survive on one-quarter of a gram of sodium per day. The Senate Diet Goals recommends less than two grams of sodium per day. However, a great many people salt their food too heavily, and as a result consume ten or more grams of sodium daily—forty times the sodium they need, and five times the recommended upper limit.

After decades of this kind of excess, the kidneys can lose their ability to excrete excess sodium and water, with the result being hypertension—or high blood pressure. To try to envision what this means, think of your blood vessels as being like a garden house. Imagine what the result would be if you connected this garden hose to a fire hydrant. Excessive pressure could cause a rupture in a weak area of the hose.

CASE HISTORY: M.J. checked into the La Costa medical offices with a voluminous medical record. At forty-five years of age, she continued to suffer from high blood pressure despite her medication. She was at least fifty pounds overweight, and she frequently had to sit down and rest because of her swollen ankles. Although her hometown physician had given her a list of foods to avoid, she usually ignored it. At age 39, she had come close to losing her life as well as that of her baby, when she developed toxemia of pregnancy.

She had come to La Costa, deciding finally to do something about her health problems, because her husband had left her.

We placed her on an 800-calorie a day diet and sent her to the women's athletic director for an exercise program. Although she complained loudly and frequently about the food she was given in the beginning, we managed to persuade her to stay for three weeks. She was very attentive at the evening lectures on diet, health, and longevity.

By the end of three weeks, J.M. had lost thirty pounds—fourteen of them in the first week. Her health and appearance had improved dramatically, with better muscle tone, lost weight, and a tan. It was even possible to see that she had ankles. But most significant was the fact that she could stop the medication she took for hypertension.

It took the full three weeks to break her of the salt habit, to convince her that it was an acquired affinity and that it was what had led her to overweight, hypertension, toxemia of pregnancy, and swollen ankles. On her last night at La Costa, she confessed that her habit had been so bad she had even salted bacon.

Six months later, M.J. returned with her husband to celebrate their twenty-fifth wedding anniversary. She had become so attractive heads turned when she walked into a room.

The average adult should never use a salt shaker to obtain sufficient sodium in the diet. All foods contain some sodium, and some are naturally high in sodium, such as dairy products. People who are not accustomed to extra salt in their foods find high-salt snack foods to be unpalatable. Conversely the heavy salter finds any food without the salty flavor tasteless. What happens with these people is that their salt taste buds have been deadened by excessive intake. However, their sense of taste can be readjusted to regain their natural functioning. It is the low salt user with the keen taste buds who has the inside track on a longer and healthier life.

Salt is not the solitary ogre that some popular books have made it out to be. Foods high in salt are often high in one or all of the other nutritional bad guys. Studies have shown that many people with high blood pressure have low calcium intake combined with high salt. It is possible that a calcium deficiency may affect the kidneys' ability to maintain proper sodium and fluid balance, thereby leading to water retention and high blood pressure.

The most recent studies seem to indicate that nutrients for a healthy functioning kidney, such as calcium and potassium, may be as important in high blood pressure as the already known relationship of high salt intake. Through ideal nutrition and lifestyle, you can keep your kidneys sufficiently healthy to reject excess sodium in the diet. It is an overall health package rather than one isolated nutrient that will help carry you into your second century of life.

---

**R<sub>X</sub>**

- Avoid high-salt foods. Check labels for salt or sodium.
- Do not salt while cooking. Let people add their own salt at the table.
- Develop a taste for alternative seasonings, such as lemon, vinegar, and herbs. Taste your food before using any salt condiments such as soy sauce or monosodium glutamate (MSG).
- Maintain optimal calcium intake to help prevent hypertension.
- Maintain optimal body weight and percent body fat to help prevent hypertension.

---

### Sugar

We are born with a sweet taste for the lactose of mother's milk. However, everything sweet is not lactose. Sugar, or sucrose, has only calories to offer us, with no vitamins, minerals, protein, or fiber at all. Yet sugar has become a major food commodity, and the average person consumes over 120 pounds of it per year.

Sugar has many aliases—corn syrup, fructose, sucrose, dextrose, levulose, and others. Some things we consume—such as soda pop, candy, jellies, and many pastries—are almost totally sugar in content. Children's breakfast cereals contain up to sixty-five percent sugar, and most other packaged food items contain at least some sugar.

Currently, one-fifth of all calories consumed in the developed nations is from refined sugar. It is recommended that we cut this at least in half, down to one-tenth of our calories.

Carbohydrates can be divided into two main categories—simple (various sugars) and complex (starch). Each of these can be divided into two categories—natural and refined. Although all four groups will eventually end up as glucose in your blood stream, it is the natural carbohydrates that are preferred for your health because of their accompanying fiber and trace elements.

It is when we expand our natural need for natural sugar into a craving for refined table sugar that we turn a valuable and pleasing sensation into an enemy. There are numerous problems that refined sugar can cause you:

- It causes cavities in teeth. There is a direct relationship between the level of sucrose intake and the incidence of cavities.
- It instigates overweight because of sugar's concentrated calories. Pastries, soda pop, candy, and snack foods are, in part, responsible for the abundance of fat people in the developed nations.
- It contributes to diabetes and heart disease through overweight and through missing nutrients.
- It can create nutritional deficiencies of thiamin and chromium, and possibly other nutrients as well.
- Because sugar is quickly absorbed, it may produce

hypoglycemia in many people. Erratic blood sugar levels may be common in people with diets high in sucrose.

- It may produce hyperactivity, especially in children, causing mood swings and learning problems.

CASE HISTORY: Upon his arrival at La Costa, W.A. told us, "This is my last desperate effort to do something about my health before I consider doing something even more desperate." For the past ten years, W.A. had experienced frequent bouts of depression, trembling hands, forgetfulness, and headaches. He had gone to a psychologist, who informed him that he was reasonably normal. W.A.'s physician had prescribed various medications for his symptoms, but the drugs were no longer effective.

We examined W.A. and did tests, suspecting hypoglycemia. His diet was marginal, and his lifestyle included no exercise. His stress level was high and poorly tolerated. Diabetes was common in his family. (Sometimes hypoglycemia is a prelude to diabetes; both indicate poor insulin control.)

W.A. told us that his doctor had also suspected hypoglycemia and had given him a three-hour glucose tolerance test. Although W.A. had developed a headache during the test, the lab results revealed no hypoglycemia.

It was obvious that there were many things wrong with W.A.'s lifestyle, not the least of which was his above-average sugar intake and his lack of exercise. Both tended to exacerbate his genetically inherited tendency toward erratic blood-sugar regulation. We tried a six-hour glucose tolerance test on him. The results showed definite hypoglycemia, with a reading of forty milligrams percent glucose at four hours—one hour after the other test had concluded normal findings.

We put W.A. on an 1,800-calorie a day diet, high in natural complex carbohydrates and proteins and with only whole fruit for simple sugars. A serious exercise program of tennis and swimming was designed for him. Two weeks later, W.A. looked and felt much better. Before leaving, he assured us that he would continue to comply with the regimen, confessing that he had secretly devoured a pastry for breakfast one day and found his old symptoms back with him.

There has been much disagreement in the health community over the subject of hypoglycemia. Some deny that it is a common disease; others insist that it is widespread among the population. Admittedly, there can be difficulties in identifying it with lab tests, but that should be no reason to discount for it. The fact that a treatment works for the patients should take precedence over cut-and-dried laboratory values.

If you will seriously reduce your refined sugar intake, you will have a leaner and more energetic body, with fewer dental bills and a greater chance of avoiding some of the common degenerative diseases of the twentieth century. (See Table 9.1.) Since all the carbohydrates in your diet will eventually end up in the blood as glucose, you have no need for simple sugars, particularly for refined sucrose.

### TABLE 9.1
### CATEGORIES OF SWEETENERS

| Nutritive (4 Calories/Gram) | Non-nutritive (No Calories) |
| --- | --- |
| Sucrose * | Cyclamates (Banned) |
| Dextrose * | Saccharin (Possibly Harmful) |
| Levulose * | Aspartame ("Equal") |
| Glucose * | |
| Fructose * | |
| Corn Syrup * | |
| Honey * | |
| Maltose * | |
| Lactose * | |
| Sorbitol | |
| Mannitol | |
| Xylitol | |

\* Will cause cavities.

# R
## X

- Minimize consumption of foods with sugar added. Check the food labels.

- Use sugar substitutes when preparing food.

- Train your taste buds to appreciate natural sweetness, such as that in fruits.

- Use alternatives for sweetening at the table. Alternatives include molasses, honey, fructose, dried fruit.

- When cooking, decrease the sugar called for in recipes. Use one-fourth or less.

## Fat

Fat is an essential, multipurpose substance. Without fat in the diet, active individuals would have a difficult time getting sufficient calories from their food. Without body fat, swimming would be difficult, living in cold climates would be intolerable, birds could not migrate long distances, and football players might suffer more serious injuries than they do.

Fat has definite purposes, both in our diet and in our bodies. In the diet, it provides concentrated energy, more than twice that of carbohydrates or protein. It aids in the absorption of the fat-soluble vitamins A, D, E, and K. It provides the essential fatty acid, linoleic acid, which is needed in many areas of the body. And it adds satiety to the diet because it tastes good and slows down digestion.

In the body, fat serves as a storehouse for energy reserves. If we had to carry all of our energy stores in the form of carbohydrates, the average adult would have to weigh an extra 130 pounds. Despite our association of "fat" with "overweight," fat is a lightweight and concentrated fuel which gives off an equal weight of water once it has been burned. Fat also provides insulation from the cold. People in colder climates have a much more efficient system for storing excess calories in the form of fat in the skin to protect their bodies from heat loss. Eskimos even have fat pads over their eyelids. Also, fat floats, so it gives us buoyancy in water, which is why muscular people have difficulty floating. Finally, fat provides us with padding to protect delicate internal organs.

But, if you are overweight or overfat, don't let this serve as a rationalization for staying that way. Fat has an ugly side to its character, as well. At best, fat is a tolerated necessity in the body. Remember that life is water-based. If you can envision an oil slick on the ocean or recall what a bottle of Italian dressing looks like unshaken, you can understand how poorly fat and water get along together.

To avoid trouble in your body's water-based blood stream, nearly all fat substances—including cholesterol, triglycerides, and vitamin A—must have an escort. Since fatty substances do not dissolve in the water medium of the blood, nature has given us lipoproteins to "escort" cholesterol and triglycerides while in the blood. Vitamin A has a retinol binding protein to keep it dissolved in the blood and prevent it from causing harm. Vitamin A becomes toxic only when it is not bound to its escort. Other fat-soluble substances in the body have similar escort systems to keep them functional rather than harmful in the water medium of the body. When fat starts sedimenting out of the blood, it forms fatty blockages that can eventually choke off the flow of oxygen and nutrients to the tissue on the other side of the fatty occlusions. Fat plugging up the arteries (atherosclerosis) is the major cause of death in the developed nations of the world. This deadly condition has taken an amazing toll in lives in this century, while it was little known before World War I. Fat and cholesterol seem to be the leading suspects in the search for the causes of heart disease. Since the heart has such a continuous flow of fat going to it to fuel its pumping action, it is highly susceptible to the effects of fatty blockage in the vessels.

But this condition—fat in the body or in the blood—does not have to result from fat in the diet. There are numerous societies in the world that consume far more fat than we do, yet do not suffer these problems. Eskimos eat more fat than we do, and they have a low incidence of heart disease. However, they get constant exercise and are exposed to lower levels of stress. Also, it has been discovered that the fatty fish the Eskimos eat contain something called eicosapentanoic acid, which may make them more resistant to heart disease.

The people of the Mediterranean region also consume high-fat diets, without the disastrous results suffered in the developed nations. Most of their fat comes from olive oil, which is high in unsaturated fats and vitamin E. In addition to these benefits, olive oil may contain a unique factor similar in effect to the eicosapentanoic acid of the cold-water fish.

The Masai people in east Africa have a diet very high in fat from meat and dairy products, but show a very low incidence of circulatory disorders. They are a very active people.

Exercise may be the key to the problem that people in the developed nations have with fat, but it is difficult for us to be as active as the Masai. We must adapt our fat consumption to meet the needs of our lifestyle. Fatty foods generally carry with them little more than calories. A high-fat diet is low in fiber, vitamins, and minerals. Therefore, we need to be aware of the differences in various fats, and adjust our consumption accordingly.

Generally polyunsaturated or plant fats are less likely to cause fatty plaque than saturated or animal fats. There is a new technologically created fat that has entered our diet as well, called hydrogenated fat. These hydrogenated fats are derived from unsaturated vegetable fats, but are exposed to a catalyst that causes them to be saturated with a very different structure. These may prove to be even more harmful to your health than the saturated fats they were designed to replace.

R̃X

- Eat less fat from all sources.

- Of the fat you do consume, eat less saturated fat and more of the polyunsaturated vegetable fats.

- Avoid hydrogenated fats. There is a concern about their safety. Choose tub margarine over butter; choose butter over stick margarine containing hydrogenated fats or coconut oil.

- Add vitamin E to your diet. The polyunsaturated fats you consume need this vitamin to keep them working safely and effectively.

- Select fats in the following order of preference: *Best*—sunflower, safflower, corn, soy, cottonseed, olive oil; *Acceptable*—peanut oil, fat from poultry, fish, and nuts; *Unacceptable*—coconut and hydrogenated oils, lard, bacon, beef, lamb, or pork drippings.

## Cholesterol

Cholesterol is a useful and flexible substance in the human body. It is used as the raw material for building steroid hormones, including sex hormones, for creating bile salts for fat digestion, for manufacturing the insulation for the nerves, and can be converted to vitamin D in the skin through the action of sunlight.

Yet it has earned for itself a very bad reputation. This is because the fatty blockages that create health problems in the blood vessels and heart are composed to a large degree of cholesterol. The higher one's blood cholesterol level and the lower the amount of low-density lipoproteins (LDL), the greater one's chance of having heart disease. There is definitely a relationship between the amount of cholesterol in one's diet and the levels in the blood, but it is one of several factors in the problem.

Cholesterol makes an easy scapegoat. Removing cholesterol from your diet—or reducing it—does not solve the problem. We manufacture far more cholesterol of our own than we could eat. The average healthy adult produces more in one day than is found in eight egg yolks. Exercise can lower the blood cholesterol, as well as elevate the high-density lipoproteins that protect against heart disease. Meditation can also improve these protective factors.

There are factors that can elevate serum cholesterol as well. Smoking does, because vitamin C is lost, and vitamin C is involved in at least three of the methods the body uses to get rid of cholesterol and fat. Vitamin C helps convert cholesterol to bile salts for fat digestion. If one has a high-fiber diet, these bile salts are bound to fiber and eliminated from the body in feces. Vitamin C also aids in the conversion of cholesterol to a form that can be excreted in the urine. And, finally, vitamin C is involved in an enzyme system in fat cells which dictates how much fat will be released into the blood stream; thus ascorbic acid helps to lower levels of fat (triglycerides) in the blood. Levels of fat are associated with levels of cholesterol in the blood.

Chromium deficiency stunts the body's ability to burn glucose normally, as in diabetes. The body then opts for the second favorite fuel—fat. It is not surprising, then, that diabetics and those with chromium deficiency have higher levels of fat and cholesterol in the blood.

It is important not to oversimplify either the dangers or the values of cholesterol. It was an oversimplification when researchers announced to the public, "Don't eat eggs, and you won't get heart disease." Although egg yolks are a very rich source of dietary cholesterol, most westerners actually get more from red meat and high-fat dairy products.

Consumption of eggs as well as other nutrients is dependent upon individual needs. Eggs can be good for pregnant women and for developing children. Because the infant has a brain growing at a rapid rate, both dietary and self-produced cholesterol are needed to build the fatty insulation for the brain and nervous system. The importance nature places on cholesterol for building brain tissue can be seen in the fact that human breast milk contains high levels of cholesterol.

It is possible that eggs are also good for healthy and active people who pursue a good program of diet, exercise, attitude, and lifestyle.

---

**R<sub>X</sub>**

- Lower your intake of red meats, especially marbled or fatty cuts. Lower your intake of high-fat dairy products, such as butter, ice cream, cream cheese, and cheese.

- If you are healthy, restrict your egg intake to seven to fourteen eggs per week. If you are not healthy, restrict your intake further. No restrictions are necessary for pregnant women or young people.

- Restrict your liver intake to one serving per week if you are healthy. If you are not healthy, restrict your liver intake further.

---

## Refined Foods

Food processing is not inherently bad for the nutritional value of food. Certainly the techniques of food preservation were a major step forward in the western ability to make good nutrition available year-round in all parts of the world. In the past, when fresh fruit and vegetables became ripe, the farmer had to rush his crop to market to prevent it from spoiling or rotting. Canning and freezing were able to prevent this terrible waste of food.

The "refining" of food, however, goes far beyond the simple process of preservation. The dictionary definition of "refining" is: "to make fine or pure; to free from imperfection, coarseness, crudeness; to make elegant or cultivated." This is what the food processors thought they were doing when they introduced the refinements of white flour and white rice. In the beginning, there were no obvious problems with the alteration of natural grains, because the western diet was varied and could compensate for the nutrient loss. It was when the Dutch took their white rice with them in their eighteenth and nineteenth century explorations that serious illness showed up among the natives of less-developed nations who consumed the imported grain.

In 1890, the Dutch physician Eijkman discovered that these natives could be cured of their beri-beri by feeding them the rice polishings, which represented the outer bran of the rice and contained the most thiamin. The thiamin, as well as other essential nutrients, had been lost in the processing. Beri-beri is still common in countries such as the Philippines, where unenriched white rice is a staple.

Wheat is equally abused in food refining. To make "enriched" white flour, twenty-five nutrients are removed and four are added back to it. The restoration of these four nutrients is what is supposed to make it enriched, but it is still inferior in nutritional value to the original whole wheat.

When fresh potatoes are processed into potato chips, the calories are increased 800 percent, fat is increased 39,800 percent, sodium is increased 33,300 percent, the fiber is eliminated almost completely, vitamin C and other nutrients are almost completely eliminated, and the price is increased 1,000 percent.

There are many kinds of foods that become nutritionally inferior when refined, including:

- Soy, corn, and other vegetable oils, when they are converted to hydrogenated oils.
- Whole wheat, when it is converted into white flour. (It loses most of the vitamin B-6, fiber, chromium, pantothenic acid, and other nutrients.)
- Apples, when they are converted to apple juice.
- Fresh fruit, when it is converted to peeled, sugared fruit.
- Cheese, when it is converted to processed cheese spread. (It seriously alters the ideal calcium-to-phosphorus ratio of the natural cheese.)

Generally, there are four serious problems that occur when a food is refined. Valuable nutrients are removed, especially vitamins, minerals, protein, and fiber. Questionable items are added, especially salt, fat, sugar, colorings, and flavorings. Prices are raised considerably over those of the original natural foods. And energy is wasted in both refining the foods and creating packages, which add to already crowded dump sites.

This is not intended as an indictment of the food industry. We cannot expect them to be paragons of virtue. They acknowledge that they have one objective in creating their food products—money. On one occasion, we heard a presentation given by a representative of a large breakfast-cereal company. There was an irate woman in the audience, who shouted at him, "How can you promote this sugar junk-food for our children?" The representative replied calmly, "Lady, we will stop making the stuff when people stop buying it."

You cannot expect the food industry to be the watchdog for your health. You must look after your own nutrition, creating the demand for safe, wholesome food. If no one buys their unwholesome processed and refined foods, the manufacturers would quickly find out how to put nourishing and safe foods into packages. Food processors do not start out with the question, "How can I destroy the nutritional value of this food?" They set out to create tastes that will attract people, and therefore money.

And there are many food companies that are concerned about the quality of their food products. Some manufacturers actually do improve the food for us, as in vitamin and mineral fortification and freezing fresh produce to make it available throughout the year. On several notable occasions, food manufacturers have helped to put an end to major health problems around the world, acting in response to scientific discoveries and government regulations.

For centuries, goiter was a common and dreaded disease. When it was discovered that this was caused by iodine deficiency, producers of table salt added iodine to their product. Rickets, another disease, was overcome by the addition of vitamin D to milk. Today, with widespread iron and zinc deficiencies throughout the western world, addition of these nutrients by food companies could effectively reduce health and longevity problems.

It is your duty to look after your own diet. Read labels to try to determine what has been removed and what has been added to the foods you buy, and remember that the good old-fashioned natural food is generally the most nutritious. As for the additives, some perform useful functions and are likely to be safe. Many are of questionable value and may actually be harmful. Some have actually been proved harmful, yet remain on your supermarket shelves. These we suggest that you leave where they are—sodium nitrite, monosodium glutamate, lead-lined cans, and many food dyes.

---

- Select foods as close to their natural form as possible.
- Minimize your intake of sugar, salt, fat, hydrogenated oils, sodium nitrite, artificial coloring, monosodium glutamate, modified starch, and saccharin.

---

## Caffeine

Coffee is one of the world's most popular drinks. Friends gather over coffee to talk. Many people end their meals with a cup of coffee. But it is in the mornings that the drink has its greatest popularity. Most offices have their coffee machines, where employees gather as they start their workdays. On freeways, commuters head to work with a coffee mug in one hand, hoping it will wake them up by the time they reach the office. Morning coffee has become so important for some people that they set timers that will start their coffee before they wake up so they will have it ready as soon as they step out of bed.

It is the stimulant caffeine, not the flavor, that makes coffee a morning ritual. It is also what many people seek when they drink tea and soda pop.

Caffeine has its blessings, and its curses. It is absorbed quickly and completely, and it does stimulate the central nervous system. It increases free fatty acids and glucose in the blood stream for added energy. In small quantities, it enhances mental and motor agility. It also causes gastric secretions, which may create heartburn. In some people it causes irritability. For most people, an intake of 400 milligrams or more per day will cause insomnia and poor performance.

In extreme cases, caffeine can have more serious effects. Studies done at the University of Kansas indicate that coffee taken during meals limits the body's ability to absorb iron by as much as 39 percent. Because caffeine is a diuretic, it increases urine production. By elevating fats in the blood, caffeine is not for those at risk for heart disease. There is also suspicion that it has some involvement in diseases of the pancreas as well.

Healthy people can drink coffee (or other caffeine products) in moderation—65 to 135 milligrams—with no serious consequences, but it must be remembered that it is a mild form of amphetamine. It should not be considered beneficial for children, and therefore should be avoided while pregnant or lactating. To be aware of how much caffeine you consume in various drinks, study the breakdown in Table 9.2.

R<sub>X</sub>

- If you drink caffeine products, do so in moderation. Keep your daily intake to less than 130 milligrams.

- If your reason for drinking warm beverages is for the warmth or for the sociability, choose green or herbal teas, since they do not contain caffeine.

- The following people should reduce or eliminate their intake of caffeine—pregnant and lactating women, young children, older people at risk for heart disease or diabetes.

- Avoid drinking caffeine products with your meal. Have them at least an hour before.

- Check the labels of medication you are taking. Caffeine is an ingredient in many nonprescription drugs.

### TABLE 9.2
### CAFFEINE CONTENT OF POPULAR DRINKS

| Product | Amount | Caffeine (in milligrams) |
|---|---|---|
| Coffee | 1 Cup | |
| Instant or Freeze-dried | | 61-70 |
| Percolator (Electric) | | 93-120 |
| Dripolator (Non Automatic) | | 137-146 |
| Tea (Brewed 5 minutes) | 1 Cup | |
| Black | | 35-46 |
| Green | | 20-33 |
| Mint or Herb | | 0 |

| Soft Drinks | 12 Ounces |
|---|---|
| Coca Cola | 65 |
| Dr. Pepper | 61 |
| Mountain Dew | 55 |
| Diet Dr. Pepper | 55 |
| Tab | 50 |
| Pepsi Cola | 43 |
| RC Cola | 34 |

## Alcohol

Legend has it that alcohol was discovered in Persia about 3,500 years ago when a despondent chambermaid attempted suicide by drinking a container of fermented grapes labeled "poison." When she awoke the next morning with a throbbing head, she began looking for more of the same, this time not to commit suicide.

Alcohol is produced by the fermentation process of yeast consuming carbohydrates. Grapes turn into wine; barley and hops into beer; rice into saki; molasses into rum. This normal fermentation process creates an alcohol content of up to twenty percent, or forty proof. In order to obtain stronger alcohol, it is necessary to boil the liquor and capture the early vapors in the distillation process. Distilled spirits are stronger than the yeast itself can stand to live in. Alcohol is not nutritious, but it is a nutrient by virtue of its calories. Four out of five adults consume some alcohol, and one-third of these consume five or more drinks at one sitting. This is a serious health issue that cannot be ignored.

CASE HISTORY: Most guests are asked to fill out a detailed diet history when they come to La Costa. This is analyzed by computer, giving us valuable information on matters of health and nutrition. When L.U. arrived, he was in poor health. He was definitely obese, but his diet history could not explain this fact. We asked him about liquor.

"You mean I was supposed to write that down, too?" he asked in surprise.

Once he had provided this additional information, we found that his problem was excess alcohol consumption. He drank at lunch with his business clients, and he had a few at dinner. There were also late-night cocktail meetings and celebrations. Relaxing on weekends, he had more than a few at home. When he traveled, he had drinks on the plane. Of the average 3,350 calories he consumed a day, nearly half were from alcohol.

L.U. seemed to be willing to change this situation. Fortunately he was not an alcoholic, at least not in the sense of having a physical addiction. His total consumption of alcohol, however, might have qualified him as one.

He was placed on an 800-calorie per day diet, with high-potency vitamin and mineral supplements, and an exercise program was worked out for him. By the end of the second week, he had lost fifteen pounds, and he looked and felt considerably better. The rest of his weight would come off more slowly.

When he left, we had a talk with him, expressing our concern about his returning to the same lifestyle and reminding him of peer pressures. We suggested that he try to find a drink that would look similar to his usual gin or vodka, but without the alcohol. He did not have to give up alcohol totally, but should limit himself to an occasional drink at nights and on weekends.

L.U. seemed determined to do something about his health.

He returned to La Costa about six months later, and we hardly recognized him. He was forty pounds lighter and looked fifteen years younger. Since leaving, he had taken up tennis with great zeal. He told us that the exercise had diminished his desire for alcohol, even on weekends. A drink of carbonated water with a lemon slice kept him comfortable in social and business situations.

His life had taken a definite upswing as a result. His marriage had returned to passionate lovemaking, probably due to improved general health and more zinc available to his body, since alcohol requires zinc to be processed in the liver. In his work, he had been promoted. His vastly improved energy level and mental alertness had brought him great respect from upper-level management.

Alcohol has a wide range of effects on the human body, some of them positive and some negative. (See Figure 9.3.) The beneficial ones are few; alcohol serves as a mild sedative, and it increases the level of high-density lipoproteins in the body, but that is the extent of the positive effects. (The high-density lipoproteins are known as "the good cholesterol," and they lower your likelihood of having heart disease.)

There are many harmful effects, especially in large amounts. Depending on your size, age, sex, health, and activity level, four or more drinks per day would be considered a large amount. Alcohol elevates fats in the blood, dehydrates the body, lowers blood sugar levels, reduces mental and motor coordination skills, promotes obesity, depletes nutrients (including thiamin and magnesium), increases stomach acid output, and is a toxin during pregnancy. While releasing social inhibitions, it decreases sexual performance.

## FIGURE 9.3
### PHYSIOLOGICAL EFFECTS OF ALCOHOL

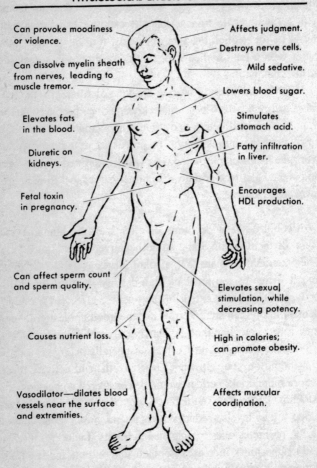

Can provoke moodiness or violence.

Can dissolve myelin sheath from nerves, leading to muscle tremor.

Elevates fats in the blood.

Diuretic on kidneys.

Fetal toxin in pregnancy.

Can affect sperm count and sperm quality.

Causes nutrient loss.

Vasodilator—dilates blood vessels near the surface and extremities.

Affects judgment.

Destroys nerve cells.

Mild sedative.

Lowers blood sugar.

Stimulates stomach acid.

Fatty infiltration in liver.

Encourages HDL production.

Elevates sexual stimulation, while decreasing potency.

High in calories; can promote obesity.

Affects muscular coordination.

In addition to the harm you can cause yourself if you are an excessive drinker, it is important to realize the numerous social problems of alcohol. Abuse of wives, husbands, and children is encouraged by drinking. Nearly half of all traffic fatalities are caused by alcohol and drug abuse, and over seventy percent of drownings and recreational accidents are caused by alcohol.

If you have serious health problems, we recommend eliminating alcohol from your diet. If you are in good health, we recommend that you limit your drinking to two or three per day maximum. Whatever your condition, you don't need the extra calories. (Refer to Table 9.4 to see the number of calories in various alcoholic beverages.)

### TABLE 9.4
#### CALORIC CONTENT OF ALCOHOLIC BEVERAGES

| Drink | Amount | Calories |
|---|---|---|
| Gin, Rum, Vodka, Whiskey | 1½ Fluid Ounce Jigger | |
| 80 Proof | | 100 |
| 90 Proof | | 110 |
| 100 Proof | | 125 |
| Beer | 12 Ounces | |
| Low Calorie | | 70-125 |
| Regular | | 150-200 |
| Wine | 4 Ounces | |
| Table, Dry | | 100 |
| Dessert, Sweet | | 160 |

R$_X$

- If you drink, do so in moderation (two to three drinks per day).

- Small doses daily are better than four sober days followed by a weekend bender.

- Make sure your blood sugar level is well regulated and your nutrient intake is at an optimal level in order to minimize the possible harmful effects of alcohol.

- If you drink, supplements of a multi-vitamin and mineral tablet along with choline may be of benefit.

- Follow the preferential order of alcoholic beverages—dry wine, beer and dessert wine, distilled spirits.

- Avoid or minimize alcohol during pregnancy.

- If you drink, don't drive.

- Eat food when you drink, in order to moderate the effect of alcohol.

- Don't use alcohol while taking medication.

- Encourage moderation among family and friends. For social events, have nonalcoholic beverages available.

- Parents, remember that you teach better by example than by instruction.

## ❄❄❄ 10 ❄❄❄
# Environment

"Millions long for immortality who do not
know what to do with themselves on a rainy
Sunday afternoon."

—SUSAN ERTZ

[• Avoiding factors in the environment that affect longevity
• The importance of immunization and sanitation in avoiding
contagious diseases • Air pollution affects everyone, even in
remote areas of the world • The dangers of tobacco smoke
• Water and soil pollution—the contamination isn't always
visible • Some common deadly toxins—lead, formaldehyde,
aluminum, nitrates, asbestos • Sunlight has risks as well as
benefits • The dangers of nuclear radiation • Avoiding accidents in the automobile and the home]

A great many things that exist outside your body can affect
your well-being—viruses, bacteria, smog, light, noise, pollutants, food additives, and cigarette smoke. Some elements
in your surroundings may be more easily avoidable than others.

Some you may not be aware of because you cannot see them. Our objective here is to make you aware of problems in your environment that can affect your health and longevity, not to make you paranoid. By being aware of these outside influences, you can more effectively avoid them.

If you live or work in a city, you may not be able to escape the problems of smog, but working together you and your neighbors may be able to alter the conditions. Noise levels in the cities are also problems that create physical and mental side effects for city dwellers. Smokers endanger not only their own lives, but also the lives of those around them. Nuclear power plants present risks to surrounding areas. And when you select your foods in the supermarket, you may or may not be subjecting your body to dangerous pesticides such as EDB (ethylene dibromide). Even sunshine in large doses can have its negative effect on you.

CASE HISTORY: B.B. was a guest at La Costa who suffered from the effects of big-city living. He looked a bit unraveled when he presented himself at the medical offices for examination. Normally he was the picture of good health. Although he was a busy and successful executive, living and working in a large city in the eastern United States, he made an effort to take care of his health. He jogged on his lunch hours, avoided tobacco and alcohol, and relaxed in the evenings by playing his video games. At age 43, he prided himself on his dynamic enthusiasm and vibrant energy level.

B.B.'s symptoms included increasing incidences of headaches, strained vision, short temper, irritability, ringing in the ears, and inability to concentrate. His examination revealed a slightly elevated blood pressure, but this was not sufficient to explain all of his symptoms. There had to be more to his problem. Occasionally, in elusive cases, we resort to a hair analysis as a means of detecting health concerns. We did a hair analysis on B.B., and it revealed an elevated level of lead in his system

B.B. was inhaling abundant lead fumes in his big-city lunch-time jog, and was suffering from lead toxicity. The ringing in his ears resulted from excessive noise pollution, and he was suffering strained nerves from the breakneck pace of his work with computers followed by evenings of video games.

To combat his problems, we placed B.B. on a 2,400-calorie per day diet that was high in fiber and legumes, with supplements of vitamins and minerals that included extra ascorbic acid. Since B.B. was already enthusiastic for exercise, he did not have to be pushed toward an exercise program. He was coerced into more than the normal number of relaxing offerings of La Costa—hot herbal wraps, jacuzzis, massages, and sunbaths. He attended the lecture on stress reduction and was advised to read books on the subject.

During his two-week stay, his headaches reduced in frequency and intensity. He returned to his big-city life with more realistic expectations from his body. Though he could not escape completely the noise, smog, exposure to cathode ray tubes (from computers), and stress, his new awareness permitted him to keep his levels to a minimum, and to avoid a serious debilitating disease.

## Contagions

Infectious organisms are no longer the menace they once were, at least in the developed nations. However, it is important for us to remember that viruses, bacteria, molds, fungus, and parasitic worms do exist in our physical environment, and they can all cause disease. For the first two million years or so of mankind's existence, they were the principal cause of death, and they are still serious problems in the underdeveloped nations.

Immunization programs must be credited, at least in part, for wiping out most of the infectious epidemics that once cut our lives short. Vaccines are administered early in life to westerners, and they are required for entering or leaving some countries of the world where these diseases are still a threat. Generally, the less developed the nation, the more shots required for travel.

Improvements in sanitation have also had much to do with winning the war against contagious diseases. To most of us, it now seems obvious that one should not drink from a water supply that is contaminated with feces, garbage, and dirt, but this was once the case for all humans, and is still the case in many parts of the world. Experienced writer and traveler Rob Schultheis advises, "In Mexico boil your drinking water. In Turkey boil it and add iodine. In Afghanistan boil it and add iodine, but drink beer."

Public health measures such as vaccination programs and sanitation do protect you. However, there are a few ailments that are still present, despite our best efforts. As yet there are no effective immunization programs against the viruses that produce colds and flu, and the average person in the West still has about six colds per year.

There is evidence that a properly nourished, well-exercised, and rested person is less susceptible to infection than one who is not well nourished, exercised, and rested. To minimize your susceptibility to contagious diseases, we recommend maintaining proper hygiene, adherence to inoculation programs, good nutrition, physical activity, proper rest, and positive attitude.

## Air Pollution

If you have ever approached Los Angeles, Rome, or Mexico City on a warm summer's day, you know what air pollution looks and feels like. Most major cities of the world face this problem to some extent. Along with the technological advancements of our modern world, we have created some rather formidable and monstrous by-products—carbon monoxide, nitrogen derivatives, diesel soot, lead, and sulfur dioxide, along with many others—that mingles with our air. In some cities, the smog can become so bad that the eyes burn, and breathing can become labored for sensitive people. Many television stations have begun to give smog reports along with the weather, making people aware of various levels of alerts for health problems. Third-stage alerts can mean danger for people with respiratory problems.

Nature has a cycle that takes care of simple air pollution. Animals give off carbon dioxide in respiration, and plants gather it and combine it with sunlight and water to make their food through photosynthesis. Carbon monoxide in the air eventually combines with oxygen to form carbon dioxide, which is why plants are so helpful alongside freeways. But even plants can do only so much to clear the air. The earth now has fewer forests than it once had, and many of those remaining are jeopardized by industrial pollutants.

Ultimately air pollution affects everyone—even the owners of factories who create the stuff. Eventually the contamination reaches even the most remote regions of the world. Industrial air pollutants from northern Europe are beginning to make noticeable deposits in arctic Siberia. Acid rain—which is created by airborne chemicals—has been dissolving great works of sculpture and architecture that have lasted for centuries. If acid rain can dissolve marble, one wonders what it can do to the human body.

The breakdown of the earth's delicate protective ozone layer is a further complication of this problem, and it is a serious one. The ozone layer protects the earth from excessive heat and solar radiation. Our smog is gradually destroying this protection, and possible repercussions of this may be weather changes, increased skin cancer, and the melting of the polar ice caps.

Some nutrients can help to dilute the effects of air pollution. Vitamin C, vitamin E, vitamin A, and the mineral selenium have been shown to have some protective properties, but they cannot entirely eliminate the risk of shortened lifespan for those who live in highly polluted areas.

If your air is not clean, the ideal solution is to move. You may consider this a drastic recommendation, but the alternatives are serious. Ask someone with lung cancer or emphysema what he or she would be willing to do to breathe well again. Or consider the effects on your children: studies have shown that there are alarming levels of lead in the bodies of inner city children. This lead toxicity can cause poor general health, or it can cause learning and behavioral disabilities.

## Tobacco Smoke

When health-care professionals concentrate on a very few recommendations that can make a big difference in the health of westerners, they always include the exclusion of tobacco products. Among the many health hazards of tobacco smoke are:

- Coal tar, a known carcinogen.
- Carbon monoxide, the deadly content of automobile exhaust.
- Nicotine, an addictive substance that works as a mild sedative, raises basal metabolism, accelerates heart rate, and causes constriction of tiny blood vessels.
- Hot temperatures, which burn the tongue and delicate lung tissue.
- Toxic trace elements, such as cadmium, which build up in the smoker.
- Destruction of vitamin C, causing subclinical vitamin C deficiency, symptoms, such as premature wrinkling of the skin, elevated fats in the blood, increased risk for infections, and cancer.

Ninety percent of people with lung cancer or emphysema have been smokers. Numerous other types of cancer appear in higher rates among smokers than nonsmokers. Pregnant women who smoke endanger the health of their unborn children, because cigarette toxins can pass through the placenta and affect the fetus. Infants of smoking mothers are more likely to suffer from small birth weight or heart defects.

The subject of maternal smoking is a serious one, considering the increasing rise in the number of women smokers. In the early part of this century, women who smoked did so clandestinely. However, the movies of the 1930s and 1940s glamorized smoking, and by the end of World War II women had begun to smoke openly. Smoking among women has increased ever since. In 1950, deaths from lung cancer among women occurred at a rate of only four per 100,000; by 1983, this rate had increased to twenty-three per 100,000. This nearly 600 percent rise in deaths from lung cancer makes it the number one killer of women, putting breast cancer into second place.

If smoking were harmful only to the smoker, it might be possible to let smokers continue their slow form of suicide. However, there is considerable evidence that secondhand smoke causes harm as well, and the issue may one day be faced: whose rights predominate, the smokers' or the nonsmokers'? The pregnant woman who smokes brings this issue into clearest focus: does a mother have the right to endanger the life and health of the fetus developing within her?

By this time you may have begun to suspect that we do not recommend smoking. Your suspicions would be correct. We do not recommend smoking, especially if you wish to live a long and healthy life. Though there may be an occasional smoker who will live beyond the given 72 years of the average male lifespan, most will not. The vast majority of smokers will die prematurely.

If you smoke, we advise you to stop. It can be done, though we acknowledge that it is difficult for many people. Despite all warnings, one-third of the adult population continues to smoke. That means there are over 52 million Americans who are either ignorant of health facts or too addicted to nicotine to stop.

A great many people give as their alibi for not quitting the fact that they would gain weight. Some people do gain weight, but they do not have to do so. If they do gain weight, that weight can quickly be lost.

It is important to understand why this weight gain may occur. One reason is that when your burned taste buds heal, food tastes more flavorful, and you find yourself wanting to eat more. Also, since smoking satisfies an oral need for many people, the ex-smoker seeks other forms of oral satisfaction. The urge to eat replaces the urge to smoke. Because smokers are rarely exercisers, it is difficult for them to get rid of the extra calories they consume when they quit. Finally, there is the fact that nicotine elevates the heart rate and thus the basal metabolism. When a smoker stops smoking, his heart is able to return to its non-drug-induced rate, with the result that fewer calories are needed for the body's basic functions.

All of these problems can be overcome, and you can easily rid yourself of the five or ten pounds you might gain, merely by following the good health prescriptions we offer. Proper diet, good exercise, and healthy lifestyle can keep you fit and energetic. If necessary, seek help to stop your habit.

If you are not a smoker, we suggest that you avoid inhaling secondhand smoke. If you are forced into a situation in which you can't avoid sharing the same breathing space, tactfully and politely request that the smoker consider your needs; most smokers will oblige.

## Water and Soil Pollution

With increasing frequency, there are news items about communities being evacuated because of dangerous chemicals in the water. At one point, it is a small town in Missouri being evacuated because of the deadly chemical dioxin in the ground water. On another occasion, it is a community in New England standing in line for water rations from a truck because their ground water has been contaminated by gasoline. At still another time, it is health officials in the San Joaquin Valley of California advising against giving well water to infants because of the seepage of nitrates from fertilizers.

The waste products of modern technology have to go someplace; ultimately they end up either in the soil or in the water. Modern agriculture has grown to become dependent upon pesticides and fertilizer, and chemicals from them also enter the soil and water. The result of all this is water and soil pollution, which eventually affects all people.

In most countries of the technological West, the large cities have grown up along major rivers, which serve as water supplies. Industries have also grown up in these cities, and they have used the rivers and streams for waste disposal. Of course, the cities use purification systems to attempt to make the water drinkable, but they are not always successful. In some cases, the chemicals used to purify the water can create problems as well. For example, most cities use chlorine to kill bacteria, but chlorine in concentrated form is a deadly toxin. Even in small quantities, it can reduce the level of vitamin C in the human system. Chlorine is the essence of bleach, a chemical that not only causes dyes to fade in clothing but can kill skin cells on contact.

When the nitrates from fertilizers manage to seep from the soil into the water supplies, they can become deadly. Nitrates can combine with proteins (amino acids) in the intestinal tracts of humans to form nitrosamines—known to be cancer-causing agents. The pesticide DDT is no longer in wide use, but we continue to use chemical means to control the insect population, and the full long-term, cumulative effects of some of these insecticides and pesticides are not fully known.

A few years ago, a man brought his very sick wife to La Costa in a desperate attempt to cure her. The cause of her illness was unknown, but she was suffering from kidney failure. For a number of years they had been living in a beautiful old southern mansion in a remote area of Louisiana. We suspected—but could not prove—that her kidneys were suffering from the long-term effects of drinking contaminated well water. The area where they lived was swampy. In such areas, the groundwater is close to the surface and is therefore highly susceptible to contamination from septic tanks and other sources. The woman died a month after leaving La Costa.

Your water may not kill you; it may not even make you obviously ill. But you should be aware of its potential for contamination, and if you have any reason to doubt its purity, try drinking bottled water or purchasing your own water purifier. Your body needs large amounts of good, clean water daily for many reasons, including flushing out the waste products of metabolism. It is essential to your good health. Also, as we have advised earlier, do not drink softened water, which is high in sodium.

## Common Deadly Toxins

It is not just the toxic waste of industry that we must be wary of. There are other toxic substances we are unwittingly exposed to in our daily lives—lead from paint and from automobile exhaust; formaldehyde from plastics, shampoo, dyes, and insulation; aluminum from cooking utensils and antacid pills; nitrates from food and water; asbestos from pipes, in insulation, and fire-retardant materials.

The body's reaction to these toxins is not always noticeable immediately, but it can be severe. For example, asbestos looks harmless enough, but it can have a deadly delayed reaction. There is an ugly form of cancer, mesothelioma, that afflicts people who are exposed to asbestos through skin contact or through breathing its fibers for even a short time. The movie actor Steve McQueen died from this form of cancer. He had worked with asbestos for only a few months when he was in his twenties in the U.S. Navy.

Researchers have found alarming levels of lead in children who live in large cities. Others who have compared the bones of today's people with those of ancient Peruvian Indians have found the lead content today is five hundred times what it was then. Lead from automobile exhaust is a major contributor to this, but there are other sources as well.

CASE HISTORY: S.K. was only twelve years old when her parents brought her to the La Costa medical offices. Although La Costa is an adult spa, S.K.'s parents had been regular guests, so we agreed to see what we could do. Their family doctor had been unable to uncover the cause of S.K.'s trouble.

The child was suffering from serious headaches, malaise, lethargy, and poor concentration. Their doctor had examined and tested, and could recommend only painkillers, sedatives, and psychological counseling. The parents had brought the physician's records, so we could avoid repeat testing.

S.K.'s diet seemed acceptable, and there was truly nothing

in the tests to indicate a source of trouble. We questioned the parents at great length about everything—friends, trips, home environment. Finally we found a clue when S.K.'s father mentioned that he had been renovating their home—an elegant, old Victorian house. "Come to think of it," he said, "I started just before her problems began." He had been belt-sanding the paint off the walls, floors, and doors.

We did a hair analysis to confirm our suspicions. S.K. did indeed suffer lead toxicity from the sanding of the lead-based paints which were commonly used before their dangers were known. For months she had been breathing leaded dust particles. Her parents had not suffered, because adults are not quite as susceptible as are the growing young, with their higher basal metabolism.

We prescribed a high-legume diet with multiple vitamin-mineral supplements and five grams of vitamin C each day to help purge the lead from S.K.'s system. She was told to spend some time each day walking, even though she didn't feel like it. Her father ceased his home repairs.

After two weeks, S.K.'s headaches were noticeably waning. After three months, she was back to her normal, playful, affectionate self.

Aluminum is the most abundant metal in the earth's outer layer. It is lightweight, won't rust, and can be recycled economically. However, when aluminum accumulates in the human system, it can wreak havoc. It is suspected as a cause of Alzheimer's disease, an affliction of the central nervous system that strikes an increasing number of elderly people with debilitating—and incurable—effects.

Many antacids contain aluminum, so they should be used

with caution, for long-term use could be cumulative and therefore hazardous. Aluminum cookware, when used with acid foods, could add considerable amounts to the body as well.

Formaldehyde is another chemical that can cause serious problems for humans. It is used in a multitude of products found throughout our modern society. Formaldehyde is in synthetic dyes and resins, embalming fluid, glues for building materials such as particle board, shampoo, insulation, and many plastic products. Since formaldehyde is normally a gas, it can be inhaled from seemingly stable products. Some people can be affected merely by having it come into contact with their skin and its damage can be considerable.

CASE HISTORY: D.W. was not a guest at La Costa, but was someone we were acquainted with. As a healthy high school teenager, she decided she would enter a convent after graduation. She would be pursuing her college education there while beginning a career as a nun. One of her college courses was biology, and one of her first undertakings in the course was the dissection of a shark.

It was shortly after this that she noticed her health began to deteriorate. She suffered from general fatigue, and was susceptible to every virus that was around. She finally became so sick that she was confined to her room.

She managed to recover sufficiently and go on to take her vows to become a nun, though her health was not what it had been in her youth. At the convent, her health again grew progressively worse. Eventually her emotions became unstable, and finally D.W. was released from the convent, a near-invalid at age 31.

Returning to her home, her health gradually began to

improve. She read extensively, questioning things in the environment of the convent, which was in the flight pattern of a major airport. She believed she had an extreme allergy, and she began to avoid certain foods and common household items to test her theory.

She managed to narrow in on one substance as the culprit—formaldehyde. Scientists know that this chemical attacks the very essence of the cell blueprint—the DNA. D.W. found that it was an ingredient of many things she had once come into contact with at the convent, from the preservative used on the dead shark to the black dye in the nuns' habits. It was also in the fumes of the jet planes that took off and landed at the nearby airport.

She was particularly allergic to formaldehyde, far more sensitive to its dangers than are most people.

You may not be allergic to formaldehyde, but you would show obvious health problems if your exposure to it were sufficient. Where possible, you should avoid formaldehyde. Use wood, steel, paper, and other time-tested products around your home. Read the labels of chemicals you use on your body, such as shampoo. Avoid inhaling fumes from diesel engines and jet planes.

## Sunlight

Without the sun, there could be no life on earth. Plants require the rays of the sun for photosynthesis, and animals need the plants for food. The needs for sunlight are countless. Sunlight upon the skin helps us produce vitamin D to prevent rickets. Our eyesight is always best in natural outdoor light, and many other biological functions seem to depend on receiving regular sunlight.

But excess sunlight seems to create problems that may be even more serious than insufficient sunlight. Dermatologists have gathered evidence that excessive sunlight not only causes premature wrinkling of the skin, but also increases the risk of skin cancer. The highest risk is for fair-skinned people who spend all week indoors, then spend the weekend trying to get an instant tan. Sunburns are all you can get instantly; suntans must be obtained slowly and gradually.

Since the sun appears to be part of nature's plan for maintaining our health, exposure to it in a rational manner cannot be all bad. In between the paleness of total sun deprivation and the leathery darkened hides of sun worshippers lies a healthy and safe level of exposure. It is important to realize that the skin of some people is more sensitive to sunlight than the skin of others. You need to be aware of the degree of sensitivity of your skin, as well as the different kinds of sunlight it may be exposed to, especially if you travel to different parts of the world.

If you are blond or red-haired with ivory skin that freckles or burns easily, you must take the sun in small doses. People with dark hair and olive skin are more tolerant of the sun's radiation. But even the blackest skin can suffer sunburn if it is exposed beyond its tolerance.

The situations in which you should be most concerned about your exposure to sunlight are: tropical and equatorial locations at any time of year; the midsummer sun in the temperate zones, especially at midday; reflective sunlight, such as in snow or near water; and high-elevation sun, because there is much less of the earth's atmosphere to absorb the sun's rays.

Almost everyone should use some kind of sun protection lotion. The SPF (Sun Protection Factor) has been established to help you select protective lotions that are right for your special needs. They are listed on commercial sunscreen products and should be heeded. Table 10.1 has a list of each of the sun protection factors, with the various skin conditions they are designed for.

The SPF number is a factor that tells you how much longer you can stay in the sun without harm than you could normally. For example, an SPF factor of 6 permits you to be exposed six times longer than you could without sunscreen protection. Conversely, it also means you can stay out your normal time with only one-sixth the amount of ultraviolet radiation.

Use these sunscreen products rationally. If you have been indoors for months without exposure to sunlight, don't expect any of them to protect you against the effects of a full day on a tropical beach. Learn to have the proper respect for your body, including your skin.

**TABLE 10.1**

**SPF FACTOR OF SUN SCREENS**

| SPF | Use For |
|-----|---------|
| 2 | Dark skin, well tanned; minimum protection. |
| 4 | Fair skin, well tanned; minimum protection. |
| 6 | Fair skin, developing a tan; dark skin untanned. |
| 8 | Fair skin, beginning a tan. |
| 10 | Fair skin, difficult to tan. |
| 15 | Total sun blockage; maximum protection. |

## Nuclear Radiation

There are few subjects that can stir up such controversy as the subject of nuclear energy. Ever since the atomic bombs were dropped on Japan to end World War II, people have been horrified by the destructive force of nuclear fission and nuclear radiation. Adaptation of this formidable power to peacetime uses—providing seemingly limitless energy—has not nullified its dangers.

There have been many questions of safety that are still not satisfactorily answered: What is to be done with nuclear waste? What happens if a truck carrying radioactive materials has an accident and spills radioactive materials in a residential district? Can radical groups obtain nuclear waste and use it to manufacture nuclear weapons? Can the massive walls of nuclear reactors really contain the many subatomic particles being produced? But the biggest question remains: When (not if) major problems occur, will they be as disastrous as some people predict?

Problems are inevitable in any industry, but the problem of a cracked reactor wall could affect thousands or even millions of people living nearby. Studies have shown that children in the area of the world's largest nuclear reprocessing plant—Windscale, in England—are dying of cancer at a higher rate than normal. Other studies of marine life within a twenty-mile radius of nuclear power stations show marked changes in breeding patterns.

Science is not infallible; scientific knowledge continues to be gained gradually through experience. It was only after nuclear power plants were in operation that scientists learned how quickly the metal walls suffered fatigue from exposure to massive radiation doses. The Three Mile Island nuclear plant in Pennsylvania was within minutes and a few degrees of meltdown, to prove the fallibility of even sophisticated safeguards used in nuclear power plants.

Mistakes happen in any human endeavor. Some mistakes are more serious than others. We must ask ourselves: Is nuclear power the best solution to our energy needs? Admittedly solar power, wind power, and geothermal power are considerably less effective than nuclear power at their current stages of development, but there are virtually no risks involved. The worst possible problem stemming from a solar collector would be occasional temporary blackouts. The worst possible problem from a nuclear power plant presents us with the ultimate horror.

What can you do about this threat to your health and life? At the most basic level, be aware of the locations of nuclear power stations and radioactive dump sites. If you live near one, keep potassium iodide pills on hand for emergency. Saturating the thyroid gland with potassium iodide helps prevent the body from absorbing radioactive iodide and incorporating it into the system. Do what you can to encourage the use of nonnuclear power sources.

## Accidents

Keeping yourself healthy doesn't insure long life; it merely makes longevity more likely. In our modern society, accidents are a major cause of deaths, with automobile deaths leading the list. In the United States, nearly 50,000 people die each year from vehicle accidents. Nearly 13,000 people die from falls, the second largest cause of accidental death. The death rate from drowning and fire is also high.

Deaths and disabilities from accidents are, in many cases, needless because they are preventable. Certainly most fires could be prevented by ordinary precautions, such as making sure of proper wiring, not letting children play with matches, not smoking in bed (or not smoking, period). Also, many lives could be saved if people were prepared for such emergency situations. Having fire drills and keeping fire extinguishers available are important in homes, apartments, and businesses, just as they are in schools. Also, have smoke detectors installed in your home; it is worth the investment.

Drownings are also avoidable in most cases. Know how to swim, and make sure everyone you love knows how. When going swimming, boating, or waterskiing, keep proper life-saving equipment handy. Nearly seventy percent of all drownings are the result of alcohol abuse. Waterskiing, scuba diving, surfing, swimming, diving, and boating, all require presence of mind to keep recreation from turning into disaster. Having a beer at the beach may not be harmful, but drunkenness around the water may be fatal.

Very little attention has been given to falling as a cause of death, even though it is the number two killer. Most people do not take proper precautions when climbing heights, the most dangerous situations being repairs around the home. If you are doing work around your home, make sure your ladder is sturdy, learn the proper procedures for walking on a roof, and find ways to secure yourself in case you should slip. If you are going to be higher than ten feet above ground, in work or play, make sure you have safe equipment.

Deaths from motor vehicles are, however, the most numerous, and many of them could be avoided. Young people, under age 25, often take daredevil risks with cars and motorcycles and end up as statistics. Half of all traffic fatalities are the result of abuse of alcohol or drugs. When you are in control of a motor vehicle, use a sober and rational mind. Drive defensively, wear seat belts, and allow plenty of room between your car and the vehicle ahead of you. And most important, obey the speed limits and other safety regulations required by law.

- Follow your physician's advice concerning inoculations and vaccinations.

- Follow good standards of hygiene, both in personal cleanliness and in food preparation.

- Know the air pollution standards where you live. If the condition of your air is potentially harmful, move. Make efforts to encourage clean air standards.

- If you smoke, quit. If you can't quit, cut down to the minimum and take recommended nutritional supplements. If you are a nonsmoker, avoid smoky enclosed areas. In contact with smokers, tactfully request consideration of your rights. If that doesn't work, become adamant.

- Be wary of your local water supply. If you are concerned about its quality, buy reputable bottled water or obtain a water purifier.

- Avoid contact with formaldehyde, lead, asbestos, nitrates, and other noxious substances.

continued

- Take sunshine in moderation. If you want a tan, obtain it gradually, over a long period of time. Use sunscreen lotions appropriate to your skin type and the intensity of sunlight exposure.

- If you live near a nuclear power station, know the steps to be taken in case of an emergency. Potassium iodide pills are good to have around.

- Drive soberly and defensively. Keep seat belts fastened. Don't tailgate, and don't speed. Keep your car's equipment in efficient, working order.

- When you climb to heights over ten feet, make sure you are using good judgment and good equipment.

- Keep fire extinguishers and smoke detectors in your home. Make efforts to prevent fires, and be prepared for emergency procedures in case they occur.

- When around water, use safety equipment and keep a sober, rational mind.

### ⇛⇛ 11 ⇚⇚
# Body Maintenance

"If I had known I was going to live this long, I
would have taken better care of myself."
—PHIL HARRIS

[• Maintaining your body so you can use it in your Golden
Years • The importance of avoiding back ailments • Learning
to stand and sit • Common back problems—osteoporosis,
stiffness, strain or injury • Your feet are necessary to maintaining mobility—pamper them • Preventing varicose veins
• Taking care of your hair • Your skin is functional as well as
beautiful • Dental caries—the most prevalent disease in
western society • Preventive medicine for teeth and gums
• Your vision—a treasure to be well guarded • Avoiding
hearing loss • Don't abuse your gastrointestinal tract • Taking
care of your sinuses • Learning relaxation techniques]

Although most of us would like to live longer, few would
look forward to years spent in a wheelchair, dependent on a
hearing aid, and wearing dentures that are ill-fitting. If we are
to add years to our lives, we would all prefer to spend those

years feeling good and having full use of our limbs and senses.

In order to keep your body working properly, it requires maintenance. Diet, exercise, and attitude can take care of your general health, but attention must be given to the details as well. Proper care of your hair, skin, nails, feet, ears, eyes, back, teeth, and gums are also important for living younger longer. We have all seen the withered, crippled older person who has little or no use of eyes, ears, legs, hands, and teeth. Most of us would prefer not to spend our Golden Years in that condition.

We do not have to end up that way, if we take care of our bodies.

CASE HISTORY: J.D. had been at La Costa numerous times, but always as a guest at the hotel, not the spa. At age 59, she decided she needed more than just a vacation; she needed some body tune-up work. She was a little late in making her decision. She had bad feet, teeth, and gums, and she was losing her hair.

Her medical examination revealed no serious ailments, but her lifestyle questionnaire and diet history revealed very bad habits. Half of her teeth were missing or capped. Her gums were swollen and bleeding, as well as receding. She smoked heavily, and brushed rarely. Her feet were in as poor condition as her mouth. Having worn fashionable but constricting pointed shoes for decades, she suffered from "hammerhead foot," bunions, and numerous other problems. And J.D.'s hair was indeed thinning. This is not an unusual problem for women after menopause, but J.D. claimed her family had always had healthy hairlines. Her hair loss was caused by the numerous dyes and permanent solutions she had used to stay in fashion for the last four decades.

We did what we could for her, and called in specialists to do what we could not. We started her on a program to stop smoking, and gave her a 1,500-calorie per day diet, with vitamin and mineral supplements and an exercise program. We called in a dental hygienist, who showed J.D. how to brush and floss her teeth and instructed her to gargle and rinse regularly with either warm salt water or hydrogen peroxide (which helps to remove food from under the gum line). We brought in a podiatrist, who performed some minor foot surgery, recommended special shoes, and gave her special foot exercises.

We asked her to stop using the dyes and permanent solutions on her hair, and recommended mild shampoos, gentle scalp massage, and niacin as a vasodilator to increase circulation to the tiny blood vessels in the scalp area.

She took all of the advice, and followed it with dedication after returning home. Five months later, she came back to see us. She was continuing to take better care of herself. Her hair had stopped falling out, and was beginning to thicken slightly in growth. Her feet were less painful, but they would probably require constant professional care. Her gums were nearly perfect, but the teeth she had lost through neglect were gone forever.

We told her our favorite Phil Harris quote: "If I had known I was going to live this long, I would have taken better care of myself."

She replied with a sigh, "Ain't that the truth."

## The Back

Mark Twain once described the human being as a "consti-pated biped with a backache." There is both humor and truth in this description.

Back ailments are very common, occurring in as much as ninety percent of the adult population. They are also very painful. There are those who point to our upright position as the reason for our back problems, but it would seem foolish to attempt to return to all fours at this stage of our development. It is true that few four-legged creatures experience the back problems of humans, but quadrupeds would have difficulty typing, playing a violin, or cooking a gourmet meal. The quad-ruped's strong back enables him to serve as a beast of burden. Most humans would prefer to have use of their hands.

Much more practical than returning to all fours would be to strengthen our backs through good posture and proper exer-cise. The bracing that we need on our upright back structures is muscle, particularly in the lower back.

Proper sitting positions are a major concern. Most sitting positions place a great strain on the lower back, which is compounded by the slumping of the upper torso. Over a long period of time, poor sitting posture can cause serious back problems. Certainly overstuffed chairs and couches are to be avoided. Sitting furniture must provide some support for keep-ing your back upright. In traditional furniture, the simple straight-backed chair accomplishes this effectively. There are several modern chair designs that are quite good for the back. The Scandinavians have created a stressless reclining easy chair that is marvelous. And there is a strange-looking sitting device developed for office use that looks more like a step stool than a chair, but it is wonderful for the back because it keeps the body in a position that resembles kneeling.

The object in sitting must be to keep your spine in an upright position, supported either by the back of the chair or by the muscles of your own back.

Because about one-third of your life will be spent in bed, it is important that you have a bed that will support your body for good posture as well as good rest. A sagging bed produces sagging spirits. A firm bed is far better for your spine and back. A therapeutic bed can be of any form you choose— waterbed, conventional mattress and boxsprings, or a foam mattress on the floor—as long as it is firm and comfortable.

Using a pillow under your head can be helpful as a support for your neck. Down pillows are generally best because they can be molded to fit the contour of your back and neck. The key for pillows as well as beds is support. If your body is supported properly, you will be comfortable, and your body can achieve rest. The best sleeping position is lying on your side in a slightly curled posture; the worst is lying on your stomach.

With a proper standing and walking posture, you can drastically improve your figure while developing the necessary muscles to maintain this upright position. Avoid the common mistakes of rounded shoulders and slumped lower back. Stand tall with head reaching for the sky. Hunch shoulders toward neck and then relax shoulders; leave them there. Initially you will need to make a conscious effort to stand erect and develop the muscles to maintain that pose. Soon it will be second nature for you to look lean, trim, elegant, and youthful with your posture.

It is not advisable to bend over from the waist, especially if you are lifting. You should keep your body in an upright position and bend from the knees. Your lower back, unless it is muscularly developed, cannot support the weight of the entire upper trunk. When you must reach to get something, use one arm to support the upper trunk so that the body's weight does not apply pressure to the lower back. If you are moving a heavy object, always push, never pull it.

To avoid back problems, it is advisable to maintain an exercise program to keep the back muscles in good shape. (See Chapter 6.) About eighty percent of the supporting strength of any bodily joint comes from the surrounding muscles. Your back has nearly two dozen joints; if your back muscles are weak from lack of exercise, you are at high risk for developing back problems.

However, it is essential that you introduce yourself gradually to your exercise program. Because few people regularly do exercises for the back, it is likely that your back muscles are not presently in top condition, and attempting a vigorous exercise program can cause injuries. Build your exercise program for the back in gradual stages, and continue it for the rest of your life. If you do so, you can likely remain among the minority of adults without back problems.

CASE HISTORY: R.O. was among the first guests at La Costa over eighteen years ago. At that time he was experiencing back problems, the result of his high school football days. Some time before we met him, surgery had been performed on his back, and he was told that he would have to live with a continuing problem of pain and stiffness.

The La Costa exercise director felt that R.O.'s condition

could be improved through exercise, and he proceeded to instruct R.O. on how to work gradually into a swimming routine. Swimming is an excellent exercise for the back, because it does not require weight to be borne by the back, and so the risk of injury is minimal. R.O. was also given a few exercises, those in Chapter 6, that he could perform when he was unable to swim.

The pain that R.O. had endured provided him with sufficient initiative to try the exercise program and to stick to it. At every opportunity, he swam. When he did not have a pool available, such as when he traveled, he substituted the exercises. Always he pampered his back with proper posture in walking, sitting, and lying.

Only a month after starting his program of swimming and exercising, he awoke one morning without pain.

From time to time, he forgets how painful his back problems were and neglects his exercise routine. The pain returns, and he has to endure it for a month until he can get back into shape. With pain, surgery, and traction as the alternatives, R.O. remains highly motivated in his program.


There are some new devices created to relieve the constant downward force of gravity and to help the vertebrae of the spine stay in alignment. Although gravity boots and inversion swings have earned praise from a small, vocal following, there is considerable concern among health-care specialists about the greatly increased blood pressure to the delicate arteries in the brain that may be caused by these devices. In the normal upright position, blood reaches the brain through the pumping action of the heart. In the inverted position, the heart continues to pump, but blood is also forced into the brain from the force of gravity. Suspending your body right-side-up by hanging onto a bar with your hands may be a decent compromise.

There are three general categories of back problems that are very common in western society:

- *Osteoporosis*, which is a hollowing or demineralization of the bones. This is common in older people and very common in women. It can lead to pain in the lower back as well as to the condition known as "dowager's hump." This widespread ailment produces pain, immobility, and fragile bones.
- *Stiffness*, from arthritis or tightening of the muscles as one ages. The natural tightening of muscles from aging can be slowed considerably with proper flexibility exercises. Arthritis is still a mysterious condition, but regular mild exercise helps slow down its takeover of the body.
- *Strain or injury*, usually resulting from overdoing physical labor or athletic activities. Once a part of the body has been strained or injured, one has a tendency to lapse into inactivity long after the need for rest has passed. For that reason, problems may become self-perpetuating, since an unused muscle or joint is more susceptible to strain or injury.

## The Feet

Your feet are as important to your body as a foundation is to a building or tires to a car. They are truly a work of masterful engineering. They contain one-fourth of all the bones in the body. They are lightweight, able to tolerate terrific stress, and capable of healing themselves. They deserve better attention and care than they get.

Your feet are critical to your ability to maintain mobility throughout your life. Fallen arches, bunions, corns, hammertoes, and athlete's foot may sound like minor matters, but unless attended to, they can become the curse of your old age. Pamper your feet. Give them the proper exercise, care, and protection they need.

Considering their importance, good shoes are an inexpensive investment. Most people select their shoes for the price, style, and appearance. Rarely do they consider that the primary reason for wearing shoes is to protect their feet, to encourage proper growth and formation, and to provide cushioning and support. The pointed toes that are frequently stylish are absurd, if you consider the natural shape of the foot. Wearing pointed shoes will force your cramped toes to grow in a pointed formation, eventually causing serious problems. The foot has a natural beauty that is functional; shoes designed to alter function or evolution merely for the sake of style should be avoided at all costs. It is also inadvisable to wear high heels for long periods of time. They may help to give your body a leaner look, but they can also damage the formation of the feet and create back problems.

Healthy shoes should have the following characteristics:

- *Good arch support*. The arch in the middle of the foot bears much of the weight of the body. Help to support it. A built-in steel arch support or molded rubber bottom can accomplish this.
- *Aeration*. The evaporation of sweat is important to help prevent athlete's foot and general foot discomfort. For

this purpose, shoes of unwaxed leather are best. The leather molds to the foot and provides firm lateral support; being unwaxed, it permits sweat to evaporate.

- *Cushioned Soles*. Since walking on concrete and asphalt can be seriously jarring to the foot, crepe or rubber soles serve as shock absorbers.
- *Lateral Support*. The firm structure of leather shoes can help to support the sides of the feet without rearranging their natural shape.

The feet suffer a degree of stress from walking, but they were designed for this purpose, and they can serve you well if you permit them to function as they were intended. A rolling heel-toe walking motion helps to buffer the stress. In recent years, foot-care specialists have seen an increasing number of foot injuries from stress. In running events, the foot is required to endure stress of up to 5,000 pounds per square inch. This stress can reach up to 20,000 pounds per square inch in certain jumping events. People who run extensively (25 miles a week or more) can experience foot problems despite precautionary measures. If you are a runner or jogger, we urge you to consult a podiatrist or physician trained in sports medicine to assist you in taking preventive measures to avoid foot damage.

Pampering your feet is not an idle luxury; it is essential. Clip your toenails regularly to avoid ingrown toenails. If you develop ingrown toenails from improper care, they will have to be corrected surgically. Treat yourself to footbaths with salt water or Epsom salts to soothe your feet after a hard day of walking. Foot massages and special wood rollers can help to relax tired muscles and bring healing circulation to the feet. Exercise your feet with toe-raises.

## Preventing Varicose Veins

Because of the heart's strong pumping action and the force of gravity, most healthy people have no problem in getting blood to their feet. However, getting the blood back to the heart is not so easy. When blood is permitted to collect in the lower legs, the pressure may force small breaks in veins near the skin surface. This condition—known as varicose veins—is not only ugly, but potentially harmful.

There are several procedures you can follow to help avoid developing varicose veins.

If you must stand for long periods of time, try to keep the muscles in your lower legs and feet moving. It is these muscles that help to direct the blood back toward the heart. To avoid standing still, do isometrics, toe-raises, or other movements. Whenever possible, take breaks to get off your feet. If you can, take some time to place your feet above heart level. One good way of doing this is to lie on your back on the floor (with a pillow under your head) and your lower legs resting on the seat of a chair. Also, support hose can help keep your lower leg from expanding with accumulated blood.

Keep your leg muscles in good shape. Perform the leg exercises in Chapter 6 to keep your legs functioning at their best.

When you sit, do not cross your legs or tuck them under you. Encourage blood flow by keeping your knees at a sixty-degree angle or more. If you don't think this is a serious rule, take a garden hose and bend it to make a tight angle. The water will slow down or stop. This is what happens with the blood in the vessels of your legs when you cross them or tuck them under you.

Eat properly. A good diet will help you to avoid overweight, hardening of the arteries, fatty occlusions in the blood vessels, and insufficient nutrients (such as ascorbic acid and rutin). Avoiding these problems will in turn help you to avoid varicose veins.

## Hair

Most adults give a great deal of attention to their hair, but often the exorbitant amounts of money they spend are misspent. Conditioners, permanent lotions, and dyes sometimes create more problems than they solve. Some hair loss is unavoidable because it is genetic; some is caused by abuse of the hair and scalp. We may not be able to guarantee you will retain your hair, but we can help you to minimize your hair loss with a few tips for hair and scalp care.

The hair of most men eventually thins; in some it thins to total baldness. After menopause, some women lose hair as well. Hair loss and baldness are stimulated by hormones. Male baldness occurs because of the male hormone testosterone; female hair loss occurs with the decrease in the female hormone estrogen. There is one sure cure for male baldness, discovered centuries ago—the enunchs in sultans' harems never went bald—but this hardly seems a satisfactory solution.

Some European doctors have experimented with a scalp lotion that neutralizes the testosterone on the scalp area, but this lotion still has not gained widespread approval. Both a herbal remedy and an antihypertensive drug are currently being tested as cures for baldness.

Our recommendation is to be grateful for what you have, and try to make the best of it. Some of you will be saved by your genetic inheritance. If you are young and curious to know what your chances are of early baldness, look to your mother's father to see if he was bald in later years.

To save what you have, we recommend the following:

- Stimulate the scalp through massage, using a soft-bristled hairbrush, a vibrator, or your fingers.
- Shampoo regularly (three to four times a week) with a mild detergent shampoo to help wash away the male hormone in the scalp. However, excessive washing will dry the scalp, which may also cause hair loss.
- Keep your hair short. Longer hair places more stress on the roots, prompting premature loss.
- Avoid wearing constricting hats. Tight hats cut off circulation to the scalp, causing death of hair follicles and early baldness.
- Avoid smoking, poor nutrition, sedentary lifestyle, and stress. All of these lifestyle factors can limit the length of time you will be able to enjoy having hair.

In washing your hair, dilute your shampoo with three parts water to one part shampoo. This will be just as effective in cleaning and will be easier to rinse out of your hair. If you suffer from scaly scalp, use a soft nylon bristle brush to brush your scalp while rinsing your hair in the shower. This helps to remove the dead outer layer of skin, which would later fall off as embarrassing dandruff.

Generally, avoid dyes, tints, permanents, harsh shampoos, and excessive sun and wind.

## Skin

Your skin is a marvel of protection, and it deserves your respect. It is sturdy, functional, beautiful, and self-repairing. Soft enough for a loving caress, it is also tough enough to keep out nearly everything in the environment while allowing sweat and waste products to be excreted. A piece of your skin the size of a postage stamp contains approximately three million cells, three feet of blood vessels, twelve feet of nerves, 100 sweat glands, fifteen oil glands, and 25 nerve endings.

To maintain healthy skin, proper nutrition and regular exercise are important. What you see of the skin is only the outer layer of dead cells, which is constantly being sloughed off as new cells grow, die, and are pushed to the surface. This is why poor internal health often shows so obviously in your skin. Psychological distress can also reveal its symptoms through the skin. Since the male hormone tends to keep the skin tight and youthful looking, women's skin naturally ages earlier unless some efforts are made to avoid the drying from overexposure to the elements.

Excessive makeup can also prevent proper breathing of skin tissue.

With proper care, you can have a good chance of avoiding the wrinkled and leathery-looking skin that is often associated with old age. Your skin should be invigorated and deep-cleaned daily by using a washcloth in your bathing routine. This helps to remove the scaling dead outer layer of skin. Although there are many soaps that claim to clean and moisturize at the same time, you would do just as well using a plain soap, then adding your own moisturizer later if you need it. (Those with oily skin do not need the moisturizer.) A thin layer of mineral oil or baby oil applied after washing is an excellent moisturizer.

Adolescents experience a special skin problem with acne, which is usually a temporary condition caused by hormonal imbalance. They can keep this to the level of a temporary inconvenience by regular cleansing with a mildly abrasive washcloth, eating a low-fat diet that is high in vitamins and minerals (with an emphasis on vitamin A and zinc), and exposing themselves to the sun for short periods of time.

It is important to remember that the skin tends to advertise your internal problems. If you are not well, your skin will show it. If you want your skin to look healthy, you have to be healthy.

CASE HISTORY: R.W. was a beautiful woman of 26 years of age when she came to La Costa. She had never suffered the agony of acne as an adolescent, but she was suffering it now. It had set in about a year before, when she had begun taking birth control pills, and it had developed into a severe case.

The emotional trauma of severe acne is far more serious than its physical risks. R.W. had gone from a cover-girl complexion to skin of numerous and ugly blotches, and she was very upset by this development. It was clear that the oral contraceptives had set off her problem by disturbing the delicate balance of the male and female hormones. She had ceased to take the pills soon after the severe reaction occurred. There was little that could be done to correct the hormonal imbalance that the contraceptive had created.

Most of R.W.'s lifestyle factors were good to normal, but we prescribed a nourishing 1,500-calorie per day diet, with high-potency vitamin and mineral supplements. We called in a dermatologist, who gave her a mildly abrasive face-scrubbing and a special anti-bacterial agent to apply to her face twice a day. He also suggested that she work on acquiring a tan, since the sun's ultraviolet radiation can kill the acne bacteria while drying out the skin.

After ten days, her condition seemed slightly better, and she left La Costa. Since she did not return, we do not know the ultimate resolution of her problem.

## Teeth and Gums

The most prevalent disease in western society is dental caries, with well over ninety percent of the population having cavities in their teeth. Chances are, we don't have to tell you about the aches and pains of dental problems. Once bacteria have eaten a hole in a tooth, you are probably aware of the slow deterioration that takes place, which progresses from a small filling, to a large filling, to a cap, to a root canal, to a false tooth.

The gums of westerners are also in bad shape. Scurvy, or vitamin C deficiency, is generally regarded as no longer existing in civilized nations; however a recent survey found that forty-five percent of Americans had gum problems, with four percent having bleeding, scorbutic gums as a result of clinical vitamin C deficiency. The condition of one's gums can be considered as a major indicator of health. And gum diseases are the main cause of excessive loss of teeth that require replacement with dentures.

Although advertisers attempt to convince us that denture wearers can do everything that people with regular teeth can do, nothing is as good as the real thing.

Prevention is the only method that makes sense in dental health. A cavity-ridden tooth can never be repaired to be as good as it once was. So we recommend that you take the best care possible of what you have, making an effort to keep your teeth. You need your teeth in good shape to be able to eat several times each day. Eating should be enjoyable as well as nourishing. When the teeth or gums hurt, the pleasure of eating is gone. That can lead to problems with nutrition.

Our teeth and gums have several major enemies:

- *Sugar*. Simple carbohydrates, especially the sticky ones, are fuel for caries. Societies with little sugar in their diets have considerably fewer cavities than westerners do.
- *Neglect*. When you allow the sugar to be metabolized by the bacteria on the teeth, there is an increased likelihood of holes developing in the enamel. Ignoring recommendations to floss, brush, and rinse will come back to haunt you.
- *Poor nutrition*. The health and sturdiness of the teeth originate in the prenatal stages. Your mother's diet and general health lifestyle, your diet as an infant or child, and your diet as an adult, all influence your overall dental health. All nutrients relate indirectly to tooth and gum formation, while some—such as calcium, vitamin A, fluoride, vitamin C, and protein—are directly responsible for proper development.
- *Abuse*. "Bruxism" is nighttime grinding of the teeth from stress. It slowly erodes the teeth, and it is quite common in our high-pressured societies. Chewing hard foods such as popcorn kernels or hard bread crusts or chewing on ice can cause teeth to crack.

There are several important procedures you should follow to take care of your teeth and gums. First, follow the precepts of good nutrition. Second, brush your teeth regularly with a soft-bristled brush. Also, floss your teeth regularly. Dentists tell us: "You don't have to floss all of your teeth, just the ones you want to keep." Dental flossing is just as important as brushing, because it reaches between the teeth to remove cavity-causing food particles. Finally, brush your teeth occasionally with baking soda, and rinse your mouth vigorously with hydrogen peroxide three times each week.

We will also repeat our advice to stop smoking. Since smoking binds vitamin C in the system, and since vitamin C is involved in maintaining the integrity of the gums, smokers more often experience the prescorbutic bleeding and sensitivity of their gums.

## Eyes

Your vision is a treasure to be well guarded. Humans are very sight-dependent creatures, taking in about ninety percent of all information for the brain through the eyes. We tend to take our sight for granted, failing to realize what a marvel of biological engineering our eyes truly are. They can respond to a wide variety of light intensities; they can focus on a wide expanse or a small area. They even have built-in windshield wipers in the form of eyelids.

We in the West also tend to abuse our eyesight, spending little time in sunlight, reading for long periods in inadequate illumination, and not giving our eyes proper rest. More than ninety percent of all people in the western nations wear corrective lenses, a percentage that is far higher than it should be.

By contrast, few people in China wear lenses, and it is not because of lack of availability. The Chinese have a practice of gently massaging the area around the eyes on a daily basis, and this may be responsible for maintaining the eye's ability to focus without help.

There are several guidelines you can use to keep your eyesight sharp.

- *Sunning*. The eyes function best in natural outdoor light. To give your eyes the benefit of sunning, close your eyes and cover them with your hand. Then face the sun and slowly remove your hand, keeping your eyes closed. Move your head back and forth for a few minutes. Do this exercise daily. You should also allow your eyes the benefit of exposure to indirect sunlight without glasses for at least an hour each day.

- *Good lighting*. Eye specialists have found that numerous problems of poor vision, especially in the elderly, can be resolved by increasing indoor lighting. Make sure there is ample lighting in your home. When you read, always use a good study lamp.

- *Nutrition*. Your eyes rely on constant high-quality nutrition for optimal functioning. Follow good dietary standards to keep your eyes healthy. There is reason to believe that erratic blood glucose levels may be a cause of glaucoma and cataracts, diseases in which matter is deposited in the clear parts of the eye. To avoid these problems, your eyes need the B vitamins and chromium. Vitamin A is also involved in functional vision, as well as in cellular maintenance of the eye tissue.

- *Exercise*. Your eyes need diverse exercise. People who

spend hours focusing on one area, such as reading or working at computer monitors, are restricting their eyes to one position. The result for the eye muscles could be compared to the result of keeping your arms in one position all day. Just as your arms would be stiff and painful, so would your eye muscles. When reading or focusing on close work, take a few minutes occasionally to scan back and forth, up and down, and around in each direction. Then focus close and shift to a distance. There is considerable concern that television addicts and people who use computer monitors regularly are losing the ability for their eye muscles to work their eyes properly.

- *Stimulation*. Follow the example of the Chinese. To help relax your eyes from the strain of reading, and to help stimulate blood flow around the eyes, gently massage around your eyes with the tips of your fingers.
- *Protection*. Be aware of risks to your eyes from the environment. If you go snowskiing or to the beach, protect your eyes from the sun and glare by wearing sunglasses. Try to shield them from wind, dust, and sand. Avoid injuries from sharp objects. If you play contact sports or racquetball, wear goggles.

## Ears

Nature has given you instruments that will receive stereophonic sound in a wide frequency range, that can detect the direction of sound origin, and that can maintain balance and detect motion. These instruments are your ears, and you can keep them functioning well into your later years as long as you treat them with proper respect and care. Even with normal abuse and neglect, most people retain decent hearing well into their sixties and seventies.

However, there are a number of factors in modern society that may alter that. Noise pollution has definitely been on the increase. Working around the excessive noise of power saws, guns, jackhammers, airplanes, and heavy traffic will slowly deaden your hearing ability. In the past, music was intended to soothe the ears; today, the excessive volume of electronically amplified music—in everything from headsets to concert halls—threatens to destroy hearing entirely. Studies have been done in which music volume has been measured; the results indicate the levels are far higher than is necessary to cause permanent hearing loss.

The other major cause of hearing loss is improper lifestyle that results in diseases of the arteries. Hardening of the arteries (arteriosclerosis) and blockage of the arteries (atherosclerosis) can both cause poor hearing.

## The Gastrointestinal Tract

Stomach upsets, indigestion, constipation, diarrhea, and hemorrhoids are very common ailments in the western world. They are so common that we have come to accept them as inevitable, merely a price paid for living in our technological age. This is a serious misconception. Your stomach is not weak at all; it is simply telling you that your diet and lifestyle are atrocious.

Your stomach is, in fact, a very tough organ. The acid it secretes for the digestion of food is so strong that it would be capable of eating a hole in the average living room carpet, yet its own mucous lining can withstand this acid, under normal conditions. Dietary abuses from alcohol, spices, fatty foods, overeating, and fasting can combine with emotional distress to prompt erosion of the stomach wall, ultimately producing peptic ulcers. These same irritants can cause ulcers in the intestines as well.

Constipation is a major complaint of the elderly, and a problem for many younger people, too. As we age, the motility of the intestinal muscles naturally slows. However, this does not have to result in constipation; it should certainly not be a cause for chronic constipation at age seventy. The true problem is with the classical western diet, which is low in fiber, high in fat, and less than adequate in fluids, and which is coupled with insufficient voluntary movements of the abdominal muscles.

Westerners also have problems at the end of the gastrointestinal tract, where hemorrhoids are a common complaint. The excretion of food wastes at the anus is regulated by the sphincter muscle, which is a relatively delicate mechanism. Abrasion of this muscle—through either hard bowel movements or improper wiping procedures—results in the painful condition of hemorrhoids. You can avoid this condition by maintaining a diet that is high in fiber and fluids and by learning to clean the anal sphincter without injuring it. Using wet toilet tissue for cleaning is helpful, drying the anus at completion by dabbing it softly with a dry tissue.

## Sinuses

Your sinuses were not devised merely to make your life miserable. Their main function is to help protect your internal passages from the threat of microbes and dust. In cold climates, they also serve to warm incoming air before sending it to the lungs. The misery they give you is usually symptomatic of the environmental problems they have to cope with.

Colds and flu fill the sinuses with fluids. Allergies or emotional problems can cause the sinuses to swell and create headaches. Air pollutants can cause irritations resulting in postnasal drip. All of these sufferings can be minimized by giving your sinuses some care and attention.

- *Protection.* Excessive dust, pollution, smoke, pollen, and sawdust can collect as tiny particles in the sinuses, causing irritation. Wear protective masks when working around excessive air particles. Otherwise, a regular nasal purge can help prevent these irritants from doing harm.

- *Nutrition.* Your sinuses rely on high-quality nutrition to build and repair themselves, and to produce the mucus that keeps out foreign irritants. Follow good nutrition practices.

- *Emotional Balance.* Your attitude can affect your sinuses. Anxiety and emotional distress can disturb the normal production of secretions. Relaxation and positive attitude can benefit.

- *Cleansing.* The water of the oceans has the same saline concentration as human blood. Ocean water has a cleansing value for the sinuses. If you live near the ocean, a daily swim or plunge can be beneficial. If you are among the majority of people who do not have an ocean handy, the following saltwater purge can be valuable for cleansing, stimulating, disinfecting, and clearing the sinus passages.

NASAL PURGE FOR SINUSES: Using a standard teacup, mix one-half teaspoon of salt (preferably sea salt) into four ounces (118 milliliters) of water that is warm to the touch. If your sinuses are tender or infected, use slightly less salt. Mix the solution thoroughly until no grains of salt are visible.

Hold the cup of saltwater to one nostril, closing the other nostril with your finger. (See Figure 11.1.) Then slowly inhale the solution into the open nostril with plenty of air to cause a gurgling sound.

---

**FIGURE 11.1**
**NASAL PURGE**

---

Once the solution begins to collect in your mouth, stop, spit out the solution, then follow the same procedure with the other nostril. Do not allow the solution to go into your lungs.

Once you have performed this operation on both nostrils, gently blow out all contents, one nostril at a time, while holding the other nostril closed.

Repeat this procedure three or more times. You may do this several times a week, especially if you are exposed to dirt, sawdust, or other offensive air pollutants.

## Body Relaxation

There is nothing sinful or decadent about occasionally pampering your body with a sauna, jacuzzi, or massage. Your mental and physical health will improve with the relaxation and the invigorating stimulation that these seemingly hedonistic pleasures provide. The moist heat of a sauna, jacuzzi, or hot herbal wrap can be therapeutic in many ways. It brings the blood to the skin surface, which can aid in healing minor ailments. It also opens pores and cleanses the skin.

Massage, especially after a moist heat treatment, can relax tense muscles and further invigorate the skin, promoting an overall feeling of well-being and improving your mental and physical performance.

- Treat your body as if it were the only one you will ever have.
- Protect your back by exercising for flexibility and strength.

continued

- Select furniture, both at home and at work, that will support your back comfortably. Practice good posture. Always sit upright.

- Wear good leather shoes, with arch supports and cushioned soles. Your shoes should fit your feet, not vice versa. Exercise and massage your feet regularly. Walk in a heel-toe fashion.

- Keep your hair, skin, and nails clean and attractive. Use mild, diluted soaps for cleansing. Use a washcloth on the skin and a soft brush on the scalp when bathing to prevent scaliness. Avoid dyes, excessive sunlight, and detergents.

- Take care of your teeth and gums. Avoid eating hard food and sugar. Brush your teeth with a soft-bristled toothbrush, and floss your teeth daily.

- Stimulate your gums with occasional baking-soda brushing and hydrogen peroxide rinse.

- Protect your eyes. Shield them from glare, dust, pollution, and smoke. Nourish them, sun them, and exercise them daily.

- Protect your sinuses from excessive dust and smoke. Cleanse them regularly with warm saltwater nasal purges.

- To take care of your gastrointestinal tract, reduce the stress in your life, avoid high-fat and spicy foods, avoid excessive alcohol, don't overeat, and maintain a high-fiber and fluid diet. Wet your tissue paper when cleaning yourself.

- Treat yourself to a massage, sauna, jacuzzi, or hot herbal wrap regularly.

- Protect your ears from excessive noise. Follow good diet, attitude, and exercise principles to prevent arterial problems.

## ❧❧❧ 12 ❧❧❧
# Sexuality

"Do married people live longer, or does life
just seem longer when you're married?"
—ANONYMOUS

[• The importance of sex—procreation, physical release, and
emotional expression • Sexual taboos—some valid, others
foolish • Encouraging a healthy attitude toward sex • Sexually
active people live longer • Sex is possible in the Golden Years
• Sexual dysfunction and nutritional problems • Physical exercise and sex • The importance of attitude in healthy sex]

Human beings have a few strong physical drives. We all
acknowledge the need to breathe, a thirst for fluids, and a
hunger for food, and we strive to satisfy those drives without
hesitation. There is one physical drive, however, that has a
way of becoming involved in complications and obstructions.
That is our sexual drive.

Without sex, there would be no human race. Most people
find it enjoyable. Some become obsessed with it, and others

suffer serious emotional problems connected with the sexual urge or with sexual performance. Views of sexuality vary widely, depending on one's social background, religion, age group, and marital or family status. At one extreme are those who consider sex to be primarily for pleasure; at the other are those who consider it harmful.

Most people, however, would agree that sexual intercourse has three functions in human beings:

1) *Procreation.* The survival of the human species depends upon sexual intercourse. For that reason it should be both frequent and enjoyable.

2) *Physical Release.* Beginning in adolescence and continuing throughout adult life, the sex hormones flow throughout the system, requiring some form of release. When this release does not occur, sexual frustration results, although some celibates have found release through exercise, meditation, or professional work. Sexual frustration can prompt reactions ranging from impatience to belligerence.

3) *Emotional Expression.* While love can exist between two people without sexual intercourse, the physical bonding gives love an added dimension.

If sexual intercourse serves one or more of these purposes without harming either partner, then it has value.

Throughout history, however, there have been numerous societal taboos placed on sex. Some of these have had a valid basis, such as those forbidding sexual contact between family members. Certainly, incest has a tendency to heighten genetic weaknesses, so it has not been in the best interest of society. In some societies, sexual promiscuity has been taboo because of the dangers of venereal disease. In others, such as Tahiti, sexual freedom was the norm until western explorers brought venereal disease to their shores.

Although there have been a few cultures whose religions worshipped sex or used sex in worship, most often it has been religion that has been responsible for sexual taboos. Frequently priests and priestesses have been required to maintain celibacy. The human body has often been treated with extreme modesty, with strict codes for both behavior and dress. The strict Moslem cultures still endorse polygamy, but consider women showing their faces in public to be a serious offense. Until the 1920s, western society frowned on women revealing their knees.

Although greater sexual freedom has been permitted—and even recommended—in the western world, sexual taboos have lingered among many people. For that reason, sexual dysfunction remains a serious problem for millions of people.

CASE HISTORY: E.R. had been to La Costa several times in the past, and she had always been a pleasant participant in most of the group activities, whether the sports or the spa meals. This time she was different—withdrawn and taciturn. Concerned about her manner, Dr. Smith spoke to her after a lecture one evening.

She confessed that she was having problems in her marriage—problems of a sexual nature. Her husband had recently had two extramarital affairs, and was now asking her for a divorce.

E.R. admitted that she had never really enjoyed sex. She had been a virgin on her honeymoon, as had her husband. Her total sex education had been a few remarks her mother had made to her as a teenager that "all men want is to use a woman in sin." Even E.R.'s college anatomy book had been censored of sexual organs by the nuns. Before her wedding night, E.R.'s mother had taken her aside to tell her: "Just tolerate it. Don't act like you enjoy sex or he'll think you're cheap."

E.R.'s fear of sex had not been allayed by her husband's lack of patience and understanding. She had borne her husband three children in five years, then moved into a separate bedroom.

After ten years of relative celibacy, her husband had become fed up and began to look elsewhere for sex.

Dr. Smith decided that E.R. needed special help, so he called in a psychiatrist, who began counseling with her. E.R. continued psychiatric counseling after returning home. Her motivation to change her attitude toward sex was good: she did love her husband deeply.

A year later, E.R. returned to La Costa with her husband. Clearly the counseling had been good for her. They were still married; both looked years younger; and both seemed definitely in love.


Some sexual taboos are foolish remnants of the prudery of the Victorian age. Others have a legitimate and sensible basis. In addition to the taboos against incest and excessive promiscuity, the taboos against rape are also valid; to violate another person is both seriously damaging and an insult to the beauty of sex. Equally as serious is child molestation, since children do not have the emotional maturity to understand sexual acts.

In contemporary society, planned parenthood—or birth-control—makes sense, though some groups have taboos against it. It is foolish to bring unwanted children into the world, where they may be abused both physically and emotionally. In some highly populated parts of the world they may face starvation and disease as well. We have a wide variety of birth-control techniques available, and we should use them until the decision is made to have children, bringing them into the world because they are wanted and when they are wanted.

Our objective is to encourage a healthy, open attitude toward sex between consenting adults. When both partners make the kind of emotional commitment that exists in marriage, there should be no sexual restraints whatsoever.

An attitude that all sex must be either harmful or unpleasant cannot be a healthy one.

There are some sexual problems that are truly physical in nature, but they are in the minority. The higher percentage of people who do not achieve sexual satisfaction suffer from problems of attitude. Gloria Steinem has said that "What's between your legs is less important than what's between your ears." She's right. The most important sexual organ in the human body is actually the mind. And the one most important ingredient in successful, enjoyable sex is to have an *interested* and *interesting* partner. If your partner is interested in you, and if you find your partner interesting, there should be no obstacles.

## Sex is Healthy

Most scientific studies indicate that sex is an important factor in long life. Whether this is because of the sexual release itself or because of the physical activity and the emotional sharing has not been determined. However, statistics have been compiled for humans and for animals as well. Married clergy generally live longer than their unmarried counterparts. Women who have children live longer than those who do not. (It is also the case that women who are sexually active have fewer physical problems from menopause than those who are not.) Married people generally live longer than single people; they even have fewer colds.

Rats allowed to mate at least once a week live longer than rats that are forced into celibacy.

This latter is the one study that suggests the sexual act itself may be a key, but it is not conclusive. Scientists have difficulty disassociating sex from the many things that accompany it. The physical activity that goes into sex is, in itself, very healthy, because it burns calories and contributes to good muscle tone. In marriage, the sharing of companionship lends both partners emotional support, which is healthy. Married people also eat better meals than single people.

Sexual intercourse provides great emotional comfort, and thus it enhances a positive attitude. It is also an excellent method for releasing tension. It definitely quickens the pulse and elevates the blood pressure.

It is this latter that causes some older people to be fearful of engaging in sexual intercourse. They have heard the stories of people suffering heart attacks during sex, and therefore abstain. These cases do occur, but it is not the sex that kills; it is the sudden exertion on a disease-ridden vascular network that causes the problem. If you maintain a healthy diet and exercise program and a good lifestyle, you can—and should—continue sexual activity well into old age. If you permit your body to fall into disuse and disrepair, it would be just as foolish to engage in sudden sexual activity as it would be to try to jog a mile or two, without working your body gradually into shape.

There is a story about a 65 year old man who goes to a

doctor for a checkup. The doctor, surprised at the patient's fitness, asked, "How old was your father when he died?"

"Who said he's dead?" the patient retorted.

"I just assumed," the doctor said in embarrassment.

"He's 87 and doing well."

"Well," the doctor pursued, "how old was his father when he died?"

"Who said he's dead?" the patient countered again.

The doctor grew more embarrassed. "I just assumed."

"He's 107 years old and getting married next month," the patient explained.

"That's remarkable," the doctor said in amazement, "a man his age wanting to get married!"

"Who said he *wants* to get married?" the patient rejoined.

This is the kind of old age most of us would like to look forward to. Not only to be alive at age 100, but to be healthy and sexually active as well is a highly appealing prospect. It is possible, but only by maintaining good physical health, optimal diet, a positive attitude, and a proper lifestyle. When these are not maintained, sexual proficiency may end far earlier than one would like.

CASE HISTORY: In his initial medical checkup at La Costa, D.K. was open about his sexual problems. Most people are reticent to discuss sex, even with a doctor, but D.K. confessed that he had experienced very few erections in the past year. His wife had been sympathetic, but he was aware that her patience was wearing thin. He was only 54 years old, and he had always enjoyed sex. He wanted to understand the reason for his problem, and he wanted to correct it.

Examination of D.K. revealed numerous physical and nutritional aspects that could have limited his ability to enjoy sex. He smoked. He was overweight and obese in his percent body fat measurements. His diet was horrible, typical of a top-level business executive who entertained a great deal on an expense account. Because of business, he was under considerable emotional pressure. His exercise was virtually nonexistent.

No single cause of his sexual dysfunction was apparent. It could have been any one of a half-dozen problems, or a combination. Rather than attempt to isolate the cause by trying to resolve one at a time, we chose to attempt to correct all of his various health concerns simultaneously, feeling confident his sexual problem would clear up in the process.

D.K.'s attitude was good. That was one hurdle we did not have to face. He was given an 800-calorie per day diet, with multi-vitamin and mineral supplements, including additional zinc. (His alcohol intake had been heavy, and that could have depleted his bodily zinc, which alone could have been the problem.) An exercise program was created for him, which gradually worked him into enjoyable swimming and handball. He was also put on a program to stop smoking.

When D.K. checked out of La Costa after two weeks, he looked much better, and his medical exam showed him to be less at risk for degenerative diseases. We were surprised to see him return to La Costa two months later, this time with his wife. They had come to spend a "second honeymoon."

When he shook our hands, he said, "I can't thank you enough." We didn't see much of D.K. the rest of that visit.

Although the sex drive does diminish somewhat in most people after age fifty, it does not automatically disappear. Sexual activity is possible throughout life. The myth that old people are somehow "asexual" should be dispelled. There is no automatic expiration date on your sex glands.

What we have in western society is a self-fulfilling myth. Society in general considers older adults to be inactive. As these same people age, they fulfill the role of the asexual adult because of this general belief, which they have accepted. In one study in which people were polled about their opinions of the elderly, the majority considered them to be "warm, friendly, and wise." Fewer respondents considered older citizens to be "contributing, active, bright, or useful." Fewer than five percent of the people polled thought of older people as "sexually active."

Western society has developed an unnatural emphasis on youth, automatically linking it with "vitality," which is a quality that should be considered possible at virtually any age. Many corporations have a mandatory retirement age of 65; some encourage retirement even earlier. This lends credence to the assumption that people are no longer useful beyond a certain number of years. For most people, depression dominates their fortieth birthdays, because they know that society now considers them "over the hill." Gray hairs and facial wrinkles create similar anxieties. This attitude has become so severe that, in some so-called "glamour" industries, executives are considered past their prime at age 35.

The values placed on youth are vigor, vitality, and attractiveness, yet these qualities are possible at any age. Accrued years have the added advantages of experience, judgment, and wisdom. Older people should be valued, given respect and admiration, not pity—especially if they have maintained their vigor, vitality, and attractiveness.

## Sex and Nutrition

Maintaining sexual vitality is dependent upon a great many factors. Nutrition is only one of the factors, despite the claims of popular writers who have touted miracle vitamins with aphrodisiac qualities in recent years. It is important to realize that none of the nutritional textbooks teach nutritional treatment for sexual dysfunctions, though researchers are aware of the role nutrients play in sexual activity.

A full understanding of all of the factors involved is important, so that you will realize there is no single nutrient that can be considered a panacea. If you suffer from sexual dysfunction, it is advisable not to diagnose yourself. Minor or temporary dysfunctions should clear up after following the various prescriptions we are offering for good health and longevity. If you suffer serious dysfunctions, we suggest you see your doctor. We do not recommend that you go to those who promise miracle cures from goat-gland injections or suppositories.

Numerous vitamins and minerals have a direct effect on sexual function; for that reason some nutritionally restricting diets can result in deficiencies that may cause sexual problems. Experiments done with both animals and humans indicate that malnourished creatures generally are uninterested in sex. Vitamin C plays a part in sexual activity, because of its importance to the adrenal glands. Since smoking binds vitamin C, smoking can be considered harmful for your sex as well as for your life.

Experiments with rats suggested that deficiency of vitamin E led to impotency and sterility. It was these experiments that made some people jump to the erroneous conclusion that E is the sex potency vitamin. Actually, if there is an antisterility vitamin in humans, it is vitamin A, which is intimately involved in the formation of sperm and the development of the egg. One cause of impotency in males is blocked blood vessels. Vitamin E deficiency symptoms in humans are less clear-cut than they are in rats.

Zinc deficiency is widespread in western society and can lead to impotency in males, which is also a problem that is widespread in western society. One cause of zinc deficiency is alcohol abuse, which affects the levels of various nutrients in the body, ultimately limiting sperm production, the quality as well as the number. The lack of pantothenic acid may also affect sexual activity, since large quantities are needed when one is under physical or emotional stress. Thus, all forty-five essential nutrients—at least indirectly—affect sexual potency, with some nutrients being very important to a healthy sex life.

Sexual activity can be an excellent form of exercise, because it burns calories and raises the pulse rate. However, your sexual prowess may be limited if your body is not in the best of shape. Strength and muscular tone not only enable you to engage in sex; they also make you more sexually attractive. A degree of physical stamina is needed for successful sexual intercourse as well. If you attempt to make love once a month, with no exercise between, your pleasure will not be what it could be if you kept yourself in good physical condition. Keeping yourself fit is one key to avoiding sexual dysfunction.

Attitude, however, is the one factor that is paramount for sexuality. No one can experience sexual satisfaction if his or her mind is not in it. The physical preparedness of each partner —the male's erection and the female's lubrication—largely depends on attitude. Even orgasm depends heavily on mental condition.

For the male, it is the mind that begins the neurochemical chain of events that results in an erection. The mind sets off chemicals that cause the penis to begin collecting blood, trapped there by an intricate network of valves. As blood is collected in the penis, the tension of a fluid-filled membrane causes stiffness.

Though women do not have to form a visible erection in order to participate in intercourse, they do have erectile tissue in the clitoris. Emotional stimulation is needed to cause the vagina to dilate and to produce the mucous secretions that help to receive the penis.

Of course, in both men and women, tactile stimulation is important, but the emotional stimulation is critical for enjoyment. Successful orgasm is dependent upon both attitude and touch, but emotional trauma can obstruct orgasm for either sex.

The foreplay of pleasant conversation and gentle touching prepares the mind and body to function well together in sexual intercourse. From a state of intense pleasure, the rhythmic movements of the body, and the chemical secretions released by the glands, an orgasm is produced.

It is unreasonable to expect an orgasm—either from yourself or your partner—with every sex act, particularly at times of overactivity or stress, during illness, or in old age. Frustrations from these expectations can affect your attitude and ultimately your performance. At such times, the emotional closeness and physical sensitivity should convey sufficient pleasure to both partners.

In essence, it appears that regular and fulfilling sex is not only possible throughout life, but it increases the likelihood of living longer. Equally as important is the fact that these extra years you gain will be worth living.

Be good to each other, and look good for one another, all of the time.

---

**R̲ₓ**

- Sex between consenting adults is a moral act, especially when conducted with loving commitment. Sex is good for you. It adds spice to life and will make your old age more enjoyable.

- Engage in sexual intercourse regularly. For different people, "regularly" may mean different things. Set your own pace to satisfy yourself and your partner.

- Sexual intercourse should be nonstressful. You should not put yourself in a situation in which nonperformance may result in frustration, embarrassment, or selfperpetuating nonperformance. Have sex in a relaxed environment, with realistic expectations.

- If you are having sexual problems, see your physician. The following are possible clues to sexual dysfunctions:
  (a) *Disease*. This may include circulatory disorders, diabetes, or venereal disease.
  (b) *Inactivity*. Everything in your body functions better when you indulge in regular exercise. Active people have more sex and more enjoyable sex.
  (c) *Nutritional Problems*. There are numerous possible malnutritive conditions, zinc deficiency and obesity being likely candidates.
  (d) *Emotional Problems*. About ninety percent of all sexual dysfunctions are caused by the mind. Investigate this possibility before trying other, more radical measures.
  (e) *Drugs*. Use of marijuana, tobacco, alcohol, sedatives, and other drugs can lead to impotency.

---

## ⊰⊱⊰ 13 ⊱⊰⊱
# Weight Control

"Then I tried the garlic diet. You don't lose any weight. But nobody will come near you, and from a distance you look thinner."

—TOMMY MOORE

[• Obesity is hazardous to your health • The dangers of fad diets • Overweight encourages serious diseases—osteoporosis, diabetes, heart disease, cancer, arthritis, gout, gallstones, kidney and liver ailments, hypertension, lower back problems • Your attitude—fat vs. thin • Adjusting your self-image • Do you really want to be thin? • The dangers of excessive weight loss—anorexia nervosa and bulimia rexia • Making the commitment for weight control • Overfat vs. overweight—the percent body fat measurement • Adopting a good weight-control program—nutrition, exercise, behavior modification, attitude]

Obesity is as hazardous to your health as exercise is beneficial to it. Most overweight people want to be thinner, but usually for the wrong reasons. They are more concerned about their appearance than they are about their health, and this makes them susceptible to the hucksters who promote supposedly instant and effortless ways to take off pounds and inches. In recent years, there have been literally hundreds of diet books published, many of which should have been placed in the fiction section of the bookstores. Some of these books have been as dangerous to health as the obesity they claimed to be able to cure.

Unfortunately, as long as there are people unwilling to assume responsibility for the present state of their own bodies, there will be clever peddlers offering gimmicks. Most of them make about as much sense as one offered in the early part of this century, known as the Tapeworm Diet. Customers were sold a capsule containing a live tapeworm larva, which they were instructed to swallow. As the tapeworm grew inside, the dieter could continue to eat as usual, allowing the tapeworm to devour the calories. When the dieter achieved the desired weight, the tapeworm was flushed out of the system by consuming a vile fluid. However, the tapeworm also removed vitamins, minerals, and protein, as well as calories. The dieters ended up malnourished, ill, and sometimes dead.

In more recent years, we have seen weight-loss programs that are comical, useless, or harmless; some that are effective but dangerous; and many that work, but are temporary. There was the Rainbow Diet, which set forth foods of certain colors for specific days of the week. There was the Drinking Man's Diet, which didn't help you lose weight, but after a few drinks you didn't care. And there was the Lover's Diet, which advised: "Reach for your mate, not your plate." This one actually made some sense; burning calories in lovemaking instead of adding calories from snacking had some merit.

Then there were the high-protein attempts to provide rapid weight loss—the Last Chance Diet, the Stillman Diet, the Atkins Diet, and the Air Force Diet—all of which removed pounds, at least temporarily, but also left the dieter nutritionally unbalanced. Most of the people who tried these diets regained their weight after returning to normal eating. In one case, the Last Chance Diet, the nutritionally unbalanced gelatin formula was actually dangerous, and a number of deaths were attributed to it before it was removed from the shelves.

The list of extreme measures for weight control go on and on—drugs as appetite suppressants, amphetamines to stimulate activity, thyroid tablets to elevate basal metabolism, surgical removal of a section of the intestines, stapling off part of the stomach, and wiring the jaws shut. Vacuuming of fat, lipectomy, is a new technique that holds great promise for critically obese people.

At some point, we hope people will realize that gimmicks ultimately will not work. While they may help to lose weight temporarily, they cannot enable you to control weight. A diet gimmick cannot be anything more than temporary, for failure is built into it. What is permanent is your lifestyle.

One important thing to remember, if you are one who has tried dieting, is that continued failure at losing weight affects your self-esteem, delays you in making needed lifestyle changes, and drains your pocketbook, pulling you downward into negative acceptance, where you will be inclined to say, "Since I tried all those diets and they didn't work, I guess I'm doomed to be fat." That can be fatal.

CASE HISTORY: By the time C.K. checked into La Costa, she had tried most of the current diets—Atkins, Stillman, and other variations on the high-protein theme. Now, at age 57, she had just recovered from a broken hip, which had to be put back together with metal bolts and plates, since she suffered from severe osteoporosis.

Her surgeon had warned her that the condition of her bones was so serious that she might suffer another break from something as simple as performing her household chores. Because her skeletal system was so fragile, it was now essential that she lose weight, and lose it permanently.

C.K.'s lifestyle ran the complete checklist for "how to acquire osteoporosis"—few dairy products, giving birth to several children, high stress, binges of high-fat diets between high-protein diets, very little exercise. Furthermore, she was a female who had been through menopause. Therefore, her age and sex put her at very high risk for osteoporosis.

We placed C.K. on a balanced 1,000-calorie per day diet, with a special emphasis on nonfat dairy products. She was given daily supplements of 1,200 milligrams of calcium and 600 milligrams of magnesium, plus a multiple vitamin-mineral supplement containing 600 international units of vitamin D. For her, exercise presented a special problem; we recommended water sports, which would give her the needed activity without the bone-breaking hazards of gravity.

She should be able to improve gradually over the next few years, if she can stay on her prescribed program.

Osteoporosis is not the only serious disease that is encouraged by overweight. Obese people are four times more likely to develop diabetes and heart disease than are people of average weight. Cancer, arthritis, gout, gallstones, kidney and liver ailments, and hypertension all occur in higher percentages among overweight people. Problems of the lower back are more common among heavy people as well, because excess weight on the belly increases the stress on the lower back. Following the accepted tenfold amplification principle, an excess of ten pounds on the stomach results in 100 pounds of extra strain on the lower back.

High blood pressure, or hypertension, is a common malady in obese people. Weight loss can be very effective in bringing down high blood pressure.

Statistics reveal that overweight people are involved in car accidents at a higher rate. It may be that they cannot respond or move as quickly because of the excess weight, or that their spatial orientation is poor.

The psychological and social effects of overweight are often overlooked, but they can be quite serious. Overweight people have a more difficult time being hired for jobs and getting job promotions. They are limited in the selection of clothes they can buy, and the love life of overweight people is not without its problems. One large dating service found that the one kind of person even fat people did not want to date was someone who was overweight. Numerous things that people of average weight take for granted—such as turnstiles, pews, bus seats, toilet seats—can be difficult to manage for fat people.

All of this affects the self-esteem of the person who is overweight, and that can create serious psychological problems.

## Your Attitude—Fat vs. Thin

What is your self-image? Do you think of yourself as thin? Just right? Pleasingly plump? Fat? Obese? Or do you think of yourself as a thin person in a fat body? Does your bathroom scale tell you one thing and your mirror another? Do you honestly know the condition of your body?

Your mind is a very powerful organ. It is capable of dealing with complex problems and able to bring about great achievements. It is also capable of allowing you to deceive yourself. This is especially true in matters of weight loss and weight control. Losing and controlling weight is actually a relatively easy mechanical process; what makes it complicated is one's attitude.

Do you really want to lose weight? Or do you make the attempts in order to show your friends and family that you are trying, while you actually don't care whether you lose or not? Are diets amusing ways to idle away the time in partnership with a friend? Are they attempts to please parents, friends, or spouse? These attitudes all tend to doom weight-loss efforts to failure.

In his book *Forever Thin*, Dr. Theodore Rubin, a psychiatrist specializing in weight loss, reveals a number of reasons fat people stay fat. We have added to his list a few others that we have discovered in our work at La Costa.

1) *Distorted Body Image.* Some people do not see their bodies as they actually appear. Some see themselves as fatter than they are, others as thinner.

2) *Need to be Insulated from the World.* Some people use fatness as a kind of shield to keep themselves from being hurt by others, sort of a "mattress" to absorb daily emotional crises.

3) *A Sign of Affluence.* There are those who consider fatness an indication of wealth or success. Their rationalization is "only poor people are thin."

**4)** *Bigger is Better.* This rationalization is usually that of a male, who thinks others respect and fear people who are bigger. They use their corpulence as a weapon for intimidation.

**5)** *Someone Else's Fault.* These people like to think they are the victims of the manipulation of others—mother, brother, sister, wife, husband. They prefer to remain helpless before a cruel fate.

**6)** *Avoidance of Sexual Commitment.* If these people were thin, they might have to make decisions on sexual situations they are afraid of. They don't want to be faced with the choice between commitment to sex and rejection of someone's sexual attention.

**7)** *Diet "Saboteurs."* These people feel that others lure them away from their sincere efforts to lose weight. They lack the ability to say "no" to family and friends when offered food.

**8)** *Alibis and Exceptions.* For these people, there are numerous excuses for straying from the straight and narrow. The calories don't count because it's health food. They're being taken out to dinner, and they don't want to insult their host. They're just nibbling while cooking. They feel they'll starve if they don't eat a big, delicious meal.

**9)** *Food as a Reward.* These people think: "Life is tough for me, and one of the few pleasures I have is eating. Leave me alone."

Any or all of these factors can help you to delude yourself into remaining overweight or overfat. If you recognize yourself at any point in the list, however, you should realize you really aren't doing yourself any favors. By taking potential years off your life, you are the only one you are harming.

One young guest at La Costa was a perfect example of point number 6—Avoidance of Sexual Commitment. After being pudgy in childhood, she had lost considerable weight at age 16 and had acquired a beautiful figure. She was unable to cope with sexual advances from her dates, so she gained the weight back purposely. She was now an obese woman in her early twenties and afraid of returning to a lean figure.

This points up the need for being honest with yourself, not only about your present condition of overweight, but also about your expectations of yourself once you have lost weight. Many people lose weight, without being prepared for thinness. Sudden weight loss in large amounts can create a kind of shock for the dieter, making him want to regain the weight. For this reason, a gradual loss of one or two pounds a week is easier to take emotionally.

Some overweight people romanticize about what their lives will be like when they are thin, creating expectations they cannot fulfill. They expect their lives to become miraculously perfect, with no more problems to face. When they discover that thin people have to go to work every day, deal with unpleasant people, and pay taxes just as overweight people do, they become severely disappointed, even depressed. Thinness is a much healthier and more enjoyable state than obesity, but it is not euphoric.

It is very important to have realistic expectations.

For marital partners losing weight, these expectations can be even more serious than for a single person. Obesity sometimes provides a link in a relationship. If both partners in a marriage are heavy and one loses weight, the heavy partner may feel threatened or insecure. Also, the thin partner may develop new directions, leaving the other behind. Realize before you start a weight-loss program that the divorce rate among successful dieters is much higher than it is among the general population. If you are married, accomplish the weight loss along with your spouse; support each other in the effort. If your partner objects to the effort or sets up obstacles, find out the reasons and try to resolve the problems.

You should not attempt to reach the emaciatingly thin appearance that the fashion magazines promote. The old saying "You can never be too thin or too rich" is dead wrong. The gaunt model's figure is not really healthy; emaciated people are at equal risk with their obese neighbors for an early grave. Remember that thinness does not necessarily indicate health. Some people are thin because they don't eat enough or they smoke or use drugs, or they drink to excess or have been sick. These are cases of what we call "unearned thinness." The only route to a lean figure that we recommend is "earned thinness"— a well-toned body that results from eating proper amounts of high-quality foods and then exercising the nutrient-dense calories into a lean physique.

In this regard, your self-image is all-important. There are two serious conditions that can result from unrealistic views of self—*anorexia nervosa* and *bulimia rexia*. Both are a form of emotional disturbance that can ultimately cause serious harm. *Anorexia nervosa* occurs largely among young women of upper middle-class background, who have a distorted image of themselves as overweight. (This usually derives from perfectionist attitudes encouraged by the family background.) They may become emaciatingly thin, but still look in the mirror and see themselves as fat compared to the model of perfection set by the fashion magazines. One-third of all anorectics die, essentially of self-inflicted starvation.

*Bulimia rexia* is a condition that is also self-inflicted. It is caused by the practice of inducing vomiting after eating heavily. As many as ten percent of today's young women practice this repulsive and dangerous procedure in order to stay thin. Extensive loss of stomach acid creates an imbalance in the body's acid base, and a potassium deficiency occurs. Without proper nutrients, the body suffers serious malnutrition, and the teeth become blackened and corroded from the strong stomach acid. Some victims of *bulimia rexia* reach a point where their stomach begins to reject food automatically, even when they do not attempt to provoke the vomiting response.

Many people with weight problems are not aware that their obesity or excessive leanness are symptoms of serious psychological problems. It is for this reason that we recommend seeing a doctor or a psychiatrist before beginning a weight-loss program. Even if you suffer no emotional problems, it is your mind that must create and perpetuate the enthusiasm to continue a weight-control program.

## Making the Commitment

We have stated that the mechanics of weight loss and weight control are simple. They are. However, we do not wish to minimize the difficulty of assessing your weight and health status and of making the commitment to the needed change.

How do you really know if you suffer from obesity—and to what extent are you overweight or overfat? Your bathroom scales are totally inadequate in giving you an indication. Based on weight scales, only about forty percent of the adult population is overweight. Based on percent body fat measurements, about eighty percent of the adult population is obese, or overfat.

The serious drawback of your bathroom scale is that it cannot tell you the quality of the mass you are weighing. Most people attempt to match their weight to figures provided by life insurance tables based on "normal" weight and height. As we have pointed out before, "normal" is not necessarily a desirable goal. The life insurance tables are statistics compiled from decades of measuring life insurance clients, usually long-legged Caucasians of European descent. This hardly allows a fair comparison for other body structures.

If everyone were in reasonably good physical condition, these tables might be useful. Some people, however, are defined as overweight by the charts, but they are actually in excellent shape because they have increased their lean mass and decreased their fat tissue through exercise. The charts would define many football players and bodybuilders as overweight, but the truth is that they are not. According to the scales, most fashion models would be underweight, while in truth many may be overfat because of lack of muscle tone. We had one male guest at La Costa who was six feet one inch tall and weighed 150 pounds. According to the charts, he was underweight, but his percent body-fat measurement showed him to be obese. He looked good in a three-piece suit, but through inactivity he had lost lean tissue and gained fat tissue.

For determining accurately the condition of your body, the percent body fat measurement is the most useful, but it is difficult for you to determine this measurement on your own. There are currently four ways for obtaining this information. One is *Circumference Measurements*. There is a relationship between the circumference of various parts of the body and the percentage of body fat. By a complex method of comparison, an approximation can be reached. It is difficult and can be inaccurate, however.

Another difficult method is *Underwater Weighing*. This requires special equipment to weigh your body underwater after all air has been exhaled. Since fat floats and muscle doesn't, the percent body fat is determined by comparing one's weight underwater with weight on land. Few people would have the bulky, expensive equipment for this method.

The *Skinfold* process is somewhat easier, but it requires practice to be accurate. Calipers are used to measure the skinfold thickness, and this measurement is used in a mathematical calculation.

The method used at La Costa is *Electrical Resistance through the Body*. Requiring special equipment, this method measures the percentage of both fat and water in the body. (Water conducts electricity and fat doesn't.) It is both accurate and easy to use.

Although as yet there is no effective way for you to determine your percent body fat at home, there are ways you can get some indication. The most common method is the *Pinch an Inch* technique. While in a sitting position, grasp your skin just above the hipbone. If, in pinching it, the amount of skin between the fingers measures one inch or more in thickness, there is some work to be done in your fitness program. If the skin measures two inches or more, you are probably in the obese category. Women can use the same test on the triceps area of the back of the arm or midthigh, since they also store fat there.

Men can also take the *Beltline Test*, but this is not accurate for women. If your waist measurement is greater than your chest measurement, you are probably overweight. Men and women can both take the *Waist Test*. To do this, subtract your waist measurement in inches from your height in inches. If the result is less than 36, you may have a problem.

Finally, you can take the *Mirror Test*. To do this, stand in front of a mirror without your clothes on. Count the number of ripples, extraneous bulges, and extra chins. Next count the number of well-formed muscles and the bones that are visible at the skin surface. If the former outnumber the latter, make an appointment to see your doctor or a weight counselor.

Each of these self-administered tests can give you an indication of the quality of mass you are carrying around, while your bathroom scale merely gives you weight. Have a qualified professional do a skinfold test, which is the most popular method, to determine your level of overweight. A very small minority of the population—about one-fifth—do not need some form of weight-control program.

Once you have been able to see yourself as you really are, you will have passed a major hurdle toward weight control, but you still may not have reached the easy part. There are numerous defense mechanisms that you may willingly or unwillingly set in your own way. The next step is to understand fully that you are the one responsible for your weight.

CASE HISTORY: J.W. had been to La Costa before. In fact, she was a regular at the women's spa, and over many visits in a period of fifteen years, she had lost a total of nearly 300 pounds. Unfortunately she had gained about 350 pounds over the same period of time. At age forty-five, J.W. admitted that the situation was out of control. She could not remember the last time she had felt healthy and energetic, and she now wore shapeless clothes as a kind of tent to cover her enormous figure. The quality of her marriage had steadily declined.

Some people require a "last straw" to force them to face their condition and do something about it. For J.W., the last straw came at a party, when someone asked her when her baby was due. She wasn't pregnant. She and her husband were both embarrassed.

We asked J.W. which weight-reduction methods she had tried. She told us it would be easier to list the ones she hadn't tried. She was a self-taught expert on how not to lose weight. Her rhythm method of girth control had actually made her problems worse. By fasting for weight loss rather than exercising, she had slowed her metabolism greatly. By relying on pills and diet products to do the work for her, she had set herself up for ultimate failure and despondency, which led to depression, which led to eating.

J.W. quoted something she had read that applied to her: "Probably nothing in the world arouses more false hopes than the first four hours of a diet."

We countered with another: "The second day of a diet isn't too hard, because by that time you're off of it."

J.W.'s obvious determination to succeed this time was not a facade. She had always been a gourmet cook—one of her talents that had betrayed her waistline—and she was eager to learn the nutrition we taught, as well as the cooking substitutes that can be used in place of salt, sugar, and fat. Made aware of the psychological aspects of weight control, she worked on developing a positive lean image of herself and on maintaining the initiative to keep going.

We placed J.W. on an 800-calorie per day diet, with multiple vitamin-mineral supplements. A gradually increasing exercise program was designed that was both practical and enjoyable for her.

In her two weeks with us, she lost thirteen pounds, then went on to lose another fifty-two pounds after returning home. The next year, when she again checked in at La Costa, she was minus a total of sixty-five pounds.

In a visit to the spa kitchen, we showed her what sixty-five pounds of fat looked and felt like. She could barely lift the burden.

Like J.W., you have to make a firm decision and commitment to set your life on a healthy course, assuming full responsibility yourself. You can't succeed if you expect someone or something else to do it for you—a pill, a book, a device, a doctor, a nurse, or a dietician. If you place the responsibility for weight loss on one of these, you will not accept the responsibility or guilt for final success or failure. Under these circumstances, you are less likely to give the effort your full commitment.

If you expect immediate results, you will also be likely to fail. It takes months or even years to gain noticeable weight. You should not expect it to come off in a few days. Anyone who goes into a weight-loss program looking at his watch rather than at his calendar is setting himself up for failure.

If you expect a diet to be a "cure," you cannot expect it ultimately to succeed. Overweight is not like the mumps or tonsillitis. Once you've had the mumps, you're immune. After your tonsils have been removed, you can't have tonsillitis again. There is no "cure" for overweight except to maintain good health with proper diet, exercise, and lifestyle.

If you are honest with yourself, have a degree of objectivity and good self-image, and are willing to take full responsibility for your commitment, you can take excess weight off and keep it off. But it does depend entirely on *you*.

## A Good Weight-Control Program

Your diet is only one of the causes of your overweight condition. For that reason, you cannot expect diet alone to resolve the problem. You must work on remedying all the causes. And if you want weight loss to become permanent, you must make your remedies permanent. A successful weight-loss and weight-control program requires altering your habits in four important areas—and altering them on a lifetime basis.

This kind of program has been used at La Costa with great success. The four components of the program are:

1) *Nutrition*. Depending upon your size, sex, and general health, and on the amount of weight to be lost, we recommend a total calorie intake between 800 and 1,200 calories per day. Calories for weight maintenance vary considerably, according to individual needs. The foods should be high in fiber and fluids, while being low in fat, cholesterol, salt, and sugar. This should be consumed in three or five meals per day, but only if the calories for the midmorning and midafternoon snacks are taken away from the other three meals.

Your diet for weight reduction and for weight control should be a balanced one. Of course few people know how to select a balanced diet; many don't even make the attempt to understand what it is. "Balanced" means merely that a meal contains a decent share—preferably one-third—of the Recommended

Daily Allowances of vitamins, minerals, and protein, and that the calorie breakdown is 58 percent carbohydrate, 30 percent fat, and 12 percent protein.

Admittedly, it would take a computer to figure out these precise percentages for every meal. To simplify this into something practical, the Exchange Program was developed, creating six food groups to replace the earlier division of four—meat, milk, bread, and fruit and vegetables. As mentioned in the chapter on Nutrition, this new grouping into dairy, vegetables, fruit, bread, meat/protein, and fat makes it easier to formulate a high-fiber diet. (The old system encouraged a high-fat diet.)

The Exchange System was developed by nutritionists and medical experts, and it is sanctioned by the American Dietetic Association, the American Diabetic Association, the American Medical Association, and the United States Public Health Service.

"Exchange" means that all selections within one given category have approximately the same calories and content of protein, fat, and carbohydrate. For example, one slice of bread (preferably whole grain) is equal in calories and protein to a small tortilla or a half cup of rice. The rice, tortilla, or bread can be exchanged freely, and you will still have the same nutritional content.

The Exchange System is delineated in Table 13.1. Table 13.2 provides a sample 1,200 calorie menu plan based upon the Exchange System. Table 13.3 is a suggested daily breakdown of exchanges that are ideal for calorie intakes between 1,000 and 2,500 per day.

We recommend that you use these tables to plan your meals. At first glance, it may appear difficult, but it is really quite simple when you get used to it. Try the 1,200 calorie menu plan to begin. To vary your meals, compare the foods on the menu with other foods in the six exchange groups, and merely substitute for one another within its own group. (Of course, portions should remain within the calorie requirements.)

Once you become familiar with the six groups and can feel comfortable with them, you should be able to select a decent meal wherever you are—at home, on an airplane, in a restaurant, or at a friend's house. From the Exchange Plan, you can determine the number of calories in your food without having to carry a lengthy calorie-counting guide to nutrients, requiring lengthy and complicated consultation.

2) *Exercise.* Before you start your exercise program, consult your physician to determine the state of your health. Select exercises to meet your level of fitness, and start slowly. For obese persons, non-weight-bearing exercises are best to begin with—such as fast walking, bike-riding, or swimming. You must exercise a minimum of three times a week at forty-five minutes a session. Monitor your heart rate, both at rest and at peak of exercise to achieve your target heart rate. Remember, for weight loss, exertion is the key; fewer calories are burned off in low-effort sports, such as recreational tennis and golf. To do your exercising, buy the right shoes for your sport; women should have a jogging bra, and men should have an athletic supporter.

3) *Behavior Modification.* Be aware of things in your environment that influence you to eat—watching television, visiting with friends, reading, driving in the car, and so on—and substitute noncaloric activities to replace them. At mealtime, use smaller plates so that smaller amounts of food will look sufficient.

Chew your food thoroughly, setting your utensils down after taking each bite. Make your mealtimes pleasant in other ways— soft music, soft lighting, dressing for dinner—and take your time eating. Leave a bit of food on your plate when you are finished to signify satisfaction. To help assuage your appetite at the table, try having nutritious *hors d'oeuvres*, such as vegetable soup, twenty minutes before mealtime. Appetizers such as these warm, high-fiber soups can significantly curtail your likelihood of overeating.

4) *Attitude*. Your attitude will make or break your weightreduction program. If emotional problems influence your eating, seek professional counseling. Keep a lean self-image. Be proud of each pound you lose, and be patient. Be firm in your commitment, and reject the attempts of others to sabotage your program.

---

**R<sub>X</sub>**

- For nutrition, eat high-quality foods, but less of them. Emphasize foods that are high in fluid and fiber, such as fresh fruits, vegetables, and homemade soups. Avoid fried foods, alcohol, pastries, and other low-nutrient-density foods. For weight loss, with a minimum of 800 calories per day for short duration and 1,200 calories per day for longer duration, include a high-quality multiple vitamin and mineral supplement daily. Drink at least five cups (1.2 liters) of water daily to help flush your system thoroughly.

- For exercise, start slowly and do exercises that you can enjoy. Check with your physician if you have any concerns about your health. Do routines for flexibility, strength, and vascular fitness. Remember that your weight-loss program will not be successful without exercise.

continued

---

- For behavior modification, be aware of the people, places, events, and moods that encourage you to overeat. Avoid these or change your response to them. Remember to eat slowly, chew food thoroughly, and enjoy your meals.

- For attitude, think of the energy you will have and the sense of well-being you will experience once you are lean. Remember that your attitude is the key to successful lifetime weight maintenance. See yourself as thin, and begin to live as a thin person would. Prepare yourself for your new image. Do not expect perfection in life once you achieve leanness. Set realistic goals for weight loss. As you achieve these goals, reward yourself with something other than food. Believe that you can do it, because you can.

## TABLE 13.1
## FOOD EXCHANGES

*General Rules:*

1) Portion control is essential for weight loss and maintenance. Be sure to weigh and measure all foods and beverages.
2) Choose fat-free methods of cooking such as boiling, broiling, baking, roasting, and poaching. Avoid frying.
3) Hidden calories count! Limit intake of sugars, fats, sweets, gravies, sauces, and alcohol.
4) Eat regular meals, slowly, in a pleasant atmosphere. Never eat standing up.

### FOODS ALLOWED AS DESIRED

Seasonings, Spices, Saccharin, and Other Artificial Non-Calorie Sweeteners, Vanilla, Vinegar, Plain Coffee or Tea, Unsweetened Gelatin.

### WEIGHTS AND MEASURES

*Calories:*

Carbohydrates . . . . . . . . . . . . . . . . . . . . . . . . . . 1 gram = 4 calories
Protein . . . . . . . . . . . . . . . . . . . . . . . . . . . . . . . . 1 gram = 4 calories
Fat . . . . . . . . . . . . . . . . . . . . . . . . . . . . . . . . . . . 1 gram = 9 calories

*Weights:*

1 ounce = 28.35 (30) grams
1 pound = 16 ounces
   (A flat top postal scale of good quality is sufficiently accurate for use in preparing meals.)

*Measures:*

Measure with a standard measuring cup or standard measuring spoon as follows:

3 teaspoons = 1 Tablespoon (Tbsp.)
8 Tablespoons = ½ cup
16 Tablespoons = 1 cup = 8 fluid ounces
16 ounces = 2 cups = 1 pint

# THE LA COSTA PRESCRIPTION FOR LONGER LIFE

*Standard Tableware:*
  Iced Tea Glass = 12 ounces = 1½ cups
  Water Goblet = 8 ounces = 1 cup
  Juice Glass = 4 ounces = ½ cup

---

## SKIM MILK EXCHANGE

*80 Calories*                    *12 grams Carbohydrate, 8 grams Protein*

  Skim milk, non-fat (1/10 of 1%) ........................ 1 cup
  Buttermilk, made from skim ............................ 1 cup
  Dry cottage cheese .................................... ½ cup
  Powdered skim milk, dry ............................. 1/3 cup
  Plain low fat yogurt ................................. ½ cup

---

## VEGETABLE EXCHANGE

---

*½ Cup Cooked Measure*
*25 Calories*                 *5 grams Carbohydrates, 2 grams Protein*

| | | |
|---|---|---|
| Artichoke | Greens | Onions |
| Asparagus | Beet | Rhubarb |
| Bean sprouts | Chard | Rutabaga |
| Beets | Collard | Sauerkraut |
| Broccoli | Dandelion | String beans |
| Cabbage | Kale | Green/Yellow |
| Carrots | Mustard | Summer Squash |
| Cauliflower | Spinach | Tomatoes |
| Celery | Turnip | Tomato Juice |
| Cucumbers | Jicama | Turnips |
| Eggplant | Mushrooms | Vegetable Juice |
| Green Pepper | Zucchini | |
| | Okra | |

The following raw vegetables may be used as desired:

| | | |
|---|---|---|
| Chicory | Escarole | Radishes |
| Chinese cabbage | Lettuce | Watercress |
| Endive | Parsley | |

---

---

## FAT EXCHANGE

---

*45 Calories*                                      *5 grams Fat*

Butter or Margarine ....................... 1 pat, 1 tsp. level
Bacon, Crisp ........................................1 slice
Coconut, Fresh ............................1 piece, 1 × 1 × ⅜
Cream Cheese .............................. 1 Tbsp. level
Neufchatel Cheese ........................... 2 Tbsp. level
Cream, Light (20%) ......................... 2 Tbsp. level
    Heavy (40%) ................................. 1 Tbsp. level
French Dressing or Oil and Vinegar .................... 1 Tbsp.
Mayonnaise ................................... 1 tsp. level
Nuts in Shell ........................................ 6 small
Salad Dressing, Mayonnaise Type .................. 2 tsp. level
Sour Cream .................................. 2 Tbsp. level
Tartar Sauce ................................. 2 Tbsp. level
Oil or Cooking Fat ................................... 1 tsp.
Olives ...................................... 5 small, 3 large
Avocado .............................. ⅛ (4-inch diameter)

---

## FRUIT EXCHANGE

---

*No Sugar Added*
*40 Calories*                      *10 grams Carbohydrates*

Apple ........................... 1 small, 2½-inch diameter
Apple Juice ...................................... 1/3 cup
Applesauce .......................................... ½ cup
Apricots, Fresh ....................................2 medium
    Cooked ....................................... ½ cup
    Dried ........................................ 4 halves
Banana ............................ ½ small, or 3 inches large
Strawberries ........................................ ¾ cup
Boysenberries, Gooseberries ...................... 2/3 cup
Loganberries, Raspberries, Blueberries ................. ½ cup
Cantaloupe............................... ¼ of 6-inch melon
Cherries ........................................ 10 large
Cider ........................................... 1/3 cup

# THE LA COSTA PRESCRIPTION FOR LONGER LIFE

| | |
|---|---|
| Cranberry Juice | ½ cup (4 ounces) |
| Currants, Fresh | 2/3 cup |
| Dried | 1 Tbsp. |
| Prune Juice | ¼ cup |
| Prunes, Fresh or Dried | 2 medium |
| Raisins | 2 Tbsp. level, 1 ounce |
| Tangerine | 1 medium |
| Watermelon | wedge, 4-inch × 1½-inch thick |

---

## MEAT EXCHANGE

---

*Lean, Low Fat. Per 1 Ounce*
*55 Calories*          *7 grams Protein, 3 grams Fat*

| | |
|---|---|
| Beef: Chuck, Flank, Steak, Tenderloin, Round, Rump, Tripe | 1 ounce |
| Lamb: Leg, Rib, Sirloin, Loin, Shank, Shoulder | 1 ounce |
| Pork: Leg (Whole Rump, Center, Shank), Ham, Smoked (Center Slice) | 1 ounce |
| Veal: Leg, Loin, Rib, Shank, Cutlet, Shoulder | 1 ounce |
| Poultry: Chicken, Turkey, Hen, Pheasant, without Skin | 1 ounce |
| Fish: Any Fresh or Frozen | 1 ounce |
| Canned Salmon, Tuna, Crab, Lobster | ¼ cup |
| Clams, Oysters, Scallops, Shrimp | 5 each |
| Sardines, Anchovies | 3 medium |
| Cottage Cheese (2% fat) | ¼ cup |
| Egg Whites | 3 each |
| Tofu | 2 ounces |
| Cheese, Containing less than 5% Butterfat | 1 ounce |

*Medium Fat, Per 1 Ounce*
*75 Calories 7 Grams Protein, 5 Grams Fat*

| | |
|---|---|
| Beef: (15% Fat) Ribeye, Round | 1 ounce |
| Pork: Loin, Shoulder, Canadian Bacon, Boiled Ham | 1 ounce |
| Liver, Heart, Kidney, Sweetbreads | 1 ounce |
| Cottage Cheese (4% Fat), Creamed | ¼ cup |
| Cheese: Mozzarella, Ricotta, Farmer's, Parmesan, Grated | 1 ounce or 3 Tbsp. |
| Egg | 1 |

## Weight Control

*High Fat, Per 1 Ounce*
*100 Calories*                  *7 grams Protein, 7 grams Fat*

Beef: Brisket, Corned Beef, Ground Beef (20% Fat),
    Roasts, Steak ..................................... 1 ounce
Lamb: Breast ..................................... 1 ounce
Pork: Spare Ribs, Loin, Pork (Ground),
    Country Style Ham ............................. 1 ounce
Veal: Breast ..................................... 1 ounce
Poultry: Capon, Duck, Goose ...................... 1 ounce
Cheese: Cheddar Types ........................... 1 ounce
Cold Cuts ........................ Slice, 4½ inches × ⅛ inch
Frankfurter ..................................... 1 small

---

## BREAD EXCHANGE

(Includes Bread, Cereal, Crackers, and Starchy Vegetables.)

---

*70 Calories*            *15 grams Carbohydrate, 2 grams Protein*

*Bread:*

White, French, Italian, Wheat, Rye, Pumpernickel,
    and Raisin ............................. 1 slice (25 grams)
Pita or Biali ............................. ½ (5-inch diameter)
Bagel ............................. ½ small (3-inch diameter)
Bread Sticks ............................. 2 (6½ inches long)
Buns, Frankfurter or Hamburger .......................... ½
Cake, Angel Food .................. 1 slice, 1½ inch at edge
Muffin, English ...................... ½ (3-inch diameter)
Tortilla, Corn ...................... 1 (6-inch diameter)

*Cereal:*

Bran Flakes .......................................... ½ cup
Other Ready-to-eat, Unsweetened Cereal .............. ¾ cup
Puffed Cereal Unfrosted ............................. 1 cup
Cereal, Cooked ...................................... ½ cup
Grits ............................................... ½ cup
Rice or Barley ...................................... ½ cup
Pasta: Spaghetti, Macaroni, Noodles, Cooked .......... ½ cup
Popcorn, Popped, Dry ............................... 1½ cups

# THE LA COSTA PRESCRIPTION FOR LONGER LIFE

| | |
|---|---|
| Cornmeal, Dry | 2 Tbsp. |
| Flour | 2½ Tbsp. |
| Wheat Germ | ¼ cup |

*Crackers:* •

| | |
|---|---|
| Arrowroot | 3 |
| Graham | 2 (2½-inch square) |
| Matzo | ½ (4-inch × 6-inch) |
| Oyster | 20 |
| Pretzels | 25 (3⅛-inch × ⅛-inch diameter) |
| Rye Wafers | 3 (2-inch × 3½-inch) |
| Saltines | 6 |
| Soda | 4 |

*Starchy Vegetables:*

| | |
|---|---|
| Corn | 1/3 cup |
| Corn, on Cob | 1 small |
| Lima Beans | ½ cup |
| Parsnips | 2/3 cup |
| Peas, Green, Canned or Frozen | ½ cup |
| Beans, Peas, Lentils, Dried and Cooked | ½ cup |
| Baked Beans, no Pork, Canned | ¼ cup |
| Potato, White | 1 small |
| Potato, Mashed | ½ cup |
| Pumpkin | ¾ cup |
| Winter Squash, Acorn or Butternut | ½ cup |
| Yam or Sweet Potato | ¼ cup |

---

**TABLE 13.2
SAMPLE MENU PLAN**

---

### 1200 Calories

*Breakfast:*

One-half Grapefruit
4 ounces Orange Juice
1 slice Toast
1 Egg
1 tsp. Margarine
8 ounces Skim Milk

*Lunch:*

Green Salad or 1 cup Raw Vegetable
1 tsp. Oil and Vinegar
2 slices Bread
2 ounces Lean Meat or 3 ounces Fish
Small Apple
4 ounces Skim Milk

*Dinner:*

Green Salad
1 tsp. Oil and Vinegar
2 ounces Lean Meat, one quarter Chicken, or 3 ounces Fish
One-half medium Baked Potato or one-half Cup Rice
1 slice Bread
One-half cup steamed Carrots
Small Wedge Melon
4 ounces Skim Milk

---

# THE LA COSTA PRESCRIPTION FOR LONGER LIFE

## TABLE 13.3
### DAILY EXCHANGE PLAN

BREAKFAST

| Calories Per Day | Fruit | Bread | Meat | Fat | Skim Milk |
|---|---|---|---|---|---|
| 1000 | 1 | 1 | 1 | 1 | ½ |
| 1100 | 2 | 1 | 1 | 1 | ½ |
| 1200 | 2 | 1 | 1 | 1 | 1 |
| 1300 | 2 | 1 | 1 | 1 | 1 |
| 1400 | 2 | 1 | 1 | 1 | 1 |
| 1500 | 2 | 2 | 1 | 1 | 1 |
| 1600 | 2 | 2 | 1 | 1 | 1 |
| 1700 | 2 | 2 | 1 | 1 | 1 |
| 1800 | 2 | 3 | 1 | 1 | 1 |
| 1900 | 2 | 3 | 2 | 1 | 1 |
| 2000 | 2 | 3 | 2 | 1 | 1 |
| 2100 | 2 | 3 | 2 | 1 | 1 |
| 2200 | 2 | 3 | 2 | 2 | 1 |
| 2300 | 3 | 3 | 2 | 2 | 1 |
| 2400 | 3 | 3 | 2 | 2 | 1 |
| 2500 | 3 | 3 | 2 | 2 | 1 |

## TABLE 13.3 (Cont.)
## DAILY EXCHANGE PLAN

LUNCH

| Calories Per Day | Vege-table | Fruit | Bread | Meat | Fat | Skim Milk |
|---|---|---|---|---|---|---|
| 1000 | 1 | 1 | 2 | 2 | — | ½ |
| 1100 | 1 | 1 | 2 | 2 | — | ½ |
| 1200 | 1 | 1 | 2 | 2 | 1 | ½ |
| 1300 | 1 | 2 | 2 | 2 | 1 | ½ |
| 1400 | 1 | 2 | 2 | 2 | 1 | ½ |
| 1500 | 1 | 2 | 2 | 2 | 1 | ½ |
| 1600 | 1 | 3 | 2 | 2 | 1 | 1 |
| 1700 | 2 | 3 | 2 | 2 | 1 | 1 |
| 1800 | 2 | 3 | 2 | 2 | 2 | 1 |
| 1900 | 2 | 3 | 2 | 2 | 2 | 1 |
| 2000 | 3 | 3 | 2 | 2 | 2 | 1 |
| 2100 | 4 | 3 | 2 | 3 | 2 | 1 |
| 2200 | 4 | 3 | 2 | 3 | 2 | 1 |
| 2300 | 4 | 3 | 2 | 3 | 2 | 1 |
| 2400 | 4 | 3 | 3 | 3 | 2 | 1 |
| 2500 | 4 | 3 | 3 | 4 | 2 | 1 |

## TABLE 13.3 (Cont.)
## DAILY EXCHANGE PLAN

### DINNER

| Calories Per Day | Vege-table | Fruit | Bread | Meat | Fat | Skim Milk |
|---|---|---|---|---|---|---|
| 1000 | 1 | 1 | 2 | 2 | — | — |
| 1100 | 1 | 1 | 2 | 2 | 1 | — |
| 1200 | 1 | 1 | 2 | 2 | 1 | ½ |
| 1300 | 2 | 1 | 2 | 2 | 1 | ½ |
| 1400 | 2 | 2 | 2 | 3 | 1 | ½ |
| 1500 | 2 | 2 | 2 | 3 | 2 | ½ |
| 1600 | 2 | 2 | 2 | 3 | 2 | ½ |
| 1700 | 2 | 2 | 2 | 4 | 2 | ½ |
| 1800 | 2 | 2 | 2 | 4 | 2 | ½ |
| 1900 | 2 | 3 | 2 | 4 | 2 | ½ |
| 2000 | 3 | 3 | 2 | 4 | 2 | 1 |
| 2100 | 3 | 3 | 2 | 4 | 2 | 1 |
| 2200 | 3 | 3 | 3 | 4 | 2 | 1 |
| 2300 | 4 | 3 | 3 | 4 | 2 | 1 |
| 2400 | 4 | 3 | 3 | 4 | 3 | 1 |
| 2500 | 4 | 3 | 4 | 4 | 3 | 1 |

## *** 14 ***

# The Grim Reapers

"Men heap together the mistakes of their lives
and create a monster they call Destiny."
—JOHN OLIVER HOBBES

[• Serious degenerative diseases are preventable • Long life
depends on avoiding degenerative disease • Exercise a critical
factor • Cardiovascular diseases—atherosclerosis and arteriosclerosis • Hope for cancer patients • Blood glucose levels
and diabetes • Alcohol abuse increases your chance of dying
young • Avoiding arthritis • An epidemic of osteoporosis]

There is increasing evidence that the serious degenerative
diseases of the twentieth century are preventable. Although
there have also been great advances toward treating these diseases, it is quite clear that prevention is still the best medicine.
It is far easier to try to avoid developing cardiovascular disease,
cancer, diabetes, alcoholism, arthritis, and osteoporosis than
it is to attempt to survive after one of these grim reapers threatens your life.

Your chances for living a long, healthy, and happy life are greatly dependent upon your ability to avoid serious degenerative disease. Only one out of twenty deaths today results from accidents. Even fewer deaths are caused by infectious disease. About fifty percent are brought on by cardiovascular disease, with twenty-one percent resulting from cancer.

Dying from these diseases is not easy or pleasant. Victims may linger in a kind of living death, their health gradually deteriorating. This "death before death" condition keeps our nursing homes and hospitals filled to capacity. It is not the kind of old age we should look forward to, especially when it is possible to spend these years as active, alert, and vigorous contributors to society.

Studies of long-lived cultures around the world—in the Georgian Mountains of Russia, the Vilcabambas of the Andes, and the Hunzas of Afghanistan—indicate that these people who remain vigorous to ages ranging between eighty and 110 years have several things in common. They ate their own unprocessed food. They lived in supportive groups and were exposed to low levels of psychological distress. They performed vigorous exercise in doing their daily chores. As they aged, they were given greater respect and reverence by their people. And they lived in surroundings that were relatively untouched by air, water, and soil pollution.

None of these groups followed any of the strange health regimens—such as fasting or consuming raw liver or handfuls of pills each day—that are often recommended by groups today.

## Cardiovascular Disease

Circulatory disorders seem to be among the major products of advanced civilization. At present, you have about a fifty-fifty chance of dying from one of the cardiovascular diseases. By altering your attitude, nutrition, and exercise habits you can considerably increase your chances of avoiding this twentieth-century "plague."

The human circulatory system is one of nature's most amazing creations. The average adult body has 60,000 miles of blood vessels that deliver oxygen and nutrients to 60 trillion cells, at the same time removing waste products from them. This activity is accomplished by the pumping of the heart, an organ about the size of a fist. In the average lifetime, a heart will pump over 55 million gallons of blood through this system.

When permitted to work properly, the circulatory system can be very durable and incredibly efficient. However, there are two problems that can interfere with the proper functioning of the circulation: fatty blockage and hardening of the arteries. Arteriosclerosis is the generic term for disease of the blood vessels, while atherosclerosis is the most prevalent of these diseses, and involves fatty obstruction of blood flow.

If the vessels become clogged with fatty deposits, atherosclerosis develops. The fatty deposits—called plaque—are high in cholesterol, and they cause the tissue on the other side of the occlusion to weaken or die. Occlusions can occur anywhere in the body, but the heart is particularly susceptible. Because the heart muscle burns fat as a primary fuel, considerable fat flows through the heart's arteries. When fatty deposits occur in the heart's vessels, the condition is known as "coronary artery disease." Seriously blocked vessels can cause angina pain. Totally blocked vessels will cause a heart attack.

When the blood vessels lose their usual flexibility, thicken, and become brittle, arteriosclerosis occurs. This disease is caused by mineral deposits, usually calcium, collecting along the walls of the vessels. This can cause a very serious problem when combined with high blood pressure. When the blood vessel walls lose their elasticity, they are likely to burst from the pressure. If this occurs in one of the vessels of the brain, it is a stroke, and the result is impairment of the bodily functions controlled by that area of the brain.

Both of these vascular problems can occur anywhere in the body, with serious consequences. Other areas that are particularly susceptible include the kidneys and eyes. These and other organs lose their effectiveness when the blood vessels in that area do not function at their best. These prevalent and deadly diseases of the vascular system are much easier to prevent than they are to treat.

*For Preventing Circulatory Disorders—*

- Maintain a positive attitude, avoiding distress, hatred, and isolation. Enjoy life, and love yourself. There is a personality type that is more likely to develop circulatory disorders—the perfectionist who is hard driving, often impatient, and too busy too often. This type produces excess stress hormones—called catecholamines—that have a harmful effect on the blood pressure and the fat levels in the blood.

- Eat a wide variety of wholesome and natural foods, in small and frequent meals. Consume less salt, sugar, and cholesterol. As a regular part of your diet, include fiber from its natural sources of fruits, vegetables, whole grains, and legumes. Unless you are extremely active, severely restrict your fat intake.

- Exercise regularly. When you are active, the blood in your vessels moves faster, burning fat and preventing it from settling into deposits along the vessel walls. Exercise reduces stress, strengthens the heart, and enlarges the blood vessels. It also creates corollary circulation, which is alternate routes of vessels that nourish a given tissue area. Exercise generally discourages the aging, blockage, and hardening of the vessels.

## Cancer

In all humans at all times in their lives, cellular division is taking place. One cell splits into two, forming a new cell. During the prenatal stages and in infancy, the new cell formation is particularly rapid and controlled. The DNA blueprints seem to know exactly what is to be done, how fast to do it, and what to build with. As one ages, cell division slows and the DNA blueprints gradually become less precise.

Cancer, or neoplasia, is an uncontrolled and abnormally rapid division of cells. Whether it is caused by virus, radiation, chemical toxins, or other agents, the results are similar—very rapid and erratic growth in cell number. It is the number two killer in the developed nations of the world. And it is probably the number one fear.

This fear continues, despite the fact that the mortality rate from cancer appears to be leveling off; in some forms of cancer it even seems to be declining. At present, there is nearly a fifty percent survival rate among those who get cancer, and medical advancements are now being made at a rapid rate. There is now considerable hope for cancer patients.

Even greater hope exists in the possibility that as much as eighty percent of all cancer may be preventable.

There is a highly credible theory that most forms of life occasionally develop small cancerous outbreaks, but are able to squelch them through special support systems that include immunoglobins, interferon, and antioxidants. For most people, most of the time, the support systems work well. For some people, for some reason, the systems may be lacking, and the cancer goes unchecked.

If the theory is correct—and we believe it is—cancer can be prevented by keeping the mind and body in optimal condition at all times.

*For Preventing Cancer—*

- Avoid environmental carcinogens such as excess sunlight, tobacco products, formaldehyde, asbestos, radiation, and other proven or suspected cancer-causing agents.

- Eat properly. Studies show that a well-nourished body can better resist cancer. Vitamin A, vitamin C, vitamin E, and selenium are nutrients your body's systems need to help prevent numerous diseases, including cancer. Fat and some food additives seem to encourage the growth of cancer cells.

- Avoid distress. There is a personality type that may be at higher risk for cancer. Many cancer victims are of the type who hold their emotions unexpressed beneath an outer appearance of calm. The body has a delicate biochemical balance, which is known to be affected by emotional distress. Positive emotional outlets do help to keep the chemical balance, and may prevent cancer cells from overwhelming the body's defenses.

- Exercise. Your body functions more efficiently with continual exercise. Also, nutrients are absorbed better and waste products are removed more effectively. Exercise, particularly if it is enjoyable, dissipates psychological distress.

## Diabetes

Most parts of the human body have a definite preference for glucose as fuel. Although fat, protein, and alcohol can be used as alternative fuels, blood glucose is the body's most efficient energizer. To help blood glucose reach the cells, you have a hormone known as insulin, which is produced by the pancreas. In some people, insulin production becomes insufficient or the body cells fail to respond to the insulin produced. In this disease, known as diabetes, the cells cannot obtain their fuel, and the glucose builds up in the blood.

Some parts of the body can adapt to use other fuels, but others—notably the brain, kidneys, and lens of the eye—function very poorly on anything but blood glucose. Hypoglycemia is the opposite of diabetes. In hypoglycemia, the blood sugar is extremely low, and in diabetes it is high. Sometimes hypoglycemia develops into diabetes.

The changes that take place in the body of a diabetic are subtle, but insidious. Blood vessels deteriorate through the body, leading to a higher incidence of gangrene, coronary heart disease, and even death to the kidneys, resulting in a patient's dependence on artificial kidney machines. The tiny capillaries in the eyes suffer greatly; uncontrolled diabetics are 25 times more likely to suffer blindness than other people. Because the glucose cannot get into the cells without insulin, the kidneys must filter the glucose out of the blood, using copious quantities of water to dilute it. (This is the reason diabetics suffer excessive thirst and have to urinate frequently.)

Though no cure is known, medical treatment is available for diabetics. Consequently, many people do not think of it as serious, compared to other diseases. However, because diabetics often develop other problems, such as kidney or cardiovascular diseases, it qualifies as the third major killer among the degenerative diseases.

The causes of diabetes are not fully understood. There seem to be numerous reasons for its occurrence: viruses attacking the pancreas, poor nutrition, psychological distress, obesity, pancreatic burnout from excessive sugar intake, and genetic predispositions. Overweight adults have a greater likelihood of becoming diabetic than people of optimal weight. Certain families are known to have a greater tendency toward diabetes than others. And recent statistics compiled in Europe indicate a decrease in juvenile diabetes apparently resulting from an increase in breast-feeding.

What is clear is that, based upon the current rate, one out of five people living today will develop diabetes sometime in their lives.

*For Preventing Diabetes—*

- Avoid overweight. Eat high-fiber meals, and eat small and frequent meals. Avoid refined sugars. If your diet is not of high caliber, take vitamin-mineral supplements, especially chromium. Breast-feed infants.

- Exercise. Regular activity improves the productivity of the pancreas and the receptivity of the cells for the insulin. Exercise prevents overweight and enhances the body's overall efficiency, while slowing aging.

- Keep a positive and enthusiastic attitude in your daily life.

## Alcoholism

An occasional alcoholic drink does not harm most healthy adults. However, in large amounts, alcohol can be harmful to your health and longevity. This applies not only to the person who is defined as an "alcoholic," but to anyone who consumes more than two or three drinks on a daily basis. Since nearly thirty percent of those who drink consume five or more drinks at a session, alcohol is a threat to the health of a great many people who may appear to be quite healthy.

Alcohol causes harm in several ways. It elevates fat levels in the blood, increasing the possibility of cardiovascular plaque formations. Intake of more than one ounce of liquor, twelve ounces of beer, or four ounces of wine in an hour's period places a strain on the body and liver, because the alcohol has to wait to be processed. In several ways, excessive alcohol can accelerate the aging process—causing deterioration of mental functions, irritating the gastrointestinal tract, and increasing chances of developing malnutrition or cirrhosis of the liver.

Alcohol abuse also increases your risk of dying young from automobile or recreational accidents or from an accident in the home.

If you aren't sure whether you abuse alcohol or not, ask yourself these questions: Do I want a drink or do I need it? Do I usually drink until drunk? Has drinking adversely affected my personal relationships or my work productivity? Do I spend considerable time during the day thinking about drinking?

If your answer to most of these questions is an affirmative, you are probably drinking more than is good for you, and you need to do something about the situation. Since it is estimated that one out of ten deaths are alcohol related, this is a subject of great concern for many people who hope to live beyond the normal lifespan.

R<sub>X</sub>

- If you are a heavy drinker, see your physician for a checkup. Long-term alcohol abuse may already have done damage that needs medical attention.

- A nutritionist may be able to offer you a high-quality diet with supplements that will help you to regulate your blood sugar and control your urges for alcohol.

- Seek psychological counseling, especially if you feel you can only be "yourself" when inebriated. Many people drink for emotional reasons—to forget problems or because they are afraid to face situations.

- Join a support group, such as Alcoholics Anonymous. It helps to know that others have faced your dilemma and have emerged victorious.

- Stay alive and involved in life. Maintain social contacts. Develop crafts and hobbies or volunteer for activities that will keep you occupied, especially if you drink out of boredom or loneliness.

- Develop a daily exercise ritual. Physical activity defuses your emotions and soothes strained nerves. Exercise can also increase your confidence and self-esteem.

- If these steps fail and you cannot keep yourself from the bottle, check into an alcohol rehabilitation hospital.

## Arthritis

It is estimated that at least ten percent of the developed nations' populations suffer from arthritis. Although it is not considered a deadly disease, it does cause great suffering. Because the pain of arthritis immobilizes the victim, the lack of exercise increases the chances of developing other degenerative diseases.

Victims of arthritis suffer from inflammation and pain in one or more of their joints, interfering with normal movement. Human joints are an amazing and complex piece of nature's engineering. Two or more bones are held together by a tough band of proteinous cartilage; to avoid friction in movement, the body produces synovial fluid for lubrication. In arthritis, the bone ends that meet in the joints become swollen and sensitive. The synovial fluid does not lubricate the joint as it should. Pain, stiffness, and inflammation become regular symptoms for the person suffering from arthritis.

Like most of the degenerative diseases, arthritis may be caused by a variety of factors. There has been considerable research on the subject, but as yet there is no proven cure. The disease may be caused by bacterial or viral infection, reaction to drugs, vitamin C deficiency, heredity, or any number of other factors, including psychological inducement.

*For Preventing Arthritis—*

- Follow rules of good nutrition. Overweight people are more likely to develop arthritis, because of the stress placed on the joints of the lower skeletal system. Excessive fat— in the "normal" intake range—can make arthritis worse. There is some evidence that minerals missing from the diet—i.e., calcium, magnesium, zinc—may be a cause of arthritis. Check for food allergies; some people have had noticeable improvement in their arthritic condition when suspected allergenic foods were omitted from their diets.

- Exercise. Active people are less likely to experience arthritis, and those who do suffer from arthritis acknowledge that their pain increases when they become sedentary, even though it is extremely painful to move initially. If you have reason to believe you are susceptible to arthritis, choose exercises that do not place severe repeated stress on joints.

- Try to avoid harboring resentment or feeling cheated by life. There is a personality type which is more likely to develop arthritis. This type may feel a subconscious need for attention or sympathy that will result from suffering. Harboring long-term grudges may be another psychological instigator of arthritis.

## Osteoporosis

Osteoporosis has reached epidemic proportions in western nations, and it is—at least indirectly—a deadly disease. In the beginning, it may appear only as a few loose teeth or a sore back, but eventually it may develop into a shrinking of skeletal structure, a dowager's hump, and brittle bones that break from the slightest stress or strain.

In addition to providing the internal support structure for the body, the bones serve as a storage depot for the body's calcium. The blood deposits calcium and phosphorous salts in the bones on a daily basis. These minerals give the bones strength by being stored there, but they are also needed by the rest of the body. For this reason, the blood makes constant withdrawals from the storage depot. When the withdrawals are greater than the deposits, demineralization of the bones begins taking place.

Without the strengthening minerals, the bones shrink, teeth loosen, and brittleness increases chances of serious breaks. In itself, this condition is not life-threatening, but the complications that can set in can be deadly. The breaks require months of recovery, and inactivity can cause other ailments.

Osteoporosis can—and should—be prevented.

*For Preventing Osteoporosis—*

- Follow rules of good nutrition, getting the right balance of vitamins and minerals and avoiding excess fat consumption. Fat in the diet combines with calcium in the intestines to form unabsorbable soaps, which are then lost in the feces. Saturated fats do this disastrous soapmaking particularly well. Excess phosphorous intake can cause leaching of calcium from the bones. Too much protein in the diet can cause calcium loss as well. Not only do you need sufficient calcium in your diet (1,000 milligrams or more per day), but also vitamin D for absorption and magnesium for mineral balance.

- Get plenty of exercise. Scientists have proven that the bones fortify themselves when the body is used regularly. Sedentary lifestyles diminish the need for a strong skeletal system, and increase the likelihood of abundant calcium loss from the bones. Regular activity helps keep the skeletal system well calcified.

- Avoid severe emotional distress. Stress diminishes the efficiency of absorbing nutrients, including calcium, vitamin D, and magnesium. Distress can cause loss of calcium from the bones.

# ⋙⋙ 15 ⋘⋘

# Long Life—Whose Responsibility?

"Responsibility—the high price of self-ownership."

—ELI SCHLEIFER

[• Doctors can't take full responsibility for your health • Your role—knowing your body and taking care of it • Observing symptoms—excretions and sensations • How not to deceive yourself • Knowing the health-care professionals and when to call them • Taking full responsibility]

Health-care costs continue to spiral upward. Medical technology becomes more advanced and complex with each passing year. Doctors increasingly specialize. The names of health conditions seem to derive from no known language. For these and other reasons, the average person finds it more difficult to understand modern health care.

Awestruck or bewildered, most people today turn over full responsibility for their health to doctors and other health-care professionals. Some feel that physical ailments are so technical that they cannot possibly understand them. Others assume that the new technology is able to perform miracles, so they don't need to keep in touch with their bodies themselves. Some few may even consider that the large medical fees entitle them to be cured of whatever exotic condition they may contract.

When guests at La Costa come for a medical examination, we ask them to tell us about their health. All too often, their response begins with, "My doctor says..." Generally, we have the reports of their doctors in our hands, and we don't need the patient to translate them for us. We want to know how the guest feels about his or her health.

Unfortunately, few people are able to tell doctors about their own bodies.

## Your Role

Your body is yours. You decide what goes into it and how it is maintained and used. You are responsible for its health and its future. Doctors and other health-care professionals are there to help you when your body has problems you cannot control, but you cannot expect them to take the major responsibility for its proper functioning. That obligation is yours, and yours alone.

Whether you are aware of it or not, your body is constantly telling you things. You have literally millions of sensors all over your body, with receptors in your brain, to keep you informed on all sorts of conditions—temperature, pressure, pain, and many others. Because some of these sensations are unpleasant or uncomfortable, the people of contemporary society endeavor to ignore them or block them out in some way. This can be a serious mistake.

For example, if you have a pain in your back, it is trying to tell you something is wrong. You may relieve the pain symptoms temporarily by taking a sedative. However, that does not deal with the problem itself, which may continue, perhaps growing more severe. If you are typical of today's society, you will wait until a more serious symptom occurs to immobilize you before doing something to correct the problem.

The mild symptom may have signaled a mild problem that could have been dealt with relatively easily. Perhaps you had been sitting too long, using incorrect posture, and all you needed was a bit of exercise. The medication enabled you to feel better and to continue your work, sitting incorrectly, causing further problems for your back. If you continue to fool your back this way, day after day, the problem may become so severe the medication no longer works. That is when you go to the doctor with a major back problem, which will probably be very difficult to treat at that point.

It is important that people reacquaint themselves with their bodies, to listen to minor symptoms and know how to respond. The reflex to reach for the pill bottle may not be the proper response. At the very least, there should be a moment to let the signal register and to understand its warning before reaching for medication to quell it. We are not suggesting that you must endure all painful symptoms—or that you should ignore your doctor's advice to take medication, which can help you heal without intolerable discomfort. We suggest only that you listen to your body, something a great many people do not do.

CASE HISTORY: R.C. spent more money on medical care than most people earn. Each time she came to La Costa, she had some new medical problems to tell us about. Invariably, she prefaced everything with, "My doctor says..."

Always we tried to get her to tell us about her problems from her viewpoint—what her specific symptoms were, how she felt about them, if she noticed anything in her lifestyle that might be connected. She either could not or would not tell us. She saw no relationship between her lifestyle and her problems. When we tried to educate her to listen to her body and to persuade her to alter her lifestyle so that she could avoid further problems, she insisted, "My doctor takes care of my health. That's what I pay him for."

Now in her late fifties, R.C.'s health is not good. The old joke, "She's had so many operations she should have zippers installed," applies very well to her. Her medical file is voluminous, and it increases each year by geometric progression. Yet she still adamantly refuses to take charge of her own health.

Most doctors prefer that their patients be actively involved in their health care. They do not want complete control, but see their role as one of professional guidance with occasional intervention. Although they would not wish to have their patients come in with every minor complaint, most would agree that people frequently ignore their symptoms until it is too late. Some people develop cancer of the colon after decades of warnings from constipation and other symptoms. Many patients develop heart disease after years of labored breathing and racing hearts from slight exertion. Most physicians would prefer to try to resolve problems such as these in the early stages.

In becoming reacquainted with your body, there are two

major categories you should begin to observe on a regular basis—excretions and sensations.

*Excretions.* The substances that flow out of your body are good indicators of what is going on inside. Feces, urine, mucus, tears, and perspiration can all serve as useful gauges of your bodily functions. By keeping track of them, you can notice when any one or more become abnormal. An isolated instance of abnormality, however, is no sign that you should rush to your doctor. For example, one day of constipation should not lead you to think you have cancer of the colon. A condition that lasts a few days indicates that you need to make a change in your lifestyle to correct a problem. If your corrective measures do not improve the situation within a reasonable time, seek medical attention.

The bodily secretions you should be aware of are:

- *Feces.* They should have a soft consistency, and your bowel movements should occur daily or more frequently, unless you are fasting. The feces should be various shades of brown.
- *Urine.* Normally your urine should be nearly clear to a slightly yellow shade, unless you are taking vitamins, in which case, it can be a deep yellow because of the riboflavin. You should have between four and ten urinations within a twenty-four hour period.
- *Mucus.* Under normal circumstances, your mucus should be clear and slightly viscous, with no serious odors. It should not be visible generally because it evaporates at the same rate at which it is produced.
- *Tears.* There should be no tearing accumulation unless

your eyes are irritated. When they appear, tears should be clear and thin in consistency, with regular flow and drainage.

- *Perspiration.* Only when the body heats up should your perspiration be visible. Otherwise it will not be obvious. It should have minimal odors.

*Sensations.* Physical sensations, such as pain, itching, swelling, chills, aching, and fever are all intended to tell you something that you must be wary of. Again, minor occurrences of these symptoms generally indicate a minor problem, one you should be able to remedy yourself. When conditions persist or increase despite your efforts, you should see your doctor. Here are just a few of the important sensations from your body that you should be keenly aware of:

- *Heartbeat.* Is it regular and subtle, or is it erratic and pounding?
- *Digestion.* Does it occur smoothly and easily, or are there burning sensations and frequent pains?
- *Feet.* Do your feet hurt when you walk? Is this a regular occurrence?
- *Gums.* Is there a sensitive spot on your gums? Does the inside of your mouth ache frequently? Are your gums generally a nice healthy pink color?

Sometimes it may require considerable thought and attention to discover the source of your physical ailments. A muscular ache after a day of unusually strenuous exercise is easily recognized. The same is true of a rash or swelling that appears consistently after eating shrimp. A constant burning sensation in your stomach that refuses to be quelled by antacid pills can be understood by your doctor. But there are extreme cases that may baffle the health-care specialist as well as you, though you might be able to uncover the cause if you really gave thought to the matter. The case of E.A. is an example of this.

CASE HISTORY: When E.A. first came to La Costa more than ten years ago, he had excellent health and a good attitude. Not long after his first visit, he was married. From that time, he returned to La Costa each year, suffering a different set of symptoms that had been treated by his hometown physicians.

One year, he had serious gastric disturbances, including burning sensations and pain; he was taking ulcer medication to quiet the symptoms and control the stomach acid. Another year he came with several skin rashes, which were controlled by sunshine, ointments, and cortisone injections. On yet another visit, he was suffering with heart palpitations and breathing problems.

Then, one year, we did not see him.

When he returned the next year, he seemed very different; his manner was subdued. He told us he had suffered a nervous breakdown, and subsequently his wife had left him. Yet his health—both mental and physical—was actually improving, though he had not yet regained the zest for life he'd had before his marriage.

E.A. revealed to us that his marriage had been arranged by his parents. His wife had not been of his choosing. He had been enduring both a hostile marriage and a submissive relationship with his parents, and this condition had been destructive to his health. The emotional stress of living with an incompatible mate and enduring the browbeating of domineering parents had manifested itself in E.A.'s digestive system, then his skin, and finally in his heart and respiratory system.

Each time the signals were sedated with drugs, and the real cause was ignored.

Assuming the responsibility for your own health is not always easy. The mind is just as capable of deceiving as it is of understanding, especially if you have a tendency toward rationalization, wishful thinking, or gullibility. In this era of science and material progress, we all have a tendency to believe in miracles and self-styled experts more than in ourselves.

Gimmicks such as ionic pillows and no-effort weight-loss pills are all too attractive, both as novelty and as credible "scientific" developments. Charlatans who offer miracle drugs with the explanation that they are "so effective the medical establishment is trying to destroy them" can sometimes make their cases sound reasonable. Ultimately, however, they encourage you to continue deceiving yourself, and they take advantage of your willingness to turn over the responsibility of your health to someone or something else.

No miracle is going to give you long life. The key to health and longevity is prevention. Up to ninety percent of all ailments today could have been prevented. There are two simple reasons they were not prevented—apathy and/or ignorance. You can avoid having your life cut short by remedying those two conditions in your own life—by caring about your health and by learning how to alter your lifestyle and respond to the needs of your body.

## The Health-Care Professionals

In assuming responsibility for your body's health, it is important to know when to seek the help of a health-care professional, as well as to understand what kind of help to seek. No matter how good the care you take of yourself, there will be times when you will need help. Even the best program for prevention requires some periodic checking by a physician. We do not recommend that you give up regular medical checkups.

If you are under forty and in good health, a checkup every two years should be sufficient. If you are age forty or over, your checkups should be once a year. After age sixty, these checkups should be in-depth with extensive blood chemistry profiles conducted.

You can take care of minor scratches and bruises yourself, but the following conditions would require immediate medical attention:

- *Major Cuts*. If a wound is pumping blood, an artery has been lacerated. Pack the wound with a clean, cold, wet towel, pressing it against the wound, and go to the nearest medical service.
- *Bone Breaks*. To get the bone properly set for mending, go to a doctor as soon as possible.
- *Loss of Consciousness*. If someone is unconscious and unable to be roused, emergency medical attention is required.
- *Concussion*. A severe blow or fall can have major complications. Concussion is a shock to delicate inter-

355

nal organs, and brain injury can be serious. If someone has suffered concussion and parts of their body are very tender, internal bleeding may have occurred. Seek expert aid promptly.

- *Continuous Vomiting or Diarrhea.* Extensive loss of bodily fluids is a definite life-threatening situation. Seek medical help.

All of these are emergency situations, because they are life-threatening. There are some situations that are not life-threatening in which you may need help. Your body's sensations or excretions may warn you of problems that you cannot deal with, and on these occasions you should not hesitate to seek help. Emotional problems, general lethargy, or lack of energy might also require some assistance. Even though you are in charge of your health, you must not feel that you are alone. You have your physician and a wide variety of health-care professionals to serve as your support group.

*General Medicine.* There are five different kinds of professionals with training in general health care. Their qualifications and treatments vary widely. The best-known, of course, is the *Medical Doctor* (M.D.), who is educated in emergency medicine and general health. In recent years, a great many medical doctors have specialized, and although there are still some general practitioners around, one is frequently faced with the need to choose among Internalists, Pediatricians, Obstetricians, Neurologists, Dermatologists, and so on, depending upon the nature of a complaint. Until ecent years, medical doctors have not been able to devote a great deal of attention to preventive medicine, because of their need to focus on emergency medical care.

The *Doctor of Osteopathy* (D.O.) is trained similarly to the medical doctor, with additional schooling in spinal manipulative therapy, which seeks to keep the spine in alignment through physical adjustments. Like the medical doctor, they can prescribe drugs and perform surgery. In some parts of the world, they are being absorbed into the general medical profession.

Like the doctor of osteopathy, the *Doctor of Chiropractic* (D.C.) performs manipulative therapy. However, his training and licensing limit him to nondrug and nonsurgical techniques of healing. In addition to manipulative therapy, the doctor of chiropractic performs massage and physical therapy.

Which of these three general health practitioners you choose depends on your health needs. If you suffer from back pain, it is possible that a chiropractor may help. But if you are not sure of the reason for your problem, you would probably need the more general medical doctor or doctor of osteopathy.

There are two other general health practitioners who can be of service to you—the *Nurse Practitioner* (N.P.) and the *Physician's Assistant* (P.A.). Although neither has the training or licensing of the medical doctor or the doctor of osteopathy, they are qualified to handle the minor complaints, such as earache, sore throat, and cuts, that constitute an estimated seventy to eighty percent of the physician's work.

*Nutrition.* For help of a nutritional nature, you can consult an M.D. who has training in nutrition or a *Registered Dietician* (R.D.). The registered dietician is probably the closest of any of the specialists to a nutritionist, but not all R.D.s are adept at clinical nutrition, since many specialize in food service management.

*Exercise.* Among medical doctors, there are a number who specialize in sports medicine and in cardiac rehabilitation who can offer considerable expertise to a program of exercise. In this field, there are several health-care professionals who may also be of help. The *Registered Physical Therapist* (R.P.T.) has considerable understanding of the muscular and skeletal systems of the human body. The *Occupational Therapist* is also trained in techniques for recuperation from strains and injuries, as well as in general physical and emotional rehabilitation. The *Exercise Physiologist* is now hired by major medical centers to incorporate exercise prescriptions into general healing and prevention approaches.

*Attitude.* There are three kinds of professionals trained to assist you with emotional problems. *Psychiatrists* are medical doctors who have specialized in the study of mental problems. They can prescribe drugs. *Psychologists* have devoted all of their study to emotional disorders, but cannot prescribe drugs. *Counselors* work in conjunction with physicians and psychiatrists to assist people in emotional distress. In some parts of the world there are telephone services in which counselors are available to talk to people with specific problems. Some *Clergy* are also trained in psychological counseling.

*Body Maintenance.* In today's society, you have specialists who are trained thoroughly in problems related to any part of the body. Medical knowledge has become so vast that no general practitioner could possibly be familiar with all the specific treatments available for every part of the body. Problems of the hair and the skin can be dealt with by a *Dermatologist.* For your eyes, you have several alternatives. An *Ophthalmologist* is an M.D. specializing in problems of the eyes. An

*Optometrist* (O.D.) has training directed only toward eye care. An *Optician* can fill prescriptions for eyeglasses and contact lenses. Problems with your sinuses can be treated by a medical doctor who is an ear, nose, and throat specialist known as an *Otolaryngologist*.

There are a great many different specialists trained to help you with problems of the teeth and gums. Dentists may be either a *Doctor of Dental Surgery* (D.D.S.) or a *Doctor of Dental Medicine* (D.M.D.), but their training is essentially the same. Dentists who specialize in the study of gums are *Periodontists*, and those who specialize in the dental problems of children are *Pedodontists*. The *Orthodontist* supervises braces for the teeth, and the *Endodontist* handles root canal work. False teeth are provided by the *Prosthodontist*. The *Oral Surgeon* can rebuild damaged face and mouth areas and can extract impacted wisdom teeth.

Problems of the stomach and the intestinal tract can be cared for by the medical doctor who specializes as a doctor of osteopathy or medical doctor who specializes as a *Gastroenterologist* or a *Proctologist*. Serious back problems should be treated by the medical doctor, the doctor of osteopathy, the doctor of chiropractic, or a registered physical therapist. However, you may take your minor back or muscular problems to a *Masseur* or *Masseuse*, or to an *Acupuncture* or *Acupressure Therapist*.

For your feet, you may seek the help of the *Doctor of Podiatric Medicine* (D.P.M.), known as a *Podiatrist* and formerly called a Chiropodist.

These health-care specialists are there to help you to prevent serious illness, as well as to take care of problems when they arise. Your program for health and longevity does not diminish the importance of doctors or the services they provide. Antibiotics, inoculations, anesthetics, painkillers, and sedatives still play a part in health care. We do hope, however, that your new awareness gives you an understanding of how, when, and why these are needed. You should also know that some drugs can present risks for some people. Antibiotics can produce allergic reactions, in some cases severe ones. Painkillers and sedatives can be addictive. Birth-control pills are useful and convenient, but they also cause chemical changes in the body. Prescription drugs can be abused just as illicit drugs are. For the patient, the risks should always be weighed against the advantages where drugs are concerned.

The same attitude should be maintained toward the subject of surgery. The deft hands and the life-support devices of surgeons have saved many lives and vastly improved the quality of many others. If death or severe impairment of life is the only alternative, surgery obviously is beneficial. Many forms of surgery performed in the past, however, have been increasingly criticized. Removal of tonsils, adenoids, and appendix used to be standard medical practice; now these surgeries are performed only when essential. The value of hysterectomies and mastectomies is now under question as perhaps not necessary in all cases. Medical authorities are now investigating the value of coronary bypass surgery, as well.

Some surgical operations definitely qualify as "elective surgery," which means that they are optional and dependent upon your choice. Your doctor is merely the advisor. You should be sufficiently familiar with your body and its problems to make the necessary decision, weighing values against risks. Ask questions; learn about problems; and get a second opinion. Your doctor will respect you and your efforts.

Our current health-care system is a dinosaur. Cumbersome

and awkward, it is doomed to extinction. The patient's lifestyle leads to numerous health breakdowns, which are treated by the frustrated physician who then bills overtaxed private and government agencies, who must then stiffen the tariff from their participants and taxpayers. No one is happy. No one wins. Various countries have experimented with health maintenance organizations, socialized medicine, and preferred provider organizations.

We need a health-care system that rewards both the patient and physician when the patient stays well. Until that relationship is established, most people are doomed to excessive illness, lackluster lives of low energy, and early death.

Always remember that you are in charge of your own body. Your physician is working for you in your efforts toward a healthier and longer life. Your chance of living decades beyond the normal lifespan is primarily dependent upon you. Whatever risks you take are your choice. You decide what you eat, where you live, how much exercise you get, what attitude you will have, and when you need the help of a health-care professional. Each decision you make has its risks and its advantages. Heed the prescriptions we have offered you.

May you make good decisions and live well past 100.

# APPENDIX A
# Sample Menus

# Breakfast Menu

| CALORIES PER SERVING | SELECTIONS |
|---|---|
| 40 | Fruit of Choice |
| 40 | Juice of Choice |
| 90 | Hot Oatmeal or Wheatena with Nonfat Milk |
| 80 | Cold Puffed Wheat or Puffed Rice with Non-fat Milk |
| 110 | Cold Spa Rice Krispies with Nonfat Milk |
| 115 | Cold Spa Corn Flakes with Nonfat Milk |
| 130 | Cold Shredded Wheat with Nonfat Milk |
| 60 | 3-egg White Omelette: Mushrooms, Herbs, Chives |
| 75 | Egg, Any Style |
| 75 | Omelette: Mushrooms, Herbs, Chives |
| 85 | Spanish Omelette |
| 150 | Petite Filet Mignon (2 ounces, cooked) |
| 155 | Spa French Toast with Diet Jam |
| 70 | Whole Wheat Toast (1 slice) |
| 70 | ½ English Muffin |
| 70 | Spa Bran Muffin |
| 35 | Toasted Rice Cake |
| 28 | 4 Bagel Thins |
| 10 | 1 teaspoon Diet Jam |
| 38 | 1½ ounces Whipped Cottage Cheese |
| 75 | 3 ounces Low-fat Cottage Cheese |
| 75 | 3 ounces Plain Yogurt, Low-fat |
| 0 | Spa Bran (1 teaspoon, zero calories) |
| 40 | Nonfat Milk, 4 ounces |

# THE LA COSTA PRESCRIPTION FOR LONGER LIFE

10        Nonfat Milk for Coffee, 1 ounce
           Coffee   Decaffeinated Coffee
           Tea with Lemon   Herbal Tea with Lemon

## BREAKFAST SUGGESTIONS FOR
## 600, 800, AND 1,000 CALORIE DIETS

|  | CALORIES ALLOWED |
|---|---|
| *600 Calorie Diet* | 180 |

- Fruit or Juice
- 1 Egg, Cottage Cheese, or Yogurt
- 1 Slice of Toast or Muffin

*800 Calorie Diet*     265

- Fruit or Juice
- 2 Eggs or Steak or 1 Egg and Cottage Cheese
- 1 Slice of Toast or Muffin, Diet Jam

*1,000 Calorie Diet*     320

- Fruit
- Juice
- 2 Eggs or 1 Egg and Cottage Cheese or Steak
- 1 Slice Toast or Muffin, Diet Jam

## Luncheon Menu

| CALORIES PER SERVING | SELECTIONS |
|---|---|
| 20 | Melon Balls Supreme |

| | |
|---|---|
| ·50 | Clam Chowder |
| 20 | Cucumbers in Yogurt with Radishes and Chives |
| 15 | Cole Slaw |
| 15 | Fresh Mushrooms Vinaigrette |
| 200 | Chef Salad with Choice of Dressing |
| 150 | Grilled Liver with Onions |
| 150 | Vegetable Quiche with Tofu |
| 150 | Baked Chicken with Herbs |
| 150 | Cold Salmon Platter |
| 35 | Whipped Hubbard Squash |
| 15 | Celery Julienne with Red Peppers |
| 40 | Strawberry Parfait |
| 40 | Orange Ambrosia |
| 40 | Frozen Banana à l'Orange |
| 14 | 2 Bagel Thins |
| 35 | Rice Cake |
| 20 | 2-ounce Pitcher Nonfat Milk |
| 40 | 4-ounce Glass Nonfat Milk or Buttermilk |
| | Tab   RC 100   Diet Coke   Iced Tea |
| | Perrier   Coffee   Decaffeinated Coffee |
| | Herbal Tea with Lemon   Tea with Lemon |

## LUNCHEON SUGGESTIONS FOR
## 600, 800, AND 1,000 CALORIE DIETS

CALORIES
ALLOWED

*600 Calorie Diet*                                                        200
- Appetizer
- 1 Entree

- 1 Vegetable or 1 Salad
- ½ Portion Dessert

*800 Calorie Diet*                                            260
- Appetizer
- 1 Salad
- 1 Entree
- Vegetable
- 1 Dessert

*1,000 Calorie Diet*                                          310
- Appetizer
- 1 Salad
- 1½ Entrees
- Vegetable
- 1 Dessert

## Dinner Menu

| CALORIES PER SERVING | SELECTIONS |
|---|---|
| 50 | Puree of Vegetable Soup |
| 20 | Mixed Fruit Supreme |
| 50 | Georgia Prawns |
| 35 | La Costa Diet Salad |
| 15 | Hearts of Romaine with Radishes, Zucchini, and Tomato |
| 150 | Beef and Chinese Vegetables |
| 150 | Roast Rack of Lamb with Mint Sauce |
| 150 | Curry of Spring Chicken |
| 150 | Broiled Swordfish |

| | |
|---|---|
| 30 | Hungarian Brussels Sprouts |
| 35 | Carrots à l'Orange |
| 40 | Pineapple Parfait |
| 40 | Hot Apple Compote |
| 40 | Fresh Papaya with Lime |
| 40 | Fresh Fruit to Go |
| 14 | 2 Bagel Thins |
| 35 | Rice Cake |
| 20 | 2-ounce Pitcher Nonfat Milk |
| 40 | 4-ounce Glass Nonfat Milk or Buttermilk |

Tab   RC 100   Diet Coke   Iced Tea
Perrier   Coffee   Decaffeinated Coffee
Herbal Tea with Lemon   Tea with Lemon

## DINNER SUGGESTIONS FOR
## 600, 800, AND 1,000 CALORIE DIETS

CALORIES
ALLOWED

*600 Calorie Diet*                                    220
- Appetizer
- 1 Entree
- 1 Vegetable or 1 Salad
- 1 Dessert

*800 Calorie Diet*                                    275
- Appetizer
- 1 Salad
- 1 Entree
- 1 Vegetable
- 1 Dessert

*1,000 Calorie Diet*                                                    370

- Appetizer
- 1 Salad
- 1½ Entree Portions
- 1 Vegetable
- 1 Dessert

*Or*

- Appetizer
- 1 Salad
- 1 Entree
- ½ Baked Potato, 70 calories
- 1 Vegetable
- 1 Dessert

# APPENDIX B
# Sample Recipes

# Soups

## Puree of Vegetable Soup

Yield: 4 servings
50 calories per serving

*Ingredients:*

2 cups unsalted, defatted chicken broth
2 medium carrots, chopped
½ cup rutabaga, chopped
¾ cup turnip, chopped
1 tablespoon onion, chopped
dash white pepper
pinch celery seed
4 ounces nonfat milk

*Method:*

Bring the chicken broth to a boil and add the carrot, rutabaga, turnip, onion, and seasonings. Bring the liquid back to a boil and cook until vegetables are tender. Cool slightly and puree in a blender. Reheat and add nonfat milk. Serve hot in bouillon cups.

## Spinach Soup

Yield: **4 servings**
35 calories per serving

*Ingredients:*

1½ cups unsalted, defatted chicken broth
8 ounces frozen spinach
1 tablespoon onion, chopped
dash white pepper
pinch nutmeg
dash celery seed
4 ounces nonfat milk

*Method:*

Bring the chicken broth to a boil and add the spinach, onion, and seasonings. Bring the liquid back to a boil and cook until spinach is done. Cool slightly and puree in a blender. Reheat and add nonfat milk. Serve hot in bouillon cups.

## Broccoli Soup

Yield: **4 servings**
35 calories per serving

*Ingredients:*

1½ cups unsalted, defatted chicken broth
6 ounces frozen broccoli spears
1 tablespoon onion, chopped
4 ounces nonfat milk
dash white pepper

*Method:*

Bring the chicken broth to a boil and add the broccoli, onion, and pepper. Bring the liquid back to a boil and cook until broccoli is tender. Cool slightly and puree in a blender. Reheat and add nonfat milk. Serve hot in bouillon cups.

## Tomato Soup

Yield: **4 servings**
**40** calories per serving

*Ingredients:*

2½ cups unsalted, defatted chicken broth
¾ cup low-sodium tomato puree
½ medium tomato, chopped
½ small carrot, chopped
1 celery stick, chopped
4 sprigs parsley
1 bay leaf
pinch oregano
pinch basil
dash garlic powder
dash white pepper
small dash dill

*Method:*

Combine all ingredients and simmer uncovered for 30 minutes. Strain. Serve hot in bouillon cups.

## Carrot Soup

Yield: **4 servings**
**50** calories per serving

*Ingredients:*

> 2 cups unsalted, defatted chicken broth
> 3 medium carrots, chopped
> 1 tablespoon onion, chopped
> pinch white pepper
> dash celery seed
> 4 ounces nonfat milk

*Method:*

Bring the chicken broth to a boil and add the carrots, onion, and seasonings. Bring the liquid back to a boil and cook until carrots are tender. Cool slightly and puree in a blender. Reheat and add nonfat milk. Serve hot in bouillon cups.

## Iced Gazpacho

Yield: 4 servings
25 calories per serving

*Ingredients:*

> 1 small zucchini
> 2 tablespoons chopped chives
> ½ green pepper, seeded and diced
> 1 cucumber, diced
> 2 small tomatoes, diced
> ½ jalapeño pepper, seeded and diced
> ½ clove garlic, minced
> pinch granulated garlic
> 1 cup unsalted tomato juice
> ½ cup beef bouillon

*Method:*

Place all the ingredients into a blender and blend for a few seconds or until the vegetables are chopped finely. Chill well. Serve in chilled soup cups.

## Mushroom Soup

Yield: 4 servings
30 calories per serving

*Ingredients:*

> 1½ cups unsalted, defatted chicken broth
> ½ pound mushrooms, sliced
> 1 tablespoon onion, chopped
> pinch white pepper

*Method:*

Bring the chicken broth to a boil and add the mushrooms, onion, and pepper. Bring the liquid back to a boil and cook until the mushrooms are tender. Cool slightly and puree in a blender. Reheat before serving; ladle into hot bouillon cups.

## Asparagus Soup

Yield: 4 servings
35 calories per serving

*Ingredients*

> 1½ cups unsalted, defatted chicken broth
> 8 ounces frozen asparagus spears
> 1 tablespoon onion, chopped
> dash white pepper

pinch celery seed
4 ounces nonfat milk

*Method:*

Bring the chicken broth to a boil and add the asparagus, onion, and seasonings. Bring the liquid back to a boil and cook until asparagus is tender. Cool slightly and puree in a blender. Reheat and add nonfat milk. Serve hot in bouillon cups.

## Cauliflower Soup

Yield: 4 servings
35 calories per serving

*Ingredients:*

1½ cups unsalted, defatted chicken broth
2 cups cauliflower, cut into flowerettes
(approximately ½ head of cauliflower)
1 tablespoon onion, chopped
pinch white pepper
dash celery seed
4 ounces nonfat milk

*Method:*

Bring the chicken broth to a boil and add the cauliflower, onion, and seasonings. Bring the liquid back to a boil and cook until cauliflower is tender. Cool slightly and puree in a blender. Reheat and add nonfat milk. Serve hot in bouillon cups.

# Dressings

## Cocktail Sauce

Yield: 2 cups
10 calories per tablespoon

*Ingredients:*

1 eleven-ounce bottle of diet catsup (prepared without
sugar or salt)
1 tablespoon freshly squeezed lemon juice
¼ cup freshly grated horseradish
¼ cup chopped chives

*Method:*

Mix ingredients except chives in the order given. Refrigerate covered. Adjust horseradish and lemon to taste. Serve very cold or very hot. Add fresh chives just before serving if desired.

## Vinaigrette Dressing

10 calories per tablespoon

*Ingredients:*

¼ cup white vinegar
1 cup pure pineapple juice
½ fresh lemon, juiced and strained

## THE LA COSTA PRESCRIPTION FOR LONGER LIFE

¼ teaspoon dry powdered mustard
1 clove garlic, bruised
coarsely ground pepper to taste
¼ cup each: finely chopped celery hearts, chives,
    or green onion tops, green and red bell peppers

*Method:*

Mix the ingredients except the chopped vegetables. Beat lightly or strain to remove all lumps. Add the chopped vegetables, place in a covered container, and refrigerate until served. Chopped fresh vegetables may be added just before serving.

## Spa Louie Dressing

Yield: 4 cups
15 calories per tablespoon

*Ingredients:*

1 carton (16-ounce) low-fat yogurt
1 bottle (11-ounce) dietetic catsup
5 chopped hard-cooked egg whites
4 scallions, cut fine (green part only)
2 bunches fresh chives, cut fine
1 green pepper, chopped
1 cucumber, peeled, seeded, and chopped
2 teaspoons prepared horseradish
juice of ½ lemon
pinch cayenne pepper

*Method:*

Combine ingredients. Cover and chill.

# Vegetables

**Eggplant Parmesan**

Yield: 6 servings
35 calories per serving

*Ingredients for Tomato Sauce:*

> 1 cup whole salt-free tomatoes, crushed
> 3 ounces tomato juice, unsalted
> ½ teaspoon oregano
> ½ teaspoon basil
> ¼ teaspoon granulated garlic
> ¼ teaspoon granulated onion
> dash rosemary
> pinch fennel seed
> dash black pepper

*Ingredients for Eggplant:*

> 2 small eggplant
> 5⅓ tablespoons parmesan cheese

*Method:*

Combine ingredients for tomato sauce and mix well. Slice eggplant into 8 slices, 2 ounces each. Cover each slice with 1 to 2 tablespoons tomato sauce and 2 teaspoons parmesan cheese.

Place in shallow baking dish and bake uncovered at 450 degrees for 15 to 20 minutes or until tender. Serve hot.

### Ratatouille

Yield: 5 servings
16 calories per serving

*Ingredients:*

> ½ small red onion, thinly sliced
> 1 clove garlic, minced
> ½ small bell pepper, sliced
> 1 16-ounce can whole tomatoes
> 1 cup zucchini, cut bite-sized
> 1 cup eggplant, cubed
> 1½ teaspoons oregano
> 1½ teaspoons chopped parsley
> black pepper
> salt substitute and artificial sweetener to taste

*Method:*

In a heavy sauce pan, mix the thin sliced onion, minced garlic, sliced green pepper, and whole tomatoes cut into bite-sized pieces. To prepare the zucchini, split in fourths lengthwise. Remove the seeds and soft center. Cut into bite-sized pieces. To prepare the eggplant, peel and cut into ½-inch cubes. Add oregano, chopped parsley, and pepper. Toss together. Bring the mixture to the boiling point, reduce the heat to simmer and cook until fork-tender. Adjust the seasoning as desired. This dish is better when held and reheated.

## Sweet and Sour Cabbage

Yield 6 one-half cup servings
25 calories per serving

*Ingredients:*

1 medium-size red cabbage
½ cup unsweetened apple juice
⅓ cup red wine vinegar, to taste
2 whole cloves

*Method:*

Core cabbage and shred. Add apple juice, vinegar, and cloves. Cover and cook slowly until tender, about 2 hours. Stir occasionally during the cooking process and add water if necessary.

To retain the vitamin C content of the cabbage, the ingredients should be cooked quickly at a high temperature.

## Carrots à l'Orange

Yield: 4 servings
35 calories per serving

*Ingredients:*

4 ounces orange juice
1 teaspoon grated orange peel
1 teaspoon lemon juice
1 teaspoon cornstarch
2 medium carrots, peeled and sliced
liquid sweetener to taste (optional)

*Method:*

Bring orange juice to a boil. Add orange peel and lemon juice. Dissolve 1 teaspoon cornstarch in 1 tablespoon cold water and add to orange juice mixture to thicken sauce. Steam carrots until tender. Add sauce and mix together. Serve hot.

# Entrees

**Bouillabaisse**

Yield: 4 servings
200 calories per serving

*Ingredients:*

4 raw clams
1 celery rib, chopped
1 small onion, chopped
2 quarts water
1 clove garlic, mashed
1 leek, thinly sliced (white part with one inch of
    green)
½ teaspoon fennel seed
pinch saffron threads
½ cup dry white wine
1 large tomato, peeled, seeded, and diced
1 rock lobster tail, quartered
¼ pound red snapper, quartered
¼ pound shrimp, shelled and deveined
¼ pound scallops
pepper to taste

*Method:*

To make clam stock, simmer clams, celery, and onion in 6 cups water for 10 minutes. Strain stock and reserve clams. In a large saucepan, heat garlic clove slightly but do not brown, discard. Slice leek and rinse carefully to remove any sediment clinging to the leaves. Soak saffron threads in white wine. Add sliced leeks, fennel seed, and wine in saucepan; saute for 3 minutes. Add diced tomatoes and saute 5 minutes longer. Add clam stock. Bring to a boil and season with pepper to taste. Add raw lobster tail, red snapper, shrimp, and scallops to stock. Simmer for 10 minutes. Add clams to heat through and serve.

## Baked Lasagna

Yield: 4 servings
200 calories per serving

*Ingredients for Tomato Sauce:*

1 small onion
1 clove garlic, minced
1 pound fresh sliced mushrooms
3 cans (16-ounce) whole salt-free tomatoes, crushed
1¼ cups tomato puree
oregano
black pepper
1 pound fresh chopped spinach

*Ingredients for Lasagna:*

2 sheets lasagna noodles (200 calories) or sliced zucchini (146 calories)
8 ounces dry curd baker's cheese or grated mozzarella cheese
½ cup grated Parmesan cheese

*Method:*

In a large saucepan, saute onions and garlic with a small amount of water or wine until well done but not brown. Add the sliced mushrooms and cook until most of the liquid is evaporated. Add the crushed tomatoes and juice, the tomato puree, and seasonings to taste. Simmer the sauce, uncovered, for 1½ to 2 hours, stirring occasionally to prevent sticking. Add the chopped spinach at the last moment.

To assemble casserole, boil the lasagna noodles in a large amount of water for 10 minutes. Drain. Spray the bottom of a 7 × 7 inch baking dish with a nonstick vegetable spray. Start with a layer of tomato sauce and lumps of baker's cheese. Cover with noodles and repeat twice. Cover the last layer of noodles with remaining sauce, the baker's cheese and Parmesan cheese. Place casserole in a 400-degree F. oven and bake for about 45 minutes, or until top is brown and sauce is bubbly.

## Red Snapper Vera Cruz

Yield: 4 servings
150 calories per serving

*Ingredients:*

1 pound red snapper
juice from 1 lime
⅛ teaspoon cayenne pepper
½ medium onion, sliced
½ small green chili, seeded and chopped
1 medium ripe tomato, chopped
1 pimiento, chopped
1 ounce light white wine (8% alcohol)
1 teaspoon lemon juice

*Method:*

Squeeze lime juice on the fish, add cayenne pepper and refrigerate for at least 2 hours. Spray a large saucepan with a nonstick vegetable spray and preheat to moderate temperature. Add onions and green chili, cook until tender. Add tomato and pimiento, cook covered for 2 minutes. Reduce temperature. Place fish on bottom of pan with vegetables on top. Combine lemon juice and wine, and pour over fish. Simmer for 6 minutes on each side or until fish is completely done. Serve hot. Garnish fish with sauce and vegetables.

## Curried Chicken Salad

Yield: 4 servings
150 calories per serving

*Ingredients:*

8 ounces cooked chicken
6 ounces plain low-fat yogurt
¼ cup fresh or canned diced red peppers
1 tablespoon green onion tops, chopped
¼ cup celery, chopped
1½ teaspoon curry powder
dash white pepper
¼ teaspoon garlic powder
Garnish: 2 medium tomatoes

*Method:*

In medium-sized bowl, blend all ingredients together and mix well. Serve 2-ounce portion of chicken salad on bed of lettuce and garnish with one-half tomato.

## Spa Lamb Stew

Yield: 4 servings
146 calories per serving

*Ingredients:*

> 12 ounces defatted lamb shoulder, cut into 1-ounce
>     cubes
> 1 clove garlic, minced
> 1 onion, diced
> ½ cup tomato puree
> ½ cup dry red wine
> 1 cup Spa Brown Sauce *(see recipe below)*
> pinch each of oregano, tarragon, rosemary, and black
>     pepper

*Method:*

Brown lamb pieces on a very hot brazier. When brown, add garlic and onion and brown lightly. Add tomato puree and cook until thick. Add the red wine and continue cooking until meat looks reddish brown. Add the brown sauce and bring to a boil. Add seasonings. Place brazier in a 325-degree F. oven. Cover and cook until lamb is tender, about 1 hour. Do not strain the sauce.

## Spa Brown Sauce

Yield: 2 cups
10 calories per tablespoon

*Ingredients:*

4 pounds cracked beef or veal bones
2 large onions, chopped
2 carrots, chopped
1 celery rib with leaves, chopped
6 parsley stems
1 can (16-ounce) tomato puree
½ cup dry red wine
water to cover
1 clove garlic, mashed
1 bay leaf
¼ teaspoon thyme
¼ teaspoon crushed peppercorns

*Method:*

Brown bones in a roasting pan in a 400-degree F. oven for 30 minutes. Stir occasionally for even browning. Add the onions, carrots, celery, parsley stems, and tomato puree, and continue browning for another 30 minutes. Transfer the browned bones and vegetables to a large pot or kettle. Deglaze the roasting pan with the wine and add to the pot.

Add the seasonings and enough water to cover by 1 inch. Bring slowly to a boil and skim foam and excess fat from the surface. Reduce the heat to a simmer and allow to simmer for 8 to 12 hours.

Strain the stock into another kettle and allow to cool to room temperature. Refrigerate overnight.

Remove the solidified fat on the surface and heat the stock slightly. Strain through a layer of dampened cheesecloth. If the sauce is too weak, bring it to a boil and reduce the liquid.

## Calorie Counter's Cheese Blintzes

Yield: 6 servings
175 calories per serving

*Ingredients for filling:*

> 1 egg, beaten
> 1½ cups pot cheese or farmer cheese
> 1 teaspoon vanilla extract
> ¼ teaspoon cinnamon

*Ingredients for Crepes:*

> 2 eggs
> 1½ cups skim milk
> 1 cup flour

*Method:*

Mix filling ingredients in a small bowl; chill.

Combine eggs and milk in a small mixing bowl. Beat with a rotary beater or whip until combined and smooth. Add flour and salt. Beat until smooth.

Preheat a 7-inch nonstick skillet over medium-high heat. Coat the surface with a nonstick vegetable spray. Pour about 2 tablespoons batter into pan, tipping and rolling the pan quickly to spread the batter evenly. Pour off any excess batter. Cook until lightly browned on the bottom and dry on top. Remove from pan. Repeat to make 12 crepes.

Spoon 2 tablespoons filling mixture on browned side of each crepe. Fold two opposite edges of crepe over filling. Fold in remaining ends, envelope style, to enclose filling completely.

Arrange blintzes, fold side down, in a shallow baking dish. (Brush lightly with melted diet margarine, if desired.) Bake in a hot 400-degree F. oven for 25 to 30 minutes. Serve hot.

## Chicken Chow Mein

Yield: 4 servings
200 calories per serving

*Ingredients:*

14 ounces chicken, deboned and cut into small pieces
2 celery sticks, chopped
½ small onion, sliced
2 ounces (¾ cup) Chinese pea pods
½ medium bell pepper, cut into long strips
¼ cup canned red peppers, diced
2 ounces (½ cup) water chestnuts, sliced
1½ cups unsalted, defatted chicken broth
1 teaspoon cornstarch
2 ounces bean sprouts
pinch ground ginger
½ teaspoon garlic powder
¼ teaspoon white pepper
Garnish: ½ cup chow mein noodles

*Method:*

Preheat a large skillet to high temperature and spray with vegetable pan spray. Saute chicken for 2 to 3 minutes, until brown. Add vegetables (except bean sprouts) and saute for 5 minutes. Add chicken broth and thicken with cornstarch. (Dissolve 1 teaspoon in 1 tablespoon cold water.) Add bean sprouts and seasonings. Mix well. Sprinkle chow mein noodles on top and serve hot.

## Chicken Cacciatore

Yield: 4 servings
145 calories per serving

*Ingredients:*

> 4 three-ounce chicken pieces, poached (allow 20% weight for bone)
> 2 shallots, chopped
> ½ small green pepper
> ½ cup sliced mushrooms
> ½ cup dry white wine
> 1 can (8-ounce) whole tomatoes
> ⅛ teaspoon garlic powder
> scant teaspoon each of black pepper, rosemary, oregano, sweet basil, and fennel seed.

*Method:*

Saute shallots, green pepper, and mushrooms in the wine. Add tomatoes, bring to a boil, then allow to simmer, uncovered, until reduced by one-half in volume. Stir occasionally. Add spices the last half-hour of cooking. Add artificial sweetener to taste, if tomatoes are bitter. Garnish each piece of chicken with ½-ounce of the cacciatore sauce.

## Beef Stroganoff

Yield: 5 servings
146 calories per serving

*Ingredients:*

> 5 three-ounce steaks of beef tenderloin, cut thin and
>    all fat and bone removed
> 2 tablespoons dry Burgundy wine
> *1 tablespoon meat glaze, if desired
> 2 minced green onion tops
> 5 whole mushrooms, sliced
> ⅛ teaspoon black pepper
> ⅛ teaspoon granulated garlic
> 1 tablespoon plain low-fat yogurt

*Method:*

Brown thin individual steaks quickly in a very hot dry pan. Remove to warm oven. Pour dry wine into the hot skillet and remove from the burner long enough to allow the alcohol to evaporate. Add the onion tops, mushrooms, and seasoning. Just prior to serving, add the yogurt and stir barely enough to mix. Place the steaks on a hot plate and garnish with 1 tablespoon of the sauce, and serve at once.

Do not overcook the sauce. Yogurt separates if stirred too much or overcooked.

*Meat glaze is a concentrated beef broth.

## Vegetable Quiche with Tofu

Yield: 6 servings
150 calories per serving

*Ingredients:*

> ¼ small onion, diced
> ½ garlic clove, minced

1 small carrot, diced
1 small crookneck squash, chopped
¼ pound mushrooms, sliced
1 small zucchini, chopped
¼ head cauliflower, cut into flowerettes
½ bunch broccoli, cut into flowerettes
½ teaspoon basil
¼ teaspoon thyme, whole
dash black pepper
3 ounces skim Swiss cheese, grated
2 eggs
½ pound tofu
1 teaspoon lemon juice
⅔ cup skim milk
¼ teaspoon ground oregano
¼ teaspoon ground sweet basil
¼ teaspoon ground tarragon
½ teaspoon garlic powder
¼ teaspoon ground nutmeg

## *Method:*

Preheat oven to 325 degrees F. Heat a large skillet to medium heat and spray with non stick vegetable spray. Add onions and garlic, cook until done. Add all vegetables and basil, thyme, and black pepper; cook until tender. Spray a 9-inch pie pan with nonstick vegetable spray. Add vegetables and grated cheese. Blend eggs, tofu, and remaining ingredients in blender until smooth. Pour egg mixture over vegetables and cheese. Cook at 325 degrees F. for 1 hour, or until knife comes out clean. Serve hot.

# Desserts

**Strawberry Parfait**

Yield: 4 servings<br>40 calories per serving

*Ingredients:*

¾ cup plain low-fat yogurt
1 cup strawberries, sliced
1 tablespoon dietetic strawberry jam
¼ teaspoon almond extract
½ teaspoon vanilla
artificial sweetener
1 teaspoon unflavored gelatin
4 ounces water

*Method:*

Combine yogurt, strawberries, jam, almond extract, vanilla, and artificial sweetener in blender and blend until smooth. In saucepan, dissolve 1 teaspoon gelatin in water over moderate heat. Mix gelatin with yogurt mixture and pour into parfait glasses. Chill until firm. Garnish with sliced strawberry and mint leaves.

# Baked Custard

Yield: 6 servings
40 calories per custard cup
No cholesterol

## *Ingredients:*

5 egg whites
2 cups nonfat milk
½ teaspoon pure flavoring extract
any liquid artificial sweetener to taste
3 drops yellow food coloring

## *Suggested Flavors:*

Cinnamon, nutmeg, mace, pumpkin*, vanilla, and mace, coconut flavoring with the top garnished with a pinch of shredded coconut, almond flavoring with 1 sliver of almond on top.

## *Method:*

Blend egg whites with a small amount of the milk, only enough to mix. Do not overbeat. Add the remainder of the milk, sweetener, and flavoring. Fill warm custard cups and place in a pan of hot water to bake for 45 minutes until set. Refrigerate at once.

*For pumpkin custard, substitute ½ cup pumpkin for 1 cup nonfat milk.

## Coupe Saint Jacques

Yield: 8 one-half cup servings
40 calories per serving

*Ingredients:*

> 1½ cups fresh churned buttermilk
> 1 cup nonfat milk
> 2 tablespoons vanilla
> 1 teaspoon plain gelatin
> 1 teaspoon grated lemon rind
> 1 cup unsweetened, pitted cherries
> artificial sweetener to taste
> Garnish: Combine ½ cup chopped watermelon,
>        cantaloupe, or honeydew melon

*Method:*

Soften the gelatin in a few drops of water until completely dissolved and combine with buttermilk, nonfat milk, and vanilla in a blender. Whip the mixture until frothy. Add remaining ingredients and blend again. Place sherbet in a shallow pan in the freezer and freeze until a mushy consistency is attained. Rewhip the sherbet with a wire whip or fork to incorporate air and keep the ice crystals small. Repeat whipping every 15 to 20 minutes until the sherbet is frozen. Remove to the refrigerator ½ hour before serving. Garnish each serving with 1 tablespoon of the chopped fruit. Serve immediately.

## Peach Melba

Yield: 4 servings
40 calories per serving

*Ingredients:*

> ½ cup raspberries, crushed
> 4 ounces unsweetened apple juice

⅛ teaspoon almond extract
2 teaspoons diet grape jelly
1 teaspoon cornstarch
4 dietetic canned peach halves

## Method:

Combine raspberries, apple juice, diet jelly, and almond extract in saucepan and bring to a boil. Simmer for 30 minutes. Dissolve 1 teaspoon cornstarch in 1 tablespoon cold water and add to sauce to thicken. Allow sauce to cool. Place peach half in sherbet glass and pour over peach. Chill. Serve with 1 teaspoon plain low-fat yogurt or 1 teaspoon low-calorie whipped topping.

## Baked Banana

Yield: 4 servings
40 calories per serving

## Ingredients:

2 small (6-inch) bananas
2 tablespoons orange juice
½ teaspoon vanilla
½ teaspoon almond extract
1 tablespoon unsweetened coconut

## Method:

Preheat oven to 350 degrees F. Peel bananas and slice in half (lengthwise). Combine orange juice, vanilla, and almond extract and mix together. Dip bananas in orange juice mixture and place on baking sheet. Sprinkle with coconut. Cover pan with foil and bake at 350 degrees F. for 20 minutes. Place under broiler to brown coconut.


## Spa Bran Muffins

Yield: 24 muffins
70 calories each

*Dry Ingredients:*

> 1½ cups whole wheat flour
> 1½ cups unprocessed miller's bran
> 2 teaspoons baking soda
> 2 teaspoons cinnamon
> 1 teaspoon nutmeg
> ½ cup honey

*Wet Ingredients:*

> 3 egg whites
> ½ cup buttermilk
> ½ cup water
> 1 small ripe banana (mashed), ½-cup
> 1 teaspoon vanilla extract

*Method:*

Mix together dry ingredients. Blend in wet ingredients.

Use muffin papers or spray tins with nonstick vegetable spray. Fill muffin tins half full. Bake for 30 to 40 minutes at 350 degrees F.or until toothpick comes out dry.

# Bibliography

## GENERAL REFERENCES

*Dorland's Illustrated Medical Dictionary*. Philadelphia: W.B. Saunders, 1974.

Holvey, D. (ed.), *The Merck Manual*. Rahway, N.J.: Merck, Sharp, & Dohme, 1972.

Mader, S.S., *Inquiry into Life*. Dubuque, Ia: W.C. Brown, 1976.

Mitchell, J. (ed.), *The Random House Encyclopedia*. New York: Random House, 1983.

*The World Almanac and Book of Facts 1983*. New York: Newspaper Enterprise Association, 1983.

United States Department of Commerce, Bureau of the Census, *Statistical Abstract of the United States 1982–83*. Washington, D.C.: Government Printing Office, 1983.

United States Department of Health and Human Services, *Promoting Health, Preventing Disease: Objectives for the Nation*. Washington, D.C.: Government Printing Office, 1980.

## HEALTH AND LONGEVITY

Alderson, M., *International Mortality Statistics*. New York: Facts on File, 1981.

Kannel, W., "The Disease of Living," *Nutrition Today*, May–June 1971.

Kasko, K., *The Great Billion Dollar Medical Swindle*. Indianapolis: Bobbs-Merrill, 1980.

Keen, H., *et al.*, "Human Insulin Produced by Recombinant DNA Technology: Safety and Hypoglycemia Potency in Healthy Men," *Lancet* (2: 8191: 398–401), Aug. 1980.

Melville, A., & C. Johnson, *Cured to Death*. New York: Stein & Day, 1982.

Musacchio, R., & D. Hough (eds.), *Socioeconomic Issues of Health 1981*. Chicago: American Medical Association, 1981.

National Health Education Committee, *The Killers and Cripplers—Facts on Major Diseases in the U.S. Today*. New York: David McKay, 1976.

United States Department of Health and Human Services, *Facts at Your Fingertips*. Hyattsville, Md.: U.S. Department of Health and Human Services, 1981.

United States Department of Health and Human Services, *An Atlas of Mortality from Selected Diseases*. Washington D.C.: U.S. Department of Health and Human Services, 1981.

United States Department of Health, Education, and Welfare, *Facts of Life and Death*. (Publication No. PHS 79-1222.) Hyattsville, Md.: U.S. Department of Health, Education, and Welfare, 1978.

Walford, R.L., *Maximum Life Span*. New York: W.W. Norton, 1983.

Wilson, F., & D. Newhauser, *Health Sciences in the U.S.* Cambridge, Mass.: Ballinger, 1982.

Wynder, E.L., & M. Kristein, "Suppose We Died Young Late in Life?" *J.A.M.A.* (238: 14: 1507), Oct. 1977.

## PREVENTIVE MEDICINE

Cassel, E., *The Healer's Art*. Philadelphia: Lippincott, 1976.

Cooper, B. & D. Rice, "The Economic Cost of Illness, Revisited," *Social Security Bulletin*, Feb. 1976.

Corder, B., J. Shirreffs, & R. Althaus, *Health—Current Perspectives*. Dubuque, Ia.: W.C. Brown, 1981.

Hatch, F., "Interactions between Nutrition and Heredity in Coronary Heart Disease," *American Journal of Clinical Nutrition* (27: 80), 1974.

La Patra, J., *Healing—The Coming Revolution in Holistic Medicine*. New York: McGraw-Hill, 1978.

Miller, B., *Family Book of Preventive Medicine*. New York: Simon & Schuster, 1971.

Pelletier, K., "Length and Quality of Life are Correlated," *Family Practice News* (15: 10: 2–57), May 1980.

Pinckney, E., *You Can Prevent Illness*, Philadelphia: Lippincott, 1960.

Rosenfeld, A., *Prolongevity*. New York: Alfred A. Knopf, 1976.

Winter, R., *How to Reduce Your Medical Bills*. New York: Crown, 1970.

## RATE YOUR HEALTH

Malcolm, R., "Playing the Longevity Game," *Wall Street Journal*, Winter 1984.

Woodruff, D., *Can You Live to Be 100?* New York: New American Library, 1978.

## GENETICS

Ayala, F., & J. Kiger, *Modern Genetics*. Menlo Park, Ca.: Benjamin-Cummings, 1980.

Moody, P., *Genetics of Man*. New York: W.W. Norton, 1975.

## ATTITUDE

Adler, R. (ed.), *Psychoneuroimmunology*. New York: Academic Press, 1981.

Agras, W., M. Norne, & C. Taylor, "Expectations and the Blood-pressure-lowering Effects of Relaxation," *Psychosomatic Medicine* (44), 1982.

Baldwin, C., *One to One*, New York: M. Evans, 1977.

Beisser, A., "Denial and Affirmation in Illness and Health," *American Journal of Psychiatry* (136), 1979.

Benson, H., *et al.*, "The Placebo Effect: A Neglected Asset in the Care of Patients," *J.A.M.A.* (232), 1975.

Benson, H., *The Relaxation Response*, New York: Morrow, 1975.

Benson, J., *The Mind/Body Effect: How Behavioral Medicine Can Show You the Way to Better Health*. New York: Simon & Schuster, 1979.

Berkman, L., "Social Network Analysis and Coronary Heart Disease," *Advanced Cardiology* (29: 37–49), 1982.

Bloomfield, H., & L. Felder, *Making Peace with Your Parents*, New York: Random House, 1983.

Bristol, C., *The Magic of Believing*. New York: Pocket Books, 1948.

Brod, J., "Psychological Influences on the Cardiovascular System," in *Modern Trends in Psychosomatic Medicine*, O. Hill (ed.), New York: Appleton-Century-Crofts, 1970.

Brown, B., *Stress and the Art of Biofeedback*. New York: Harper & Row, 1977.

Bruhn, J., *et al.*, "Psychological Predictors of Sudden Death in Myocardial Infarction," *Journal of Psychosomatic Research* (18: 187–91), 1974.

Buell, J., & R. Eliot, "Stress and Cardiovascular Disease," *Modern Concepts of Cardiovascular Disease* (48: 4: 19–24), 1979.

Carnegie, D., *How to Win Friends and Influence People*. New York: Pocket Books, 1964.

Cousins, N., "A Layman Looks at Truth Telling in Medicine," *J.A.M.A.* (244: 1929–30), 1980.

Cousins, N., *The Healing Heart*. New York: W.W. Norton, 1983.

Dyer, W., *The Sky's the Limit*. New York: Simon & Schuster, 1980.

Dyer, W., *Your Erroneous Zones*. New York: Avon Books, 1976.

Engel, G., *Psychological Development in Health and Disease*. Philadelphia: W.B. Saunders, 1962.

Frank, J., "The Faith that Heals," *Johns Hopkins Medical Journal* (137: 127–31), 1975.

Frankl, V., *The Unconscious God*. New York: Simon & Schuster, 1975.

## Bibliography

Freedman, J., *Happy People*. New York: Harcourt, Brace, Jovanovich, 1978.

Friedman, M., & R. Rosenman, *Type A Behavior and Your Heart*. New York: Fawcett, 1974.

Glass, D., *et al.*, "Effect of Harassment and Competition upon Cardiovascular and Plasma Catecholamine Responses in Type A and B Individuals," *Psychophysiology* (17: 453–63), 1980.

Greenwald, J., *Be the Person You Were Meant to Be*. New York: Dell, 1973.

Hammer, S., "The Mind as Healer," *Science Digest*, April 1984.

Hardison, J., *Let's Touch*. Englewood Cliffs, N.J.: Prentice-Hall, 1980.

Harvey, W., & S. Levine, "Paroxysmal Ventricular Tachycardia Due to Emotion: Possible Mechanism of Death from Fright," *J.A.M.A.* (160: 49), 1952.

Hilgard, E., R. Atkinson, & R. Atkinson, *Introduction to Psychology*. New York: Harcourt, Brace, Jovanovich, 1975.

Kiecolt-Glaser, J., *et al.*, "Psychosocial Modifiers of Immunocompetence in Medical Students," *Psychosomatic Medicine* (66: 1: 7–14), Jan.–Feb. 1984.

Lynch, J., *The Broken Heart*. New York: Basic Books, 1979.

Maltz, M., *Psycho-Cybernetics*. New York: Parker House, 1960.

Martin, L., *Mental Health/Mental Illness*. New York: McGraw-Hill, 1970.

Mathis, J., "A Sophisticated Version of Voodoo Death: Report of a Case," *Psychosomatic Medicine* (26: 104–7), 1964.

McGrath, J. (ed.), *Psychological Factors in Stress*. New York: Holt, Rinehart & Winston, 1970.

Menninger, K., M. Mayman, & P. Pruyser, *The Vital Balance: The Life Process in Mental Health and Illness*. New York: Viking, 1963.

Monjan, A., & M. Collector, "Stress Induced Modulation of the Immune Response," *Science* (196: 307–8), 1977.

Ornish, D., *Stress, Diet, and Your Heart*. New York: Holt, Rinehart, & Winston, 1982.

Peale, N., *The Power of Positive Thinking*. New York: Fawcett Crest, 1956.

Pelletier, K., *Mind as Healer, Mind as Slayer*. New York: Delacorte, 1977.

Peter, L., & D. Dana, *The Laughter Prescription*. New York: Ballantine, 1982.

Restak, R., *The Brain: The Last Frontier*. Garden City, N.Y.: Doubleday, 1979.

Rodgers, J., "Brain Triggers: Biochemistry and Behavior," *Science Digest* (pp. 60–65), Jan. 1983.

Rohrlich, J., *Work and Love: The Crucial Balance*. New York: Summit, 1980.

Selye, H., *From Dream to Discovery*. New York: McGraw-Hill, 1964.

Selye, H., *Stress without Distress*. New York: New American Library, 1974.

Selye, H., *The Stress of Life*. New York: McGraw-Hill, 1956.

Smith, A., *Powers of the Mind*. New York: Random House, 1975.

Vaillant, G., *Adaptation of Life*. New York: Little, Brown, 1982.

Walker, J., *Everybody's Guide to Emotional Well-Being*. San Francisco: Harbor, 1982.

Weddington, W., "Psychogenic Explanation of Symptoms as a Denial of Physical Illness," *Psychosomatics* (21: 805–12), 1980.

Wolff, H., *Stress and Disease*. Springfield, Ill.: C.C Thomas, 1968.

Yates, A., *Biofeedback and the Modification of Behavior*. New York: Plenum, 1980.

## NUTRITION

Akgmun, D., & N. Ertel, "A Comparison of Carbohydrate Metabolism after Sucrose, Sorbitol, and Fructose Meals in Normal and Diabetic Subjects," *Diabetes Care* (3: 5: 582–5), Sept.–Oct. 1980.

American Academy of Pediatrics, Committee on Nutrition, "Megavitamin Therapy for Childhood Psychoses and Learning Disabilities," *Pediatrics* (58: 910–12), 1976.

Ames, B., "Dietary Carcinogens and Anti-carcinogens," *Science* (211: 1256–64), Sept. 1983.

Anderson, G., & J. Johnston, "Nutrient Control of Brain Neurotransmitter Synthesis and Function," *Canadian Journal of Physiology and Pharmacology* (61: 3: 271–81), March 1983.

Anderson, J., "Dietary Carbohydrate and Serum Triglycerides," *American Journal of Clinical Nutrition* (20: 168), 1967.

Baker, G.J., *et al.*, "Bronchospasm Induced by Metabisulfite-containing Foods and Drugs," *Medical Journal of Australia* (2: 614–6), 1981.

Baker, H., & O. Frank, *World Review of Nutrition and Dietetics: Vitamin Status in Metabolic Upsets* (vol. 9). New York: Karger, 1968.

Barnes, B., & C. Barnes, *Hope for Hypoglycemia*. Colorado: Robinson, 1978.

Bass, L., "More Fiber—Less Constipation," *American Journal of Nursing* (pp. 254–5), Feb. 1977.

Bell, I., & D. King, "Psychological and Physiological Research Relevant to Clinical Ecology: An Overview of the Current Literature," Paper presented at the Society for Clinical Ecology, 16th Annual Meeting, Hershey, Pa. Oct. 4, 1981.

Bennion, M., & O. Hughes, *Introductory Foods*. New York: Macmillan, 1975.

Biernbaum, M.L., *et al.*, "Ten-year Experience of Modified-fat Diets on Younger Men with Coronary Heart Disease," *Lancet* (1: 1404), 1973.

Bland, J., *Your Health Under Siege: Using Nutrition to Fight Back*. Brattleboro, Vt.: Stephen Greene, 1981.

Bloom, W., "Carbohydrates and Water Balance," *American Journal of Clinical Nutrition* (20: 2: 157–62), Feb. 1967.

Bosello, O., *et al.*, "Glucose Tolerance and Blood Lipids in Bran-fed Patients with Impaired Glucose Tolerance," *Diabetics Care* (3: 1: 46–49), Jan.–Feb. 1980.

Breneman, J., "Could Food Allergy Explain Those Unexplained Symptoms?" *Diagnosis* (pp. 77–81), March 1980.

Brown, G., *et al.*, "Aggression, Suicide, and Serotonin: Relationships to CSF Amine Metabolites," *American Journal of Psychiatry* (139: 6), 1982.

Brown, H., *et al.*, "Design of Practical Fat-controlled Diets: Foods, Fat Composition, and Serum Cholesterol Content," *J.A.M.A.* (196: 205), 1966.

Brown, H., "Food Patterns that Lower Lipids in Man," *Journal of American Dietetics Association* (58: 303), 1971.

Brunzell, J., *et al.*, "Improved Glucose Tolerance with High Carbohydrate Feeding in Mild Diabetes," *New England Journal of Medicine* (284: 10: 521–4), March 1971.

Butterworth, C., & G. Blackburn, "Hospital Malnutrition," *Nutrition Today* (pp. 8–18), March 1975.

Chafetz, M., *Liquor: The Servant of Man*. Boston: Little, Brown, 1965.

Cheraskin, E., & W. Ringsdorf (eds.), *Psychodietetics*. New York: Bantam, 1977.

Church, C., & H. Church, *Food Values of Portions Commonly Used* (12th ed.). Philadelphia: Lippincott, 1975.

Clark, M., *et al.*, "Allergy: New Insights," *Newsweek* (pp. 40–45), Aug. 23, 1982.

Combs, G., & M. Scott, "Nutritional Interrelationships of Vitamin E and Selenium," *Bioscience* (27: 7: 467–72), July 1977.

Consumer Report Editors, "Caffeine: What It Does," *Consumer Report* (pp. 595–9), Oct. 1981.

Cook, J., & E. Monsen, "Vitamin C, the Common Cold, and Iron Absorption," *American Journal of Clinical Nutrition* (30: 235–41), Feb. 1977.

Crocetti, A., & H. Guthrie, "Food Consumption Patterns and Nutritional Quality of U.S. Diets: A Preliminary Report," *Food Technology* (35: 9: 40–49), Sept. 1981.

Dayton, S., *et al.*, "A Controlled Clinical Trial of a Diet High in Saturated Fat," *Circulation* (39–40: supplement 2), 1969.

Dubrick, M., & R. Rucker, "Dietary Supplements and Health Aids—A Critical Evaluation, Part 1," *Vitamins and Minerals* (15: 2: 47–53).

Eagle, R., *Eating and Allergy*. Garden City, N.Y.: Doubleday, 1981.

Editors of Executive Health, "On the B Vitamins," *Executive Health* (19: 7), April 1983.

Fabry, P., & J. Tepperman, "Meal Frequency—A Possible Factor in Human Pathology," *American Journal of Clinical Nutrition* (23: 8: 1059–68), Aug. 1970.

Fahim, M., *et al.*, "Zinc Treatment for Reduction of Hyperplasia of Prostate." *Federal Proceedings* (35: 3: 361), March 1, 1976.

Feingold, B., *Why Your Child is Hyper-Active*. New York: Random House, 1975.

Fernstrom, J., & R. Wurtman, "Nutrition and the Brains," *Scientific American* (230: 2: 84–91), Feb. 1974.

Food and Nutrition Board, "Toward Healthful Diets," *Nutrition Today* (pp. 7–11), May-June 1980.

Fredericks, D., & H. Goodman, *Low Blood Sugar and You*. New York: Constellation, 1969.

Fredericks, C., *Psycho-Nutrition*. New York: Grosset & Dunlap, 1976.

Freifeld, K., & S. Engelmayer, "Hair Analysis—Are You Being Scalped?" *Health Magazine*, June 1983.

Fuller, J., *et al.*, "Coronary Heart Disease Risk and Impaired Glucose Tolerance: The Whitehall Study," *Lancet* (1: 8183: 1373–6), June 1980.

Ginsberg, H., *et al.*, "Moderate Ethanol Ingestion and Plasma Triglyceride Levels," *Annals of Internal Medicine* (80: 143), 1974.

Glueck, E., *et al.*, "Diet and Atherosclerosis: Past, Present and Future," *Western Journal of Medicine* (130: 117–22), 1979.

Gold, L. *et al.*, "Pectin: An Examination in Normal Subjects," *Diabetes Care* (3: 1: 50–52), Jan.–Feb. 1980.

Gonzalez, E., "Vitamin E Relieves Most Cystic Breast Disease: May Alter Lipids, Hormones," *J.A.M.A.* (244: 10: 1077–8), Sept. 5, 1980.

Goodhart, R., & M. Shils, *Modern Nutrition in Health and Disease*. Philadelphia: Lea & Febiger, 1976.

Grande, F., "Sugar and Cardiovascular Disease," *World Review of Nutrition and Dietetics* (22: 248), 1975.

Green, E., & H. Appledorf, "Proximate and Minteral Content of Restaurant Steak Meals," *Journal of the American Dietetics Association* (82: 2: 142–7), Feb. 1983.

Greengard, P., "Introduction: The Vitamins," L.S. Goodman and A. Gilman (eds.), *Pharmacological Basis of Therapeutics* (5th ed.). New York: Macmillan, 1975.

Greger, J., & B. Sciscoe, "Zinc Nutriture of Elderly Participants in an Urban Feeding Program," *Journal of the American Dietetics Association* (70: 37–41), Jan. 1977.

Grieco, M., "Controversial Practices in Allergy," *J.A.M.A.* (247: 22: 3106–10), 1982.

Gsell, D., & J. Mayer, "Low Blood Cholesterol Associated with High Calorie, High Saturated Fat Intakes in a Swiss Alpine Village Population," *American Journal of Clinical Nutrition* (10: 471), 1962.

Guthrie, H., *Introductory Nutrition* (5th ed.). St. Louis: C.V. Mosby, 1983.

Guthrie, H., & J. Scheer, "Nutritional Adequacy of Self-selected Diets that Satisfy the Four Food Groups Guide," *Journal of Nutrition Education* (13: 2: 46–49), June 1981.

Hambridge, K., "Chromium Nutrition in Man." *American Journal of Clinical Nutrition* (27: 505–14), 1974.

Hanley, D., "Athletic Training—And How Diet Affects It," *Nutrition Today* (pp. 5–9), Nov.–Dec. 1979.

Harper, A., "Recommended Dietary Allowances for the Elderly," *Geriatrics* (pp. 73–80), May 1978.

Harper, H., V. Rodwell, & P. Mayes, *Review of Physiological Chemistry* (16th ed.). Los Altos, Ca.: Lange Medical Publications, 1977.

Hartung, G., *et al.*, "Relation of Diet to High Density Lipoprotein Cholesterol in Middle Aged Marathon Runners, Joggers, and Inactive Men," *New England Journal of Medicine* (302: 7: 357–61), Feb. 14, 1980.

Heffley, J., "The Role of Food Supplements," *Journal of Applied*

*Nutrition* (35: 1: 58–66), Spring 1983.

Hegsted, D.M., *et al.*, "Quantitative Effects of Dietary Fat on Serum Cholesterol in Man," *American Journal of Clinical Nutrition* (17: 281), 1965.

Hepner, G., *et al.*, "Hypocholesterolemic Effect of Yogurt and Milk," *American Journal of Clinical Nutrition* (32: 19–24), Jan. 1979.

Hippchen, L., *Ecologic-Biochemical Approaches to Treatment of Delinquents and Criminals*. New York: Van Nostrand Reinhold, 1978.

Hoffer, A., & M. Walker, *Orthomolecular Nutrition*. New Canaan, Conn.: 1978.

Hunter, B., *How Safe is Food in Your Kitchen?* New York: Scribner's, 1981.

Hutton, C., & R. Hayes-Davis, "Assessment of the Zinc Nutritional Status of Selected Elderly Subjects," *Journal of the American Dietetics Association* (82: 2: 148–52), Feb. 1983.

Isselbacher, K., "Metabolic and Hepatic Effects of Alcohol," *New England Journal of Medicine* (296: 612), 1977.

Ivy, J., *et al.*, "Influence of Caffeine and Carbohydrate Feedings on Endurance Performance," *Medicine Science in Sports* (11: 1: 6–11), 1979.

James, W., & H. Coore, "Persistent Impairment of Insulin Secretion and Glucose Tolerance after Malnutrition," *American Journal of Clinical Nutrition* (23: 4: 386–9), April 1970.

Jenkins, D., *et al.*, "Effect of Pectin, Guar Gum, and Wheat Fiber on Serum Cholesterol," *Lancet* (1: 1116), 1975.

Jenkins, D., *et al.*, "Glycemic Index of Foods: A Physiological Basis for Carbohydrate Exchange," *American Journal of Clinical Nutrition* (34: 362–5), March 1981.

Jensen, J., *et al.*, "Nutrition in Orthopaedic Surgery," *Journal of Bone and Joint Surgery* (64-A: 9: 1263–72), Dec. 1982.

Johnson, D., *et al.*, "Reactive Hypoglycemia," *J.A.M.A.* (243: 11: 1151–5), March 1980.

Kanter, Y., *et al.*, "Improved Glucose Tolerance and Insulin Response in Obese and Diabetic Patients on a Fiber-enriched

Diet," *Israeli Journal of Medical Science* (16: 1: 1–6), Jan. 1980.

King, D., "Can Allergic Exposure Provoke Psychological Symptoms? A Double Blind Test," *Biological Psychiatry* (16: 1), 1981.

King, J., *et al.*, "Evaluation and Modification of the Basic Four Food Guide," *Journal of Nutrition Education* (10: 1), 1978.

Klevay, L., "Coronary Heart Disease: The Zinc/Copper Hypothesis," *American Journal of Clinical Nutrition* (29: 764), 1975.

Kolata, G., "Food Affects Human Behavior," *Science* (218: 1209–10), 1982.

Krehl, W.A., "Nutritional Significance of Dietary Imbalance," *Federal Proceedings* (23: 1059), 1964.

Krehl, W., "The Influence of Nutritional Environment on Aging," *Geriatrics* (pp. 65–78), May 1974.

Kritchevsky, D., "Dietary Fiber and Other Dietary Factors in Hypercholesteremia," *American Journal of Clinical Nutrition* (30: 979), 1977.

Kunin, R., *Mega Nutrition*. New York: New American Library, 1980.

Larsson-Cohn, U., "Oral Contraceptives and Vitamins: A Review," *American Journal of Obstetrics and Gynecology* (121: 1: 84–90), Jan. 1, 1975.

Leevy, C., *et al.*, "B-complex Vitamins in Liver Disease of the Alcoholic," *American Journal of Clinical Nutrition* (16: 4: 339–46), April 1965.

Lehninger, A., *Biochemistry*. New York: Worth, 1975.

Lesser, M., *Nutrition and Vitamin Therapy*. New York: Grove Press, 1980.

Leveille, G., "Adipose Tissue Metabolism: Influence of Periodicity of Eating and Diet Composition," *Federal Proceedings* (29: 3: 1294–1301), May–June 1970.

Leveille, G., & D. Romsos, "Meal Eating and Obesity," *Nutrition Today* (pp. 4–9), Nov.–Dec. 1974.

Levitt, N., *et al.*, "The Effect of Dietary Fiber on Glucose and Hormone Responses to a Mixed Meal in Normal Subjects and

Diabetic Subjects with and without Autonomic Neuropathy," *Diabetes Care* (3: 4: 515–9), July–Aug. 1980.

Lieber, C., "Alcohol and Malnutrition in the Pathogenesis of Liver Disease," *J.A.M.A.* (233: 1077–82), 1975.

Lieber, C., "The Metabolism of Alcohol," *Scientific American* (234: 3: 25–33), March 1976.

Liszewske, R., "The Effect of Zinc on Wound Healing: A Collective Review," *J.A.M.A.* (81: 2: 104–6), Oct. 1981.

Lozy, M. (ed.), *Nutrition*. Kalamazoo, Mich.: Upjohn, 1980.

Lutjens, A., *et al.*, "Glucose and Insulin Levels on Loading with Different Carbohydrates," *Clinica Chimica Acta* (62: 239–43), 1975.

Maruhama, Y., *et al.*, "Hasty Eating as a Cause of Unstable Blood Glucose in Patients with Maturity Onset Diabetes," *Tohoku Journal of Experimental Medicine* (130: 4: 411–12), April 1980.

Mattson, F., B. Etickson, & A. Kligman, "Effect of Dietary Cholesterol on Serum Cholesterol in Man," *American Journal of Clinical Nutrition* (25: 589), 1972.

Mattson, G., E. Hollenbach, & A. Kligman, "Effect of Hydrogenated Fat on the Plasma Cholesterol and Triglyceride Levels of Man," *American Journal of Clinical Nutrition* (28: 726), 1975.

Mayer, J., *A Diet for Living*. New York: David McKay, 1975.

Mayo Clinic, *The Mayo Clinic Diet Manual*. Philadelphia: W.B. Saunders, 1971.

McGovern, J., "Letter to the Editor," *Annals of Allergy* (46: 45), 1981.

Mead, J., & A. Fulco, *The Unsaturated and Polyunsaturated Fatty Acids in Health and Disease*, Springfield, Ill.: C.C Thomas, 1976.

Mertz, W., "Effects and Metabolism of Glucose Tolerance Factor," *Nutrition Review* (33: 5: 129–35), 1975.

Messerli, E., *et al.*, "Obesity and Essential Hypertension: Hemodynamics, Intravascular Volume, Sodium Excretion, and Plasma Renin Activity," *Archives of Internal Medicine* (141: 81), 1981.

Metzner, H., *et al.*, "The Relationship between Frequency of Eating and Adiposity in Adult Men and Women in the Tecumseh Community Health Study," *American Journal of Clinical Nutrition* (30: 712–15), 1977.

Mitchell, Rynbergen, Anderson, & Dibble, *Nutrition in Health & Disease* (16th ed.). Philadelphia: Lippincott, 1976.

Morrison, L., "Serum Cholesterol Reduction with Lecithin," *Geriatrics* (13: 12), 1958.

Moynahan, E., "Acrodermatitis Enteropathica: A Lethal Inherited Human Zinc-deficiency Disorder," *Lancet* (11: 399–400), 1974.

National Academy of Sciences, *Diet, Nutrition, and Cancer*. Washington D.C.: National Academy Press, 1982.

National Academy of Sciences, *Recommended Dietary Allowances*. Washington D.C.: National Academy Press, 1980.

Ney, D., & D. Hollingsworth, "Nutritional Management of Pregnancy Complicated by Diabetes: Historical Perspective," *Diabetes Care* (4: 6: 647–55), Nov. 1981.

Offenbacher, E., & F. Pi-sunyer, "Beneficial Effect of Chromium-rich Yeast in Glucose Tolerance and Blood Lipids in Elderly Subjects," *Diabetes* (29: 11: 919–25), Nov. 1980.

Ornish, D., *Stress, Diet, and Your Heart*. New York: Holt, Rinehart, & Winston, 1982.

Ovesen, L., "Drugs and Vitamin Deficiency," *Drugs* (18: 4: 278–98), 1979.

Pao, E., & S. Mickle, "Problem Nutrients in the United States," *Food Technology* (35: 9: 58–69, 79), Sept. 1981.

Passwater, R., *Selenium as Food and Medicine*. New Canaan, Conn.: Keats, 1980.

Pauling, L., & D. Hawkins (eds.), *Orthomolecular Psychiatry*. San Francisco: W.H. Freeman, 1973.

Pauling, L. *Vitamin C, the Common Cold and the Flu*, San Francisco: W.H. Freeman, 1976.

Pearce, M., & S. Dayton, "Incidence of Cancer in Men on a Diet High in Polyunsaturated Fat," *Lancet* (1: 464), 1971.

Pelletier, O., "Cigarette Smoking and Vitamin C," *Nutrition Today* (pp. 12–15), Autumn 1970.

Pfeiffer, C., *Zinc and Other Micro-nutrients*. New Canaan, Conn.: Keats, 1978.

Phillips, R., *et al.*, "Coronary Heart Disease Mortality among Seventh Day Adventists with Differing Dietary Habits: A Preliminary Report," *American Journal of Clinical Nutrition* (31: S191–8), Oct. 1978.

Pleuss, J., & M. Kochar, "Dietary Considerations in Hypertension," *Hypertension* (69: 6: 34–43), June 1981.

Pottenger, F., & B. Krohn, "Reduction of Hypercholesterolemia by High Fat Plus Soybean Phospholipids," *American Journal of Digestive Diseases* (19: 107, 142).

Ram, M., & M. Bamji, "Serum Vitamin A and Retinol-binding Protein in Malnourished Women Treated with Oral Contraceptives: Effects of Estrogen Dose and Duration of Treatment," *American Journal of Obstetrics and Gynecology* (135: 4: 470–2), Oct. 15, 1979.

Reed, P., *Nutrition, and Applied Science*. St. Paul, Minn.: West, 1980.

Ringsdorf, W., & E. Cheraskin, "Vitamin C and Human Wound Healing," *Oral Surgery* (pp. 231–6), March 1982.

Rivellese, A., *et al.*, "Effect of Dietary Fiber on Glucose Control and Serum Lipoproteins in Diabetic Patients," *Lancet* (2: 8192: 447–50), Aug. 1980.

Roe, D., *Drug Induced Nutritional Deficiencies*. Westport, Conn.: Avi, 1978.

Ronaghy, H., *et al.*, "Zinc Supplementation of Malnourished School Boys in Iran. Increased Growth and Other Effects," *American Journal of Clinical Nutrition* (27: 112–21), 1974.

Rosenberg, L., *et al.*, "Coffee Drinking and Myocardial Infarction in Young Women," *American Journal of Epidemiology* (111: 6: 675–81), 1980.

Ross Laboratories, *Aging and Nutrition*, 1977.

Rubin, J., "Food Allergies," *Hospital Medicine* (pp. 86–8), March 1982.

Ryan, A., *et al.*, "Balancing Heat Stress, Fluids and Electrolytes," *The Physician and Sports Medicine* (pp. 43–52), Aug. 1975.

Sandstead, H., "Zinc Nutrition in the United States." *American Journal of Clinical Nutrition* (261251–60), 1973.

Schauss, A., *Diet, Crime, and Delinquency*. Berkeley, Ca.: Parker House, 1981.

Schneider, A., C. Anderson & D. Coursin, *Nutritional Support of Medical Practice*, Hagerstown, Md.: Harper & Row, 1977.

Schroeder, H., *et al.*, "Chromium Deficiency as a Factor in Atherosclerosis," *Journal of Chronic Diseases* (23: 123), 1970.

Schroeder, H., "Losses of Vitamins and Trace Minerals Resulting from Processing and Preservation of Foods," *American Journal of Clinical Nutrition* (24: 562–73), May 1971.

Schroeder, H., *The Trace Elements and Man*, Old Greenwich, Conn.: Devin-Adair, 1973.

Shute, W., *Dr. Wilfred E. Shute's Complete Updated Vitamin E Book*. New Canaan, Conn.: Keats, 1975.

Simons, L., *et al.*, "Treatment of Hypercholesterolemia with Oral Lecithin," *Australia and New Zealand Journal of Medicine* (7: 262–6), 1977.

Smith, L., *Improving Your Child's Behavior Chemistry*. Englewood Cliffs, N.J.: Prentice-Hall, 1976.

Sperling, M., & A. Drash, "Evolution of Diabetes Mellitus from Hypoglycemia," *American Journal of the Diseases of Childhood* (121: 5–9), Jan. 1971.

Staff of Select Committee on Nutrition and Human Needs, *Diet and Killer Diseases*. Washington D.C.: Government Printing Office, 1977.

Steincroh, P., *Low Blood Sugar—The Most Common Misdiagnosed Disease*, Chicago: Regnery, 1972.

Timmreck, T., "Nutrition Problems: A Survey of the Rural Elderly," *Geriatrics* (pp. 137–40), Oct. 1977.

Todhunter, E., & W. Darby, "Guidelines for Maintaining Adequate Nutrition in Old Age," *Geriatrics* (pp. 49–56), June 1978.

United States Department of Agriculture, "Food is More than Just Something to Eat," *Bulletin 216*. Washington D.C.: U.S. Department of Agriculture, 1976.

United States Department of Agriculture, Department of Health,

Education, and Welfare, "Nutrition and Your Health—Dietary Guidelines for Americans," *Nutrition Today* (15: 2: 14–18), March–April 1980.

United States Senate, *Nutrition and Mental Health, Hearing before the Select Committee on Nutrition and Human Needs*. Berkeley, Ca.: Parker House, 1980.

Verrett, J., & J. Carper, *Eating May Be Hazardous to Your Health*. New York: Simon & Schuster, 1974.

Walczak, M., & B. Ehrich, *Nutrition and Well-Being*. Reseda, Ca.: Mojave Books, 1976.

Whitney, E., & M. Hamilton, *Understanding Nutrition*. St. Paul, Minn.: West, 1977.

Willett, W., *et al.*, "Alcohol Consumption and High Density Lipoprotein Cholesterol in Marathon Runners," *New England Journal of Medicine* (303: 20: 1159–61), Nov. 13, 1980.

Williams, R., *Biochemical Individuality*. New York: Wiley, 1963.

Williams, R., *Nutrition Against Disease*. New York: Bantam, 1973.

Williams, R., *Physician's Handbook of Nutritional Science*. Springfield, Ill.: C.C Thomas, 1975.

Williams, S., *Essentials of Nutrition and Diet Therapy*. St. Louis: C.V. Mosby, 1978.

Winick, M. (ed.), *Nutrition: Pre- and Post-natal Development*. New York: Plenum, 1979.

Winick, M., "Slow the Process of Aging and Quash Its Problems with Diet," *Modern Medicine* (pp. 68–74), Feb. 15, 1978.

Winston, F., "Oral Contraceptives, Pyridoxine, and Depression," *American Journal of Psychiatry* (pp. 1217–21), Nov. 1973.

Worthington, Vermeersch, & Williams, *Nutrition in Pregnancy and Lactation*. St. Louis: C.V. Mosby, 1977.

Wurtman, J., *Eating Your Way Through Life*. New York: Raven Press, 1979.

Wynder, E., "The Dietary Environment and Cancer," *Journal of the American Dietetics Association* (71: 4: 385–91), Oct. 1977.

Young, C., *et al.*, "Frequency of Feeding, Weight Reduction, and Body Composition," *Journal of the American Dietetics Asso-*

*ciation* (59: 466–72), Nov. 1971.

Yudkin, J., *Sweet and Dangerous*. New York: Bantam, 1973.


## EXERCISE

Allen, M., "Activity-generated Endorphins: A Review of Their Role in Sports Science," *Canadian Journal of Applied Sport Science* (8: 3: 115–33), Sept. 1983.

American Heart Association Committee on Exercise, *Exercise Testing and Training of Apparently Healthy Individuals: A Handbook for Physicians*. New York: American Heart Association, 1972.

Bentivegna, A., *et al.*, "Diet, Fitness, and Athletic Performance," *The Physician and Sports Medicine* (7: 10: 99–105), Oct. 1979.

Blaun, R., "Exercise: The Versatile Medicine of Choice," *Medical Month* (p. 16), Feb. 1984.

Boyer, J., & F. Kasch, "Exercise Therapy in Hypertensive Men," *J.A.M.A.* (211: 1668–71), March 9, 1970.

Brody, J., "Exercise Outstrips Dieting in Shaping Your Future," *San Diego Union* (p. D-5), Aug. 28, 1983.

Cooper, K., "Guidelines in the Management of the Exercising Patient," *J.A.M.A.* (pp. 1663–4), March 9, 1970.

Cooper, K.H., *The Aerobics Way*. New York: M. Evans, 1977.

Crews, E., *et al.*, "Weight, Food Intake, and Body Composition: Effects of Exercise and of Protein Deficiency," *American Journal of Physiology* (16: 2: 359–63), Feb. 1969.

Cureton, T., *Physiological Effects of Exercise Programs on Adults*. Springfield, Ill.: C.C Thomas, 1969.

Davis, J.T., *Walking!* New York: Bantam, 1979.

Driscoll, R., *Exertion Therapy: Rapid Anxiety Reduction Using Physical Exertion and Positive Imagery*. Boulder: University of Colorado (Ph.D. dissertation), 1973.

Elman, R., *The Hiker's Bible*, Garden City, N.Y.: Doubleday, 1973.

Fardy, P.S., "Isometric Exercise and the Cardiovascular System," *The Physician and Sports Medicine* (9: 9: 43–53), Sept. 1981.

Fletcher, C., *The New Complete Walker*. New York: Alfred A. Knopf, 1976.

Fletcher, G, *et al.*, *Exercise in the Practice of Medicine*. Mount Kisco, N.Y.: Futura, 1982.

Frankel, L., & B. Richard, *Be Alive As Long As You Live*. New York: Lippincott and Crowell, 1980.

Gibbs, R., "Living Longer and Growing Younger—Exercise Prescription for the Elderly," *Australian Family Physician* (11: 10: 775), Oct. 1982.

Ismail, A., & L. Trachtman, "Jogging the Imagination," *Psychology Today* (pp. 78–88), April 1973.

Jesse, J.P., "Misuse of Strength Development Programs in Athletic Training," *The Physician and Sports Medicine* (7: 10: 46–52), Oct. 1979.

Kasch, F., "The Effects of Exercise on the Aging Process," *The Physician and Sports Medicine* (p. 68), June 1976.

Kuntzleman, C., and Consumer Guide Editors, *Rating the Exercises*. New York: William Morrow, 1978.

Kuntzleman, C.T., *The Complete Book of Walking: Total Fitness Step-by-Step*. New York: Simon & Schuster, 1979.

Lifson, A., *Taming the Tornado in Your Classroom and at Home*. Costa Mesa. Ca.: Educational Consultant Group Publications, 1980.

Lohmann, D., *et al.*, "Diminished Insulin Response in Highly Trained Athletes," *Metabolism* (27: 5: 521–3), May 1978.

Markoff, R., P. Ryan, & T. Young, "Endorphins and Mood Changes in Long Distance Running," *Medicine and Science in Sports and Exercise* (14: 1: 11–15), 1982.

*Metropolitan Life's Exercise Guide*. Metropolitan Life Insurance Company, 1966.

Montoye, H., *et al.*, "Glucose Tolerance and Physical Fitness: An Epidemiologic Study in an Entire Community," *European Journal of Applied Physiology* (37: 237–42), 1977.

Paffenbarger, R., *et al.*, "Work Activity of Longshoremen as Related to Death from Coronary Heart Disease and Stroke." *New England Journal of Medicine* (20: 1109), 1970.

Pollock, M., *et al.*, "Effects of Walking on Body Composition and Cardiovascular Function of Middle-aged Men," *Journal of Applied Physiology* (pp. 126–30), Jan. 1970.

President's Council on Physical Fitness, *Adult Physical Fitness*. Washington D.C.: Government Printing Office, 1965.

President's Council on Physical Fitness and Sports, *Walking for Exercise and Pleasure*. Washington D.C.: Government Printing Office.

President's Council on Physical Fitness and Sports and the Administration on Aging, *The Fitness Challenge in the Later Years*. Washington D.C.: Government Printing Office, 1973.

Roskamm, H., "Optimum Patterns of Exercise for Healthy Adults," *Canadian Medical Association Journal* (96, p. 895), 1967.

Schultz, P., "Walking for Fitness: Slow but Sure," *The Physician and Sports Medicine* (8: 9: 24–27), Sept. 1980.

Shangold, M., "Menstrual Irregularities Increasingly Linked to Exercise," *Family Practice News* (11: 13: 10), July 1981.

Smith, E., & R. Serfass, *Exercise and Aging, the Scientific Basis*. Hillside, N.J.: Enslow, 1981.

White, P., & T. Mondeika, *Diet & Exercise: Synergism in Health Maintenance*. Chicago: American Medical Association, 1982.

Whitten, P., "Old Masters of Swimming," *Parade Magazine* (pp. 12–14), May 20, 1979.

Zuti, B., & L. Golding, "Comparing Diet and Exercise as Weight Reduction Tools," *The Physician and Sports Medicine* (p. 49), Jan. 1976.

## PHYSICAL ENVIRONMENT

Ackerman, B., & W. Hassler, *Clean Coal/Dirty Air*. New Haven, Conn.: Yale University Press, 1981.

Baron, A., *Man Against Germs*. New York: E.P. Dutton, 1957.

Baron, R., *The Tyranny of Noise*. New York: Harper & Row, 1970.

Becklake, M.R., "State of the Art Asbestos Related Disease of the Lung and Other Organs," *American Review of Respiratory Diseases* (114: 187), 1976.

Budiansky, D., "Formaldehyde Cancer Risk—Court not Convinced of Dangers," *Nature* (304: 5922: 105), July 1983.

Farber, S., *Air We Breathe*, Springfield, Ill.: C.C Thomas, 1961.

Lowrance, W., *Of Acceptable Risk: Science and the Determination of Safety*, Los Altos, Ca.: W. Kaufmann, 1976.

Ott, J., *Health and Light*, New York: Pocket Books, 1976.

Rama, S., *et al.*, *Science of Breath*. Honesdale, Penn.: The Himalayan International Institute of Yoga Science and Philosophy, 1979.

Regunathan, D., & R. Sundaresan, "Incorporation of 14C Form Glucose into Amino Acids in Brain In Vitro in the Presence of Organo- and Inorganic Lead and Pyridoxal Phosphate," *Life Science* (33: 23: 2277–82), Dec. 1983.

Selikoff, I., & D. Lee, *Asbestos and Disease*. New York: Academic Press, 1978.

Sheppard, D., *et al.*, "Lower Threshold and Greater Bronchomotor Responsiveness of Asthmatic Subjects to Sulfur Dioxide," *American Review of Respiratory Diseases* (122: 873–78), 1980.

Shore, D., & R. Wyatt, "Aluminum and Alzheimer's Disease," *Journal of Nervous and Mental Disorders* (1: 9: 553–8), Sept. 1983.

United States Congressional Senate Committee on Public Works, *Noise Pollution*. Washington D.C.: Government Printing Office, 1972.

United States Department of Health, Education and Welfare. *The Health Consequences of Smoking*. Washington D.C.: Government Printing Office, 1967.

Whorton, M., *et al.*, "Feasibility of Identifying High-risk Occupations through Tumor Registries," *Journal of Occupational Medicine* (9: 657–60), Sept. 1983.

## BODY MAINTENANCE

Bates, W., *Better Eyesight without Glasses*. New York: Pyramid, 1943.

Bete, C., *About Foot Care*. South Deerfield, Mass.: C. L. Bete, 1980.

Cranin, N., *The Modern Family Guide to Dental Health*. New York: Stein & Day, 1971.

Dotz, W., & B. Berman, "The Facts about Treatment of Dry Skin," *Geriatrics* (38: 9: 93–100), Sept. 1983.

Downing, G., *The Massage Book*. New York: Random House, 1972.

Freese, A., *You and Your Hearing*. New York: Scribner's, 1979.

Hass, F., & E. Dolan, *The Foot Book*. Chicago: Regnery, 1973.

Huxley, A., *The Art of Seeing*. New York: Harper, 1942.

LeMarr, J., L. Golding, & K. Crehan, "Cardiorespiratory Responses to Inversion," *The Physician and Sports Medicine* (11: 11: 51–57), Nov. 1983.

Martin, R., & R. Klatz, "Gravity Inversion: How Effective, How Safe?" *Aches and Pains* (4: 11: 6–12), Nov. 1983.

Moss, S. (ed.), *Preventive Dentistry*. New York: Medcom, 1972.

Nason, A., *Textbook of Modern Biology*. New York: John Wiley, 1965.

Zizmor, J., *Skin Care Book*. New York: Holt, Rinehart, & Winston, 1977.

## WEIGHT CONTROL

Alexander, J., & K. Peterson, "Cardiovascular Effects of Weight Reduction," *Circulation* (45: 310–18), 1972.

Amad, K., *et al.*, "The Cardiac Pathology of Chronic Exogenous Obesity," *Circulation* (32: 740), 1965.

Angel, A., & D. Roncari, "Medical Complications of Obesity," *Canadian Medical Association Journal* (119: 1408–11), 1978.

Apfelbaum, M., "The Effects of Very Restrictive High Protein Diets," *Clinical Endocrinology and Metabolism* (5: 2: 417–30), July 1976.

Beller, A., *Fat and Thin: A Natural History of Obesity*. New York: McGraw-Hill, 1978.

Bennett, W., & J. Gurin, *The Dieter's Dilemma*. New York: Basic Books, 1982.

Berland, T., *Rating the Diets*. New York: Consumer Guide, 1983.

Bloom, W., "Carbohydrates and Water Balance," *American Jour-*

*nal of Clinical Nutrition* (20: 2: 157–62), Feb. 1967.

Bray, G., *et al.*, "Obesity: A Serious Symptom," *Annals of Internal Medicine* (77: 779–805), 1972.

Chaing, B., *et al.*, "Overweight and Hypertension: A Review," *Circulation* (39: 403–21), 1969.

Committee of American Diabetes Association, American Dietetics Association, National Institute of Arthritis, Metabolism & Digestive Diseases, and National Heart & Lung Institute of Health, Department of Health, Education and Welfare, *Exchange Lists for Meal Planning*. Chicago: American Dietetics Association, 1976.

Council on Foods and Nutrition, "A Critique of Low-carbohydrate Ketogenic Weight Reduction Regimes," *J.A.M.A.* (244: 10: 1415–9), June 4, 1973.

deDivitiis, O., *et al.*, "Obesity and Cardiac Function," *Circulation* (64: 477), 1981.

Flatt, J., "The Metabolic Costs of Energy Storage, from a Symposium on Obesity, Thermogenesis, and the Regulations of Energy Balance," *Meducation*, Wyeth Laboratories, July 1982.

Gordon, T., & W. Kannel, "The Effects of Overweight on Cardiovascular Diseases," *Geriatrics* (28: 80–88), 1973.

Hoyt, C., & F. Billson, "Low Carbohydrate Diet Optic Neuropathy," *Medical Journal of Australia* (1: 65–66), 1977.

Nordan, H., & L. Levitz, *Eating is Okay*. New York: Rawson, 1977.

Kannel, W.B., *et al.*, "The Relation of Adiposity to Blood Pressure and Development of Hypertension: The Framingham Study," *Annals of Internal Medicine* (67: 48), 1967.

Katahn, M., *The 200 Calorie Solution*. New York: W.W. Norton, 1983.

Knittle, J., "Early Influences on Development of Adipose Tissue," in B.A. Bray (ed.), *Obesity in Perspective*. Washington D.C.: Department of Health, Education and Welfare (Publication Number NIH 75-708; Ch. 29, p. 241), 1975.

Kolterman, O., *et al.*, "Mechanisms of Insulin Resistance in Human Obesity: Evidence for Receptor and Postreceptor Defects," *Journal of Clinical Investigation* (65: 6: 1272–84), June 1980.

Reisin, E., *et al.*, "Effect of Weight Loss without Salt Restriction on the Reduction of Blood Pressure in Overweight Hypertensive Patients," *New England Journal of Medicine* (298: 1), 1978.

Rubin, T., *Forever Thin*. New York: Gramercy, 1970.

Stuart, R., & B. Davis, *Slim Chance in a Fat World*. Champaign, Ill.: Research Press, 1977.

Stunkard, A., "The Management of Obesity," *New York State Journal of Medicine* (58: 79), 1958.

Weltman, A., *et al.*, "Caloric Restriction and/or Mild Exercise: Effects on Serum Lipids and Body Composition," *American Journal of Clinical Nutrition* (33: 1002–9), May 1980.

Wilmore, J., *et al.*, "Body Composition Changes with a 10 Week Jogging Program," *Medical Science and Sports* (2: 113–7), 1970.

Wise, J., & S. Wise, *The Overeaters*. New York: Humane Sciences, 1979.

Worthington, B., & L. Taylor, "Balanced Low Calorie vs. High Protein Low Carbohydrate Reducing Diets," *Journal of the American Dietetics Association* (64: 47–51), Jan. 1974.

Yang, M., & T. VanItallie, "Composition of Weight Lost During Short Term Weight Reduction," *Journal of Clinical Investigation* (58: 722–30), Sept. 1976.

## SEXUALITY

Genevay, B., "Age Kills Us Softly When We Deny Our Sexual Identity," in R. Solnick (ed.), *Sexuality and Aging*. Los Angeles: Unversity of Southern California, 1978.

Hastings, D., *Impotence and Frigidity*, Boston: Little, Brown, 1963.

McGrady, P., *The Youth Doctors*. New York: Coward-McCann, 1968.

Schneider, E., *The Aging Reproductive System*. New York: Raven Press, 1978.

Thomas, L., "Sexuality and Aging: Essential Vitamin or Popcorn?" *Gerontologist* (22: 3: 240–43), 1982.

## THE GRIM REAPERS

Arthritis Health Professions, The Arthritis Foundation, *Self-Help Manual for Patients with Arthritis*. Atlanta: Arthritis Foundation, 1980.

Benditt, E., "The Origin of Atherosclerosis," *Scientific American* (236: 2: 74–85), Feb. 1977.

Casdorph, R., "EDTA Chelation Therapy II, Efficacy in Brain Disorders," *Journal of Holistic Medicine* (3: 2: 101–17).

Christakis, G., *Update: Cardiovascular Risk Factors*. Puerto Rico: Roche Products, 1982.

Dolger, H., & B. Seeman, *How to Live with Diabetes*. New York: Pyramid, 1963.

Fagerberg, S., "Control of Blood Glucose and Diabetic Vascular Disease," *Acta Endocrinologica Supplement* (Copenhagen) (239: 42–43), Sept. 1979.

Freis, E., *Risk Assessment in Hypertension*. Philadelphia: Smith, Klien, and French Laboratories, 1981.

Hartung, G., "Environmental and Dietary Influences on the HDL Cholesterol Ratio" (9: 11: 61–68), Oct. 1983.

Hayflick, L., "Human Cells and Aging," *Scientific American* (218: 32–37), March 1968.

Kannel, W., & T. Dawber, "Atherosclerosis as a Pediatric Problem," *Journal of Pediatrics* (80: 544), 1972.

Kannel, W., & T. Gordon (eds.), *The Framingham Study: An Epidemiological Investigation of Cardiovascular Disease*. Washington D.C.: Department of Health, Education and Welfare (Publication Number NIH 176–1083, Section 31), April 1976.

Keys, A., "Probability of Middle-aged Men Developing Coronary Heart Disease in Five Years," *Circulation* (45: 815), 1972.

Koffler, D., "The Immunology of Rheumatoid Diseases," *Clinical Symposia* (31: 4: 2–9), 1979.

Leren, P., "The Oslo Diet-heart Study: Eleven Year Report," *Circulation* (42: 935), 1970.

Lorig, K., & J. Fries, *The Arthritis Help Book*. Reading, Penn.: Addison-Wesley, 1980.

Monte, T., "An M.D. Heals Himself of Cancer," *East West Journal* (pp. 35–39), March 1980.

Multiple Risk Factor Intervention Trial Research Group, "Multiple Risk Factor Intervention Trial: Factor Changes and Mortality Results," *J.A.M.A.* (248: 1465–77), Sept. 1980.

Nordin, B., "Prevention and Treatment of Postmenopausal Osteoporosis," *Geriatric Medicine Today* (pp. 54–70), July 1983.

Notkins, A., "The Causes of Diabetes," *Scientific American* (241: 5: 62–73), Nov. 1979.

Rockstein, M., M. Sussman, & J. Chesky (eds.), *Theoretical Aspects of Aging*. New York: Academic Press, 1974.

Schaap, D., "Meet the Oldest Man," *Parade Magazine* (pp. 4–6), Nov. 20, 1983.

Smart, C., "Preventing Cancer in the United States," *Bulletin, American College of Surgeons* (67: 9: 2–8), Sept. 1982.

Stare, F. (ed.), *Atherosclerosis*. New York: Medcom, 1974.

## COOKBOOKS

American Diabetes Association and the American Dietetic Association, *The Family Cookbook*. Englewood Cliffs, N.J.: Prentice-Hall, 1980.

*Betty Crocker's How to Feed Your Family to Keep Them Fit and Happy . . . No Matter What*. New York: Golden Press, 1972.

Brown, J., *et al.*, *Cook to Your Heart's Content on a Low-fat, Low-salt Diet*. New York: Van Nostrand Reinhold, 1976.

Coulson, Z., *The Good Housekeeping Illustrated Cookbook*. New York: Hearst Books, 1980.

Hoshijo, K., *Kathy Cooks Naturally*. San Francisco: Harbor, 1981.

Jones, D., *The Soybean Cookbook*. New York: Arc Books, 1968.

Kidushim-Allen, D., *Light Desserts*. San Francisco: Harper & Row, 1978.

Lowenthal, A., *The Great Cook's Guide to Breads*. New York: Random House, 1977.

Margie, J., & J. Hunt, *Living with High Blood Pressure: The Hypertension Diet Cookbook*. Bloomfield, N.J.: HLS Press, 1978.

## Bibliography

Morash, M., *The Victory Garden Cookbook*. New York: Alfred A. Knopf, 1982.

Omel, M., *The Diet Chef's Gourmet Cookbook*. New York: Frederick Fell, 1981.

Robertson, L., *et al.*, *Laurel's Kitchen, A Handbook for Vegetarian Cookery and Nutrition*. Ca.: Nilgiri Press, 1976.

Shurtleff, W., & A. Aoyagi, *The Book of Tofu*. New York: Ballantine, 1977.

*The American Heart Association Cookbook*. New York: Ballantine, 1981.

# INDEX

## About the Authors

R. Philip Smith, M.D., is one of America's leading experts on preventive medicine. He is Medical Director of the La Costa Spa and has been associated with it since its inception. Before joining La Costa, he was Clinical Professor at the University of Washington Medical School. He has received numerous awards and honors for his work in health care. He is the author of THE LA COSTA DIET AND EXERCISE BOOK, which is recognized as the safest and most successful weight-loss book on the market.

Patrick Quillin, Ph.D., R.D., is a recognized authority on nutrition and preventive medicine. He teaches nutrition at the university level and has served as consultant to Scripps Clinic, La Costa Spa, government nutrition education programs, weight control facilities and private industry. He has authored numerous articles on nutrition and is a registered dietician.

# HERE'S TO YOUR HEALTH!

## A compendium of useful titles from Fawcett Books.